# THE INFLUENCE OF THE FAMILY

GARLAND LIBRARY OF SOCIOLOGY
General Editor Dan A. Chekki
(Vol. 9)

GARLAND REFERENCE LIBRARY
OF SOCIAL SCIENCE
(Vol. 353)

# GARLAND LIBRARY OF SOCIOLOGY

## General Editor: Dan A. Chekki

# THE INFLUENCE OF THE FAMILY
*A Review and Annotated Bibliography
of Socialization, Ethnicity, and
Delinquency, 1975–1986*

Alan C. Acock
Jeffrey M. Clair

Department of Sociology
Louisiana State University

GARLAND PUBLISHING, INC. · NEW YORK & LONDON
1986

**Library of Congress Cataloging-in-Publication Data**

Acock, Alan C., 1944–
The influence of the family.

(Garland bibliographies in sociology ; vol. 9)
(Garland reference library of social science ; vol. 340)
Includes indexes.
1. Youth—Bibliography.   2. Family—Bibliography.
3. Ethnicity—Bibliography   4. Juvenile delinquency—
Bibliography.   I. Clair, Jeffrey M., 1958–      .
II. Title.   III. Series: Garland bibliographies in
sociology ; v. 9.   IV. Series: Garland reference
library of social science ; v. 340.
Z7164.Y8A26   1986   [HQ796]   016.3033′23      86-15005
ISBN 0-8240-8567-1 (alk. paper)

Printed on acid-free, 250-year-life paper
Manufactured in the United States of America

# CONTENTS

# PREFACE OF THE GENERAL EDITOR

Adolescence is generally characterized as a critical phase in growth: a period of transition from dependence on parents to independence, and from school to work. It is difficult to underestimate the importance of these two great transitions for both individual well-being and societal welfare. Ambivalence, confusion, inner turmoil, frustration may be associated with adolescent's conscious strivings for independence. During this period of storm and stress, the adolescent needs help from the family to guide him properly in solving his problems.

Overall, a majority of adolescents seems to be making a reasonably smooth transition from dependence to independence. However, the high rate of divorce and alternate family forms raise questions about the positive role of the family. The appropriate environment can be successfully achieved when the family environment is conducive to the development of a balanced mature personality.

Probably every generation views the adolescent as a problem. However, in recent decades the mass media has been presenting the adolescent as the cause of problems. Educators and psychologists tend to view the adolescent as suffering from problems created by the adult world. Sociologists have been discussing the issues related to intergenerational relations, generation gap, and parent-youth conflict.

For many, youth marks the end cycle of direct dependence on one's parents and the beginning of a new cycle, by becoming parents themselves. Young people who are parents face a very different world from those who do not have children. The launching stage—the period when children are ending adolescence and about to leave the parental home for college, work, and marriage—symbolizes a critical stage of transition from adolescence to young adulthood. In other words, the launching stage represents a transition from the family of orientation to the establishment of the family of procreation.

In North America, ethnic diversity has given rise to variations in family lifestyles and life chances. Besides promoting conformity to a great extent through socialization of the young, the family also seems to contribute toward deviant behavior and problems such as alcoholism, drug use, teenage pregnancy, abortion, juvenile delinquency, depression, and suicide. The problems of growth and finding meaningful activities for young people are challenges that face governments and community leaders.

While studies of ethnic families before 1970 in the United States were subject to negative stereotypes, the family literature of the past decade depicted the positive aspects of their family life. This reference volume by Alan C. Acock and Jeffrey M. Clair, Louisiana State University, is a good indicator of an increase in both the quantity and quality of research and theory on adolescence, ethnic families, and juvenile delinquency. This book, I hope, will aid social scientists, policy makers, and administrators interested in issues related to youth and families.

DAN A. CHEKKI
University of Winnipeg

# PREFACE

Families and their adolescent to young adult children are the centerpiece of this book. The theme is intergenerational influence. While the breath of substantive issues is enormous, there are special sections focusing on ethnic families and on delinquency. Because the potential literature is vast, we have concentrated on work published between 1975 and 1986 in the United States.

There are articles, papers presented at meetings, and chapters as well as books. Given the nature of the scholarly work in this area, the preponderance of publications are articles in academic journals. Publications are divided into three sections. First, there is a general section called "Family Influence." This is followed by a section on "Ethnicity" and one on "Delinquency."

Publications are listed in alphabetical sequence by author within each section. The first section contains references numbering up to 344. The second section includes references 345 to 525. The last section includes references 526 to 796. An author index gives the number of each publication for the author. This is followed by a detailed subject matter index which also provides the number of each publication.

We have received considerable help in preparing this book. We wish to thank Susan King for word processing, Mark Dugas for assisting with computer work, as well as Gloria Martinez and Kevil Duhon for library assistance. D. Antonia Acock and Krisenda Morrison-Clair deserve special thanks for their editorial help. Although these people are not responsible for any errors we may have made, the book would not have been possible without their assistance.

# The Influence of the Family

# CHAPTER ONE:

## INTRODUCTION

There is a vast literature dealing with family influence on adolescent and young adult children. We confine this book to works published since 1975 on how the family influences adolescent and post-adolescent children. The first section covers general issues in family influence while the second deals strictly at family influence among ethnic families. The last section examines the issue of family factors related to delinquency.

The many key issues stressed in our selection of references concern transmission of attitudes, beliefs, values, and behaviors across generations. While much of this work concerns the influence parents have on children, some of it compares the role of mothers to fathers, or the role of family members to the role of those outside the family. The citations reflect the increasing sensitivity of researchers to reciprocal influence in which the children are active agents in their own socialization as well as influencing their parents. These studies cover a variety of substantive topics ranging from political beliefs to work values and include religion, self-esteem, sex beliefs, social problems, and sports.

Not all of the research covered in the three sections concerns transmission. Other topics we cover include birth order differences, divorce effects, genetics, social class effects, status attainment, racial differences, drug use, economic deprivation, language, labeling, number of children, and social control.

A sampling of work done on the broader topic of generations is included. This work does not examine the issue of transmission along lineage lines.

Its concern is with issues of stability and instability across generations. Most of the work from
this vein is in the section on Family Influence.
Family influence is important to these works, but
is not their central theme.

We include some work using data sets from outside of the United States. Many of these studies
are reported in journals published in the United
States but have a cross-cultural character. Due to
the difficulty locating many of the studies published in journals outside of the United States,
we have included few of these studies. We have
identified a few studies (without an annotation)
that were unavailable to us.

While the research we cite here displays an
impressive assembly of ideas, it tends to have one
or the other of two major restrictions. First,
some of it is not developed in terms of theoretical
issues. Second, some of it is based on weak
measurement or poor research design. Therefore, we
include a number of methodological and theoretical
works that are only indirectly related to our
theme. Such additional items, in our opinion, will
be useful to researchers on the general issue of
how families influence adolescent members.

The choice of 1975-1986 keeps the focus on
current research issues. An enormous literature
from the 1960s and early 1970s is excluded. That
research addressed the generational cleavages
associated with the post-WWII baby boomers (U.S.
involvement in Vietnam, campus violence, and the
great gap of the baby boomers). It is important in
a historical sense as it portrays one of many
historical instances of inter-generational conflict
during periods of rapid social and cultural change.
However, there has been a considerable shift in
research interests since that time. Readers interested in earlier publications should see any of
several reviews that provide references to the work
of the 1960s and early 1970s. References that have
excellent literature reviews are noted by the
KEYWORD, "review." Review is a term that appears
in the index as well.

While highlighting the period since 1975, we still include a few references from prior to 1975. Most of these are classics. It is here that we are the least systematic in our rationale. Important literature prior to 1975 is excluded. To cite but one example, we do not have James Coleman's **The Adolescent Society** (New York: The Free Press, 1961). We rationalize its exclusion by its date and the fact that it did not focus on family factors. A large literature on status attainment from this early period could be included. Given such limitations, readers should not interpret the exclusion of a publication prior to 1975 as an indication that it is unimportant. Readers who examine the relevant literature we do cite will find their references cover much of the pre-1975 literature.

The distribution of publications across the 1975 to 1986 time period is remarkably consistent. Although we do not assert that our selections are a precise reflection of the actual research in any probability sense, the consistency suggests that the level of research on inter-generational influence has been stable. This is true even though individual scholars have moved into and out of this area of scholarship in terms of their own careers. Some authors, such as Thomas Smith, have a persistent interest across the entire period (at least one publication in 1976, 1977, 1979, 1981, 1982, 1983, and 1984). A few investigators were exceptionally active at the start of the time period but have since moved to other areas of research. Young scholars are emerging to fill these gaps. For example, Gary Peterson has a strong collection of papers beginning in 1982 (at least one publication in 1982, 1983, 1984, 1985, and 1986).

The net effect of this is a constant level of output. Figure 1 shows the number of references for each year from 1975 to 1986. The slight fall for 1985 and 1986 is attributed to the limited access we had to this literature while preparing this annotated bibliography.

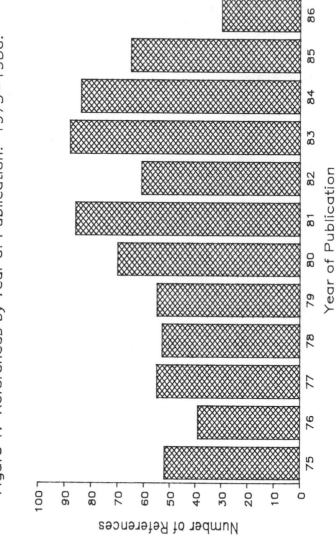

Figure 1. References by Year of Publication: 1975–1986.

Our decision to focus on adolescent and post adolescent issues has caused us to restrict the publications we catalog. This is especially evident with the massive amount of work done on early childhood socialization. There is also a thriving and developing literature on socialization at the later stages of the life cycle. We include a few references from each of these groups on a highly selective basis. Those chosen contain information, theories, or methods that are vital to research on adolescents.

## Procedures

The preparation of this book is premised on the goal of providing a carefully selected set of publications. An idea of the scope of potential literature we have considered is evidenced by the David Olson and Roxanne Markoff, **Inventory of Marriage and Family Literature, Vol 11** (Beverly Hills: Sage, 1986). This set of 11 volumes provides a huge listing of publications arranged under relevant topics. For example, volume 11 by itself lists 244 citations of parent-child relationships, 101 citations on parent-adolescent relationships, 29 dealing with socialization and a host of references on many of the more specific issues we have examined. By being selective, we are able to contribute a collection of references we consider among the best and furnish a brief annotation to provide the reader with information on which to decide if the citation is germane to his or her interests.

The choice of these references began by generating a large pool of publications for possible inclusions. This entailed both computer and manual searches through prominent journals for possible articles to include. The second step involved going over the bibliographies in each of these publications we cataloged. This process continued until we no longer found new sources.

Once the initial pool of works was gathered, the third step was the deletion of publications that did not fit into one of the three areas we identified. This was extremely subjective. In our

struggle to keep the list manageable and focused,
we may have omitted potentially valuable work.  A
more exhaustive listing is beyond the scope of this
project.

     In the fourth stage we mailed letters to
selected authors.  This was problematic since some
journals do not give addresses, and researchers on
our theme are a highly mobile lot.  Still, we
received over 100 replies to our letters suggesting
additional publications that might be included.
Some of these suggestions were already included,
some were not directly relevant, but many of them
were very helpful.

     We have annotations for over 95% of the referen-
ces.  Authors of citations for which we lack an
annotation may feel that we have wronged them, but
this is not our intention.  Most citations which
lack an annotation are publications we could not
locate given our time constraints, or they are
publications that have come to our attention by
other authors who indicate they are important.  The
preponderance of other references that are missing
a citation are those for which one was not felt
necessary.  A paper that makes a single point and
states that point in the title, does not need a
brief annotation.

     It should be noted that the annotations are
terse.  They are not intended to be critiques of
the publications, nor even abstracts.  We hope
they are enough to indicate to the reader whether
he or she should go through the trouble of locating
the publication and reading it.  Several of the
authors we contacted indicated that the annotations
for their own work were too brief.  A few suggested
we replace an annotation with the abstract
published in the original paper.  To include original abstracts would greatly lengthen this book
and it was decided to keep the annotations as brief
as possible.

     There will be readers who feel that we have
unfairly excluded crucial work.  We hope, however,
that our highly focused strategy is useful for the
majority of our readers.  Thus, while this set of

references in not exhaustive, it should be a useful complement to the references many readers already have.

## Distribution of Publications

Publications from 175 different journals are included. In Table 1 we present a list of the 25 most frequently appearing journals along with the number of articles coming from each.

The **Journal of Marriage and the Family** is by far the dominant journal for research for the general section on Family influence (45 articles) and for the Ethnicity section (11 articles). Indeed, it is the most frequently cited journal for both of these sections. However, there is little research on how the family influences delinquent behavior in this journal (only a single article in our Delinquency section).

Since both of the authors are sociologists, there is a strong representation of works from general journals of sociology. Having at least five publications in this book are many of the best known sociology journals. These include: **American Sociological Review** (19), **American Journal of Sociology** (14), **Social Forces** (9), **Social Science Quarterly** (5), **Social Psychology** (6), **Sociological Quarterly** (6), and **Sociology and Social Research** (5).

Still, there are many publications from child development, family studies, education, political science, psychology, and other social science fields. This diversity of disciplines reflects the inter-disciplinary nature of this inquiry.

Family Studies is represented by journals other than the **Journal of Marriage and the Family**. The **Journal of Comparative Family Studies** is represented by five articles. Additional family journals include the **Family Coordinator, Family Perspective, Family Planning Perspective, Family Relations, Journal of Family Issues, Journal of Divorce,** and **Journal of Marital and Family Therapy.**

Investigators outside the field of political science may be surprised by the depth of interest in political science literature. Both the **American Political Science Review** (5) and the **European Journal of Political Research** (5) appear among the top 25 journals in Table 1. While there is little political science work on Ethnicity and none on Delinquency, **American Journal of Political Science, Comparative Political Studies, Comparative Politics,** and the **Journal of Politics, provide** contributions to the section on Family Influence.

Psychology has several journals represented. Had more attention been given to pre-adolescent research, of course, this representation would be much greater than it is. Psychology journals having at least five references are **Psychological Reports** (8), **Child Development** (8), **Journal of Genetic Psychology** (6), and **Developmental Psychology** (6). Also represented are **Journal of Personality and Social Psychology, Journal of Abnormal Psychology, Journal of Psychology,** and the **American Psychologist.**

Finally, there is a variety of the interdisciplinary specialty journals including **Adolescence** (31), **British Journal of Criminology** (17), **Criminology** (16), **Youth and Society** (16), **Journal of Youth and Adolescence** (9), **Social Problems** (7), **Journal of Negro Education** (7), **Journal of Social Issues** (6), and **Sex Roles** (5).

These are the journals with the heaviest representation in our work. Two important points should be noted. First, the literature included in this book covers an extremely wide variety of sources. There are 508 journal articles and the average number of references per journal is only 2.9. In fact, most journals have only a single publication over the period of 1975 to 1986 that we have selected for inclusion.

Second, we suspect that researchers with backgrounds in education or psychology would have produced a significantly different selection of sources. Thus, while our search has been extensive, it has not been truly exhaustive.

Table 1.   25 Most Frequently Cited Journals

| JOURNAL | NUMBER OF REFERENCES |
|---|---|
| Journal of Marriage and the Family | 57 |
| Adolescence | 31 |
| American Sociological Review | 19 |
| British Journal of Criminology | 17 |
| Youth and Society | 16 |
| Criminology | 16 |
| American Journal of Sociology | 14 |
| Social Forces | 9 |
| Journal of Youth and Adolescence | 9 |
| Psychological Reports | 8 |
| Child Development | 8 |
| Social Problems | 7 |
| Journal of Negro Education | 7 |
| Journal of Social Psychology | 7 |
| Social Psychology Quarterly (Sociometry) | 6 |
| Journal of Genetic Psychology | 6 |
| Developmental Psychology | 6 |
| Journal of Social Issues | 6 |
| Sociological Quarterly | 6 |
| American Political Science Review | 5 |
| European Journal of Political Research | 5 |
| Social Science Quarterly | 5 |
| Sex Roles | 5 |
| Journal of Comparative Family Studies | 5 |
| Sociology and Social Research | 5 |

| | |
|---|---|
| Total Number of Different Journals | 175 |
| Total Number of Journal References | 508 |
| Mean Number of References per Journal | 2.9 |

## Using This Book

Each reference is numbered.  A brief annotation
is provided for over 95% of the references.  To
facilitate browsing, KEYWORDS are provided as
appropriate.  These KEYWORDS are not exhaustive,
but do include some of the frequently occurring
themes of research.  They are not a substitute for
the more extensive subject matter index.

Some KEYWORDS require explanation.  A number of
studies focus on theoretical issues or involve
particular theoretical issues.  KEYWORDS used to
identify these studies include: "identification,"
"interaction," "labeling," and "theory."
Theoretical issues are often covered in studies
with such KEYWORDS as: "historical," "perceptions,"
"reciprocal influence," and "social structure."

Several KEYWORDS are used for studies that cover
special conceptual distinctions.  These include:
"affect," "birth order," "divorce effects," "family
cohesion," "genetics," "generations," "mother-
father agreement," "mother vs. father," "peers vs.
parents," "perceptions," "power," "reciprocal
influence," "sex-specification," and "social
class."  Another set of conceptual distinctions
concern parental relations to the child including
"parental attachment," "control," "deprivation,"
"discipline," "involvement," "modeling," "rejection," "support," and "supervision."

"Cross-cultural" is a catch all for those studies that use data sets from outside of the United
States.  Some of these are truly cross-cultural
while others are cross-cultural only in the meaning
of not being done on a United States sample.
"Father absence" and "divorce effects" are used for
those studies that concern these important issues.
The term "historical" indicates a study uses data
that goes beyond the immediate context of the 1970s
and 1980s.  Only a few of these studies cover
issues that are more than a few decades old.  One
cannot read this literature without growing concerned with the ahistorical quality of most analysis.

Several publications are noteworthy because of their methods. Some of these have exemplary methodologies while others are about methodological issues facing those doing inter-generational research. Most of these use the KEYWORD, "methods," but some are more specific, using such terms as: "both parents" (if both are included), "cohort vs. lineage," "experiment," "longitudinal." Missing from the KEYWORDS, but included in the subject index is "measurement."

Some studies are noteworthy as reviews of the literature. These provide references to much of the literature from before 1975 as well as many studies we excluded from this book. These are noted by the KEYWORD "review." "Transmission" signifies that the study centers on the influence parents have on their children.

There are many substantive areas that are covered. Not all of these are included in the KEYWORDS, but many are obvious from the titles. The following substantive areas are included as KEYWORDS: "conformity," "discrimination," "economic deprivation" "education," "father absence," "political," "recidivism," "rehabilitation," "religion," "self-esteem," "sexual beliefs," "sex roles," "social problems," "sports," "status attainment," "values," "vocational interest," "work," and "rural."

The term "family background" is a catch all term for certain factors within the family that play a role in the socialization process and in the production of delinquent behavior. Many times this keyword is utilized when the authors do not refer to any of the other keywords but talk about the family background in general terms. Basically, the information provided is in reference to socio-demographic variables that are assumed to be related to research issues.

A single subject index is provided for the three sections combined. The numbers after each word in the index refer to the citations. This listing should be useful for systematic searches. The terms used in the index include the KEYWORDS, but also include many terms that are far more specific.

A single **author index** is also provided. This is particularly useful for locating work on which the individual is **not** the senior author.

## Division Into Three Sections

The publications are grouped into three sections, namely: Family Influence, Ethnicity, and Delinquency. The most general section is simply labeled Family Influence. It includes 344 references. The Ethnicity section is the most focused and, thereby limited. It has 181 references. Delinquency concerns the work that is particularly concerned with delinquency and has 271 citations.

While most readers may want to browse the entire listing of references, the division into sections will help those with specialized interests. The rationale for placement of individual publications in particular sections is subjective. We had to determine which references to place in the Ethnicity and Delinquency sections since they also concern Family Influence in general. Some placement decisions were obvious; others were more difficult. Thus, when the major thrust of the research was on a delinquency issue, the publication was placed in the delinquency section. When the major point concerned an ethnicity issue then the publication was placed in that section. All other publications went into the Family Influence section. A large number of papers involved a mixture of issues, such as, a study involving both delinquency and ethnicity issues, or, a study that has one section dealing with ethnicity, but does not have that as the major point of the publication. We hope the division will be helpful, but ultimately the reader will need to peruse all three sections.

CHAPTER TWO:

FAMILY INFLUENCE ON THE ADOLESCENT


From the mid-1980s it is possible to draw some
conclusions about the research on family factors
that influence youth. While there are several
detailed discussions of major research issues in
the bibliography that follows, we would like to
introduce it by noting a few of the topics we found
especially important. We begin with a discussion
of methodological concerns.


## Methodological Issues

The decade of research we present shows an
increasing sensitivity to methodological issues.
The research in this section shows considerable
progress in methodological design. Where early
research confused similarities between generations
with evidence of family influence or vice versa,
most contemporary research avoids such pitfalls.
Still, there are a number of methodological issues.

**Measurement.** A fundamental problem is inadequate measurement. If we are not able to measure
concepts with both reliability and validity, then
it is impossible to say much about family factors
that influence adolescents. While much of the
research in the 1970s relied on single item indicators of enormously complex concepts, more recent
research has used multiple indicators and paid
considerably more attention to issues of unidimen-
sionality, reliability, and validity. Most recent
studies routinely use such procedures as factor
analysis and report reliability coefficients. It
is unusual, however, to see much in the way of
assessing the validity of measures. Perhaps the
most promising technique to be used since about
1980 is LISREL which allows incorporation of random

measurement error into models and has the potential
for dealing with some non-random sources of error.
Dalton's (1980) publication in political science is
one of the earliest examples of this approach, but
use of the technique is becoming widespread. This
research indicates that some of the weak associations found between parental views and those of
their offspring are simply because we have measured
both sets of views with much error. By statis-
tically controlling this error, the estimates of
the intergenerational association are much stronger.

The timing of measurement is as much a problem
as the measurement itself. Typically family factors are measured at the time the child is already
an adolescent. Little information is gathered
about the attitudes and practices of the family
when the child was younger. For example, a mother
who was not religious when her son was four years
old may have become more religious when the son was
an adolescent. If the adolescent son does not
report being very religious is this continuity in
terms of what was taught in his early childhood
years? Is it discontinuity with the mother's
current religiosity? This is a most perplexing
issue. The lack of longitudinal data makes it
impossible for existing research to provide a
trustworthy answer.

**Representative Samples.** Next to measurement,
obtaining representative samples provides the most
serious barrier to adequate research. This is an
area where progress is being made, but the work is
still grossly inadequate. Many early studies used
questionnaires that were mailed to a single parent
of a convenience sample of college students. Some
early studies even used samples of unrelated parents and children. Compared to such samples, great
progress has been made. Still, there is a litany
of remaining sampling problems.

Most samples restrict the ability to generalize
findings. Much of the work of Bengtson and his
associates has been based on a three generation
sample. When we limit ourselves to families for
which we can obtain responses from each generation,
we have eliminated a large proportion of the popu-

lation.   Such families are be more homogeneous,
more traditional, less mobile, and have a family
proclivity to return completed questionnaires.
Under represented by this process are families with
several divorces, poor inter-generational
relations, and members who do not like to complete
questionnaires.   Also under-represented are poor
and minority families.

It is difficult to exaggerate the problem of low
response rate in sample designs involving several
related individuals.   The unit of analysis is not
the individual but the intergenerational family
unit.   While modern sampling strategies can produce
response rates of 70% or more on individuals, this
is virtually impossible when the primary unit of
analysis requires the simultaneous completion of
questionnaires by three family members (child-
mother-father).   Add the responses of siblings,
teachers, peers, and others, the response rate
becomes extremely low.   To illustrate this, consider the responses of three individuals to be
independent.   If the study has a response rate of
70% for individuals, the response rate for triads
will be 34%.

To make matters worse, there is no reason to
think the responses are independent.   If the responses were independent, the probability of a
daughter answering would be the same whether or not
either or both of her parents answered the ques-
tionnaire.   While there is no systematic research
on this, we assume that such probabilities are
highly dependent.

**Use of Mailed Questionnaires.**   A common method
of collecting data is mailed questionnaires.   When
doing this, it is impossible to insure family
members do not share their answers with each other.
Asking a child to estimate how his or her mother
would answer a question is likely to get the child
to ask her.   Having the mother and father complete
questions about their own relationship may produce
different results if they do this together than if
they answer them independently.

Those using mailed questionnaires usually mini-
mize such confounding of results by instructing
individuals to answer their questionnaires alone
and admonishing them not to share their answers
with other family members.  We know little about
how effective such instructions are.  Researchers
who make separate mailings and have separate return
envelopes are taking steps in the right direction,
but even these measures are limited.

The cost of face-to-face interviews make them
impractical for intergenerational research.  This
is especially true for young adult children who may
live great distances from their parents.  Telephone
surveys may be the best solution to the problem of
answers being confounded.  We suspect that telephone surveys will become much more common in the
future research on intergenerational relations.

**Unstable Families.**  Problems with including
unstable families are enormous.  Most researchers
take the simple way out by restricting their sample
to intact families.  This is not a problem for
their studies so long as they recognize this re-
striction on the population to which they seek to
generalize.  However, as a collective endeavor the
cumulative impact of these individual decisions is
that little is known about unstable families.
This is an increasingly serious qualification as we
have more and more unstable and single parent
families.  How much influence does a biological
father have as opposed to a step-father?  What
happens in single parent households?  What allows
step-parents to have a maximum influence?  We have
drawn attention to work done with unstable families
by using the KEYWORD "Divorce," but much more work
is needed.  There is, of course, a huge body of
literature on children of divorced families compared to children of intact families.  Most of this
has not been included because it either focuses on
young children or it does not deal with the
influence process explicitly.

**Reciprocal Influence.**  An always present methodological issue is the direction of influence.  Most
causal models are recursive, allowing parents to
influence children but not the reverse.  But--Do
children influence parents?  This seems like a

given to most parents of adolescents. Surprisingly,
most research we cover assumes that the influence
is all going in one direction--parent to child.  We
made a special effort to include research suggesting that the influence goes both ways.  We report
19 studies that deal with reciprocal influence in
an explicit fashion.  While this number of studies
suggests the importance of this, these studies are
extremely disappointing.  They tend to be
advocating reciprocal influence rather than esti-
mating it or explaining it.  Certainly, this area
needs more empirical research.

These comments only touch on the methodological
issues that are problematic.  The index to this
section provides nearly fifty references which are
important in terms of these issues (see methods in
the index).

## The Missing Great Gap

By focusing on publications since 1975, this
bibliography largely bypasses the earlier research
that concerned itself with the issue of the Great
Generation Gap.  The pioneering work of Kinsley
Davis (1940) argued that parents and adolescent
youth were experiencing an ever widening isolation
from one another.  Much later, Margret Mead (1978)
concerned herself with the worldwide change
brought on by the realization of the ever present
potential for nuclear disaster.  She saw this as
producing a chasm between generations.  This chasm
erupted after WWII dividing all generations that
were raised prior to WWII from all that were born
after it.

A little of this Great Gap debate appears in our
bibliography of recent work, but neither the advocates nor the debunkers of the Great Gap receive
much attention.  The notion of a unitary Great Gap
is replaced by careful efforts to find issues that
involve either a great deal of change or relative
continuity.

## Mother vs. Father

A considerable effort has been given to the role of the mother as compared to the role of the father in the socialization of adolescents. Some of this responds to the instrumental-expressive distinction through which mothers are "supposed" to be specialist in expressive and supportive aspects while fathers link the adolescent with the larger institutions of society (work, government, education).

A related issue in the mother versus father comparisons concerns the concept of identification. This position suggests that adolescent youth identify with the same sex parent regardless of the question involved. Thus, daughters are expected to be most influenced by their mother's attitudes and sons most influenced by the attitudes of their father.

In contrast to these two theoretical predictions is the consistent conclusion in empirical research that mothers are the most important factor in family influence. This seems to be true regardless of the area being investigated—religion, work, feelings, etc. It is also clear that this dominance continues even when the mother is employed.

It appears that the arguments for the father having a substantial role in socialization are more image than reality. Some maintain that the importance of the father in the family will continue to decline so long as their non-monetary participation in its day to day activities are trivial. Perhaps the re-emergence of fathers who are involved in home related activities and do interact regularly with children will modify these results.

## Perceived and Actual Opinions

Over the ten years of research we have inventoried, there has been a renewed interest in perceived attitudes as opposed to actual attitudes. Part of this may be little more than a ruse for a

failure to measure both parents and children. That
is not our interest at this point. Research that
compares perceptions and actual attitudes as stated
by family members has shown that perceptions are
very important. Symbolic interactionist, from
Cooley to the present will hardly be surprised that
families influence members largely in terms of
perceptions. Our actual opinions have little
impact unless they are accurately perceived.

This says a great deal about the importance of
communication. Perhaps, the limited influence of
fathers is that they spend too little time on
communication with family members. It is not
enough to be hard working, highly motivated, very
religious, and politically responsible. If other
family members are not certain that these are one's
beliefs and behaviors, then they are not influen-
tial. More cynically, parents can be poor workers,
unethical, and politically irresponsible and still
influence their children to be the opposite if the
parents can instill perceptions to the contrary.
Either way, perceptions, and their communication,
are the keys to family members influencing one
another.

While the perceptions are highly predictive,
there is another explanation of this that has
received little attention. Cognitive consistency
theories argue that we will perceive (or misper-
ceive) those we like as similar to ourselves in
attitudes and beliefs. Thus, a child's perceptions
may be the best predictor of the child's attitude
solely because the child misperceives the parents
to agree with him or her. It has not been possible
to disentangle the symbolic interactionist explanation and the cognitive consistency explanation.

One final area about perceptions is that the
children perceive both parents as having the same
attitudes, even when they do not. In fact, the
correlations reported between the attitudes of
mothers and fathers are not much higher than those
between either parent and his or her children.

## Substantive Content Areas

It is beyond the scope of this summary section to review the findings for the various content areas. It is evident that researchers on how families influence each other across generations have examined a wide variety of topics. While we will not review each of these topics, it is likely that many readers will have concerns with only one or a few special areas of influence.

There are several areas that are extensively examined. Affection, liking and love are topics considered in over 50 of the publications listed in this section. The effects of divorce receives considerable interest and there are 35 studies reported here on that issue. Self-esteem of adolescents is a topic of a great deal of work. Nearly forty of the publications are concerned with family factors that influence the level of self-esteem of adolescents and young adults. A number of these studies examine the role of parental support as opposed to parental control.

The aging literature shows considerable interest in the research using three generation families. This focuses on the role of grandparents in dealing with their grandchildren as well as parents as mediators in this process.

A great deal of work has to do with major institutions. There are over 60 studies dealing with political socialization. Over 30 of the studies concern religion in terms of beliefs, practice, and membership. One of the most frequently researched areas is education. While we have not included a great deal of the status attainment literature that is certainly relevant to education, we have included over 30 studies that consider family factors influencing education of adolescent and young adult children.

Along these same lines, a lot of work is done on work and occupations. We include studies of family influence on occupational achievement, aspirations, mobility, status, and orientations toward work.

There is also a large group of researchers
concerned with significant social issues. Sex
roles and changes in sex roles is emphasized by
over 40 studies. Interestingly, a lot of this work
focuses on a particular dyad, namely the mother-
daughter dyad (nearly 30 studies) while there is
much less attention given to the father-son dyad.

Quite a bit of the research concerns the general
area of social problems. This body of research
covers a wide variety of topics from smoking
behavior to pregnancy risk. Some of these studies
are indexed in terms of the particular issue, but a
lot of them are simply indexed under the title of
social problems.

One area that needs a great deal more attention
is the relationship between the parents. A great
deal more similarity is attributed to parents than
is actual the case (Acock and Bengtson, 1980). We
reference 13 studies that consider mother-father
agreement. Along with these there are problems of
mother-father relations, parental conflict, and
parental power.

While there is a large body of work done on
college students and their parents, there is much
less done on other groups. In particular, the
blue-collar families have been largely ignored.
Receiving some attention has been rural families,
but even here there are only seven publications.
Future research needs to examine family factors as
they vary across different segments of society.

### Some of the Major Scholars

It is beyond the scope of this project to
identify the key scholars working in this area. A
simple counting of the number of publications
included can be very misleading. For example,
Reuben Hill appears only four times but his work
prior to 1975 was pioneering. Moreover, a simple
counting can be misleading because a lot of routine
articles are less important than a smaller amount
of work that is pivotal. Additionally, a counting
is biased by our own research interest and
disciplinary blinders. Finally, even a slight

change in our focus would result in some dramatic
shifts.  For example, we only include four of
Melvin L. Kohn's references.

Given all of these limitations, we will not
attempt to identify the major figures.  A brief
scanning of the Index of Authors will clearly
identify those who are most prolific.  It is inter-
esting that the most prolific researchers come from
a variety of fields.  For example, Vern L. Bengtson
is a sociologist specializing in the life cycle
while M. Kent Jennings and Richard G. Niemi are
political scientists.  Thomas S. Parish is a
psychologist while Gary W. Peterson is in family
studies.

## REFERENCES: FAMILY INFLUENCE

1. Abrams, Philip. **Historical Sociology.**
   Ithaca: Cornell University Press, 1982,
   pp. 227-66.

   A review of the concept of generation.
   Includes a detailed historical analysis of
   how the concept has been used.

   KEYWORDS: cross-cultural, generations,
   historical, political, review, values

2. Abramson, Paul R. **Generational Change in
   American Politics.** Lexington, Mass.:
   Lexington Books, D.C. Heath, 1975.

   An analysis of age-group differences and
   their effect on changing class composition
   of the Democratic presidential coalition.
   Also examines the declining strength of
   party identification resulting from generational change.

   KEYWORDS: generations, political, social
   class, values

3. ————. "Generational Change and the Decline
   of Party Identification in America: 1952-
   1974." **American Political Science Review**
   70(1976):469-78.

   An analysis of the decline of party loyal-
   ties after WWII. Emphasis is on a cohort
   rather than life-cycle explanation. Shows
   little evidence of family influence.

   KEYWORDS: cohort vs. lineage, generations,
   historical, political

4.   ———. "Developing Party Identification:   A
     Further Examination of Life-Cycle, Genera-
     tional, and Period Effects."  **American
     Journal of Political Science** 23(1979):78-
     96.

     Supports cohort effects over life-cycle
     explanations of changes in partisanship.

     KEYWORDS:  blacks, cohort vs. lineage,
     generations, longitudinal, political


5.   Acock, Alan C.   "Progress in the Study of
     Generations."   **Sociology and Social Re-
     search** 69(1984):151-71.

     A review of the literature on intergenera-
     tional influence.   Covers theoretical,
     definitional, and methodological issues.

     KEYWORDS:  both parents, generations,
     methods, review, theory, transmission


6.   Acock, Alan C., Deborah Barker, and Vern
     Bengtson.   "Mother's Work and Parental
     Influence on Post Adolescent Children."
     **Journal of Marriage and the Family** 44
     (1982):441-55.

     Analyzes the effect of maternal employment
     on the relative influence mothers and
     fathers have on post-adolescent children.
     Finds that mothers who work in low status
     positions have significantly less influence
     than other categories of mother.

     KEYWORDS:  both parents, methods, mother
     vs. father, religion, sex-specification,
     sexual beliefs, social class, social prob-
     lems, transmission, work

7.  Acock, Alan C. and Vern L. Bengtson. "On the
    Relative Influence of Mothers and Fathers:
    A Covariance Analysis of Political and
    Religious Socialization." **Journal of
    Marriage and the Family** 40(1978):519-30.

    Authors find that mothers have more in-
    fluence across a broad range of political
    and social attitudes and beliefs than do
    fathers.

    KEYWORDS:  both parents, cohort vs.
    lineage, methods, political, religion, sex-
    specification, sexual beliefs, social
    problems, transmission, work


8.  ————. "Socialization and Attribution
    Processes:  Actual Versus Perceived Simi-
    larity Among Parents and Youth." **Journal
    of Marriage and the Family** 42(1980):501-
    15.

    Study finds that the attitudes post-adoles-
    cent children attribute to their parents
    are better predictors of the children's own
    attitudes than are the actual opinions of
    parents.  Children attribute far more
    similarity to parents than is actually the
    case.  Mothers more influential than
    fathers across a wide range of attitudes
    and beliefs.  The attitudes that children
    attribute to their parents tend to exag-
    gerate the actual generation gap.

    KEYWORDS:  both parents, cohort vs.
    lineage, methods, mother vs. father,
    perceptions, religion, sex-specification,
    sexual beliefs, social problems, transmis-
    sion, work


9.  Acock, Alan C. and Melvin L. DeFleur.  "A
    Configurational Approach to Contingent
    Consistency in the Attitude-Behavior Rela-
    tionship." **American Sociological Review** 37
    (1972):714-26.

An experiment showing that the correspondence between the attitudes and behaviors
of post-adolescents is contingent on their
perceptions of peers and parents.  Consistency between peers, parents, and self
attitudes results in highly accurate predictions of behavior.

KEYWORDS:  experiment, peers vs. parents,
perceptions, social problems

10.   Acock, Alan C. and Theodore Fuller.  "The
      Attitude-Behavior Relationship and Parental
      Influence:  Circular Mobility in Thailand."
      **Social Forces** 62(1984):973-94.

      Shows very little transmission of attitude
      toward mobility in Thailand.  Parental
      views are irrelevant in the context of this
      developing nation.

      KEYWORDS:  cross-cultural, generations,
      longitudinal, methods, stability, transmis-
      sion

11.   Acock, Alan C. and Wen S. Yang.  "Parental
      Power and Adolescents' Identification."
      **Journal of Marriage and the Family** 46
      (1984):487-95.

      Daughters identify with mothers and through
      her indirectly with their fathers; sons
      identify with father and indirectly through
      him with their mothers.  Power variables
      are only modest predictors of the identi-
      fication of either sons or daughters with
      either parent.

      KEYWORDS:  identification, methods, mother
      vs. father, perceptions, power, sex-
      specification

12.  Adamski, Wladyslaw W.  "The Life Orientations
     of the Younger and Older Generations of
     Poles."  **International Journal of Political
     Education** 3(1980):255-69.

     Survey of 17-30-year-old employees and 45-
     plus employees in Poland shows younger
     generation displaying more open and innova-
     tive life attitude.

     KEYWORDS:  cohort vs. lineage, cross-cul-
     tural, generations, values


13.  Aldous, Joan and Reuben Hill.  "Social Cohe-
     sion, Lineage Type, and Intergenerational
     Transmission."  **Social Forces** 43(1965):
     471-82.

     Classic study presenting evidence that
     cultural transmission through the family is
     greater in same-sex than cross-sex dyads.
     Utilizes three generation data set.

     KEYWORDS:  affect, both parents, mother vs.
     father, same sex parents, sex-specifica-
     tion, transmission


14.  Allerbeck, K.R., M. Kent Jennings, and L.
     Rosenmayr.  "Generations and Families:
     Political Action."  **Political Action**.
     Edited by S.H. Barnes and M. Kaase, et al.
     Beverly Hills, Calif.:  Sage, 1979, pp.
     487-522.

     Examines eight nation data (U.S. and seven
     liberal democracies in Europe).  Finds
     consistent support for an important family
     role in socialization.  Addresses a variety
     of political attitudes and concerns itself
     with such issues as generation gap, lineage
     effects, and affect for parents versus
     affect for peers.

KEYWORDS: affect, cohort vs. lineage,
cross-cultural, generations, peers vs.
parents, perceptions, political, transmission, values

15. Alwin, Duane F. and Arland Thornton. "Family
    Origins and the Schooling Process: Early
    Versus Late Influence of Parental
    Characteristics." **American Sociological
    Review** 49(1984):784-802.

    Using an 18-year longitudinal study of
    families and children, this study relates
    parental socioeconomic characteristics to
    school achievement. Both parental socio-
    economic characteristics and family size
    are related to achievement level.

    KEYWORDS: education, longitudinal,
    methods, social class, social structure,
    status attainment

16. Amato, Paul R. and Gay Ochiltree. "Family
    Resources and the Development of Child
    Competence." **Journal of Marriage and the
    Family** 48(1986): in press.

17. Andersen, Kristi. **The Creation of a Demo-
    cratic Majority 1928-36.** Chicago: Univer-
    sity of Chicago Press, 1979.

    Chapter Five discusses how parents fail to
    present partisan cues to their children.

    KEYWORDS: historical, perceptions, politi-
    cal

18. Anthony, E.J. "Children at Risk from Di-
    vorce: A Review." **The Child in His Fam-
    ily: Children at Psychiatric Risk,** Vol. 3.
    Edited by E.J. Anthony. New York: Wiley,
    1974, pp. 461-77.

Review of effects of divorce. Notes that
children's attitudes toward marriage are
affected by divorce and they are less
confident in their own ability to have a
successful marriage.

KEYWORDS:  divorce effects, review

19.  Antonucci, Toni C., Nancy Gillett, and
     Frances W. Hoyer.  "Values and Self-Esteem
     in Three Generations of Men and Women."
     **Journal of Gerontology** 34(1979):415-22.

     Small availability sample from three gener-
     ations is used to compare terminal values
     of three generations and examine the role
     of self-esteem.

     KEYWORDS:  affect, grandparents, same sex
     parents, self-esteem, transmission

20.  Armsden, Gay G. and Mark T. Greenberg.  "The
     Inventory of Parent and Peer Attachment:
     Individual Differences and Their Relation-
     ship to Psychological Well-Being in Adoles-
     cence."  Unpublished Manuscript.  Depart-
     ment of Psychology, University of Washing-
     ton, Seattle, 1986.

     Develops a measure of parent and peer
     attachment.  This is related to self-es-
     teem, life-satisfaction, and affective
     status.

     KEYWORDS:  affect, methods, peers vs.
     parents, self-esteem

21.  Aron, Arthur, Rosanne Ain, Jo Ann Anderson,
     Hilary Burd, Gail Filman, Rich McCallum,
     Elaine O'Reilly, Ava Rose, Lawrence
     Stichman, Zippora Tamari, John Wawro, Linda
     Weinberg, and Joan Winesauker.  "Relation-
     ships with Opposite-Sexed Parents and Mate
     Choice."  **Human Relations** 27(1974):17-24.

Study indicates that the mother is most
important for both sons and daughters in
terms of mate selection. This is at odds
with the psychoanalytic theory prediction
that sons seek a wife like their mother and
daughters seek a husband like their father.

KEYWORDS: mother vs. father, perceptions,
sex-specification, theory, transmission

22. Backman, Jerald G., Patrick M. O'Malley, and
    Jerome Johnston. **Youth in Transition:
    Adolescence to Adulthood, Change and Sta-
    bility in the Lives of Young Men**, Vol. 6.
    Ann Arbor, Mich.: Institute for Social
    Research, 1978.

    A longitudinal study of young men conducted
    by the Survey Research Center. Emphasis is
    on education and occupation. This volume
    focuses on adolescence.

    KEYWORDS: affect, education, longitudinal,
    social problems, status attainment, values,
    vocational interest, work

23. Bacon, Carolyn and Richard M. Lerner. "Ef-
    fects of Maternal Employment Status on the
    Development of Vocational-Role Perceptions
    in Females." **Journal of Genetic Psychology**
    126(1975):187-93.

    Study shows that daughters of working
    mothers see more occupations as open to
    both sexes than do daughters whose mothers
    do not work outside of the home.

    KEYWORDS: mother-daughter, sex roles,
    vocational interest, work

24. Baltes, P.B., S.W. Cornelius and J.R.
    Nesselroade. "Cohort Effects in Develop-
    mental Psychology." **Longitudinal Research**

in the Study of Behavior and Development.
Edited by J.R. Nesselroade and P.B. Baltes.
New York: Academic Press, 1979, pp. 61-87.

Reviews theory and methods surrounding the
concept of cohort as it is used in developmental psychology.

KEYWORDS: cohort vs. lineage, generations,
historical, longitudinal, methods, social
structure, theory, values

25.  Baranowski, Marc D.  "Adolescents' Attempted
     Influence on Parental Behaviors."  **Adoles-
     cence** 13(1978):585-604.

     Small sample used to show that adolescents
     attempt to influence their parents.  More
     influence attempts are directed toward the
     mother than toward the father.

     KEYWORDS: both parents, mother vs. father,
     perceptions, reciprocal influence

26.  ———.  "Grandparent-Adolescent Relations:
     Beyond the Nuclear Family."  **Adolescence** 17
     (1982):575-584.

     Reviews research on role of grandparents in
     adolescent socialization and the factors
     that influence the quality of the relation-
     ship between adolescents and grandparents.

     KEYWORDS: affect, grandparents, review

27.  Barnes, Grace M., Michael P. Farrell, and
     Allen Cairns.  "Parental Socialization
     Factors and Adolescent Drinking Behaviors."
     **Journal of Marriage and the Family** 48
     (1986): in press.

     KEYWORDS: affect, both parents, alcohol

28.  Barnes, S.H., and M. Kaase, et al. **Political
     Action.** Beverly Hills, Calif.: Sage,
     1979.

     Describes a major study involving surveys
     in eight different nations including the
     United States and seven European countries.
     Survey includes a subsample of a single
     parent and his or her child in which the
     children are pre-adults. Survey focuses on
     political issues but includes a wide var-
     iety of scales. This is a major data set
     which can be obtained from the Survey
     Research Center at Michigan.
     KEYWORDS: cross-cultural, education,
     generations, historical, political,
     religion, social class, social structure,
     theory, transmission, values

29.  Baumrind, D. "New Directions in Socializa-
     tion Research." **American Psychologist** 35
     (1980):639-52.

     Examines the need for a feminist approach
     to socialization. Specific concern is with
     reproduction of gender related
     insufficiencies by the organizational
     asymmetry of family structure. This is
     because children of both sexes are raised
     by their mother. Also criticizes "positi-
     vistic" methods.

     KEYWORDS: both parents, child rearing,
     interaction, methods, mother vs. father,
     reciprocal influence, review, sex roles,
     transmission

30.  Beck, P.A. and M.K. Jennings. "Parents as
     'Middlepersons' in Political Socializa-
     tion." **Journal of Politics** 37(1975):83-
     107.

     An examination of the role of the parents
     in political socialization that
     incorporates such issues as the consensus

of the parents, the comparison of the
mother's and father's relative influence,
and genotypic versus phenotypic continuity.

KEYWORDS: both parents, mother vs. father,
mother-father agreement, both parents,
political, theory, transmission

31.  Becker, George.  "The Wandervogel Movement:
     A Challenge to the Generational Conflict
     Model."  **Conflict and Consensus:  A
     Festschrift in Honor of Lewis A. Coser.**
     Edited by Walter W. Powell and Richard
     Robbins.  New York:  Free Press, 1984, pp.
     71-94.

     Reviews theory and literature on concept of
     generation in a cross-cultural context.
     Identifies the relationship of stratum-
     specific interests to the development of
     youth movement with conservative and lib-
     eral orientations.

     KEYWORDS:  cross-cultural, generations,
     political, review, theory

32.  Bell, Richard Q.  "A Reinterpretation of the
     Direction of Effects in Studies of Sociali-
     zation."  **Psychological Review** 75(1968):81-
     95.

     Classic statement of argument that rela-
     tionship is reciprocal with the child
     influencing the parent.  Notes that a
     correlation does not demonstrate the
     direction of the effect.

     KEYWORDS:  methods, reciprocal influence,
     transmission

33.  Bell, Richard Q. and L.V. Harper.  **Child
     Effects on Adults.**  Hillsdale, N.J.: Law-
     rence Erlbaum Associates, 1977.

States how children influence their
parents. Although this focuses on the
influence of very young children on their
parents, it is important in that it re-
verses the usual intergenerational analysis
in which the direction of influence is
assumed to be coming only from the parents.

KEYWORDS: child rearing, cross-cultural,
experiment, historical, reciprocal
influence, review, theory, values

34.    Bengtson, Vern L.  "Generation and Family
       Effects in Value Socialization."  **American
       Sociological Review** 40(1975):358-71.

       Compares cohort and lineage influences in
       the shaping of core values based on a data
       set of three generations of related indi-
       viduals (Total N = 2,044).

       KEYWORDS: cohort vs. lineage, generations,
       transmission, values

35.    Bengtson, Vern L. and Neal Cutler.  "Genera-
       tions and Intergenerational Relations:
       Perspectives on Age Groups and Social
       Change."  **Handbook on Aging and the Social
       Sciences.**  Edited by Robert H. Binstock and
       Ethel Shanas.  New York:  Van Nostrand,
       1976, pp. 79-145.

36.    Bengtson, Vern L., Neal E. Cutler, David J.
       Mangen, and Victor W. Marshall.  "Genera-
       tions, Cohorts, and Relations Between Age
       Groups."  **Handbook of Aging and the Social
       Sciences.**  Edited by R. Binstock and E.
       Shanas.  New York:  Van Nostrand, 1985, pp.
       304-33.

       Although this is directed toward relations
       among older segments of the population, it
       provides an extensive review of the litera-
       ture and issues as well as methodological
       and theoretical concerns.

KEYWORDS:  affect, age of parent, cohort
vs. lineage, generations, historical,
interaction, longitudinal, methods, political, reciprocal influence, review, social
class, social problems, social structure,
theory, transmission, values

37.  Bengtson, Vern L. and J.A. Kuypers.  "Genera-
     tional Differences and the 'Developmental
     Stake.'"  **Aging and Human Development** 2
     (1971):249-60.
     Classic statement of how generational
     differences in perceptions are a function
     of each generation's developmental stake.

     KEYWORDS:  generations, theory

38.  Bengtson, Vern L. and Robert S. Laufer.  **The
     Journal of Social Issues** 30(1974). Special
     Issue on Youth, Generations, and Social
     Change.

     This is a special issue of the journal that
     includes articles on generations and
     emergent life styles.

     KEYWORDS:  generations, rural, sexual
     beliefs, social problems, theory, transmis-
     sion

39.  Bengtson, Vern L., David J. Mangen, and
     Pierre H. Landry, Jr.  "The Multi-Genera-
     tion Family:  Concepts and Findings."
     **Intergenerational Relationships.**  Edited by
     V. Garms-Homolova, E.M. Hoerning, and D.
     Schaefer.  New York:  C.J. Hogrefe, 1984,
     pp. 63-79.

     Outlines a model of intergenerational
     solidarity within families and reviews
     findings from several U.S. surveys.

     KEYWORDS:  affect, cohort vs. lineage,
     generations, methods, review, theory,
     transmission, values

40.   Bengtson, Vern L., E. Olander, and E. Haddad.
      "The 'Generation Gap' and Aging Family
      Members:  Toward a Conceptual Model."
      **Time, Roles and Self In Old Age.**  Edited by
      J.F. Gubrium.  New York:  Human Sciences
      Press, 1976, pp. 237-63.


41.   Bengtson, Vern L. and J.M. Starr.  "Contrast
      and Consensus:  A Generational Analysis of
      Youth in the 1970s."  **Youth:  The Seventy-
      Fourth Yearbook of the National Society for
      the Study of Education** (Part 1).  Edited by
      R.J. Havighurst and P.H. Dreyer.  Chicago:
      University of Chicago Press, 1975, pp. 224-
      66.

      Reviews literature on issues concerning age
      groups, religion, sex roles, and work as a
      way of discussing generational differences
      during the 1970s.

      KEYWORDS:  cohort vs. lineage, generations,
      historical, religion, review, sex roles,
      values, work


42.   Bengtson, Vern L. and Lillian E. Troll.
      "Youth and Their Parents:  Feedback and
      Intergenerational Influence in Socializa-
      tion."  **Child Influence in Marital and
      Family Interaction.**  Edited by R.M. Lerner
      and G.B. Spanier.  New York:  Academic
      Press, 1978, pp. 215-40.

      Reviews theory and research on the degree
      of the generation gap and the direction of
      the influence, i.e., parent to child vs.
      child to parent.

      KEYWORDS:  generations, methods, percep-
      tions, reciprocal influence, review,
      theory, values

43.  Bernard, J.  "Adolescence and Socialization
     for Motherhood."  **Adolescence in the Life
     Cycle.**  Edited by S.E. Dragastin and G.H.
     Elder, Jr.  Washington, D.C.: Hemisphere
     Publishing, 1975, pp. 79-95.


44.  Bielby, D.  "Maternal Employment and Socio-
     economic Status as Factors in Daughters'
     Career Salience:  Some Substantive Refine-
     ments."  **Sex Roles** 4(1978):249-65.
     A study of the effects of maternal employ-
     ment on career salience of adult daughters
     under 30 years of age.

     KEYWORDS:  education, mother-daughter,
     social class, status attainment, transmis-
     sion, values, vocational interest, work


45.  Biller, H.B. and A. Davis.  "Parent-Child
     Relations, Personality Development and
     Psychopathology."  **Issues in Abnormal Child
     Psychology.**  Edited by A. Davids.  Belmont,
     Calif.: Brooks/Cole, 1973, pp. 48-77.

     Review of theory and research on parent-
     child relations.  Covers specific dyad
     relationships.

     KEYWORDS:  affect, child rearing, inter-
     action, review, sex specification, theory


46.  Booth, Alan, David B. Brinkerhoff, Lynn K.
     White.  "The Impact of Parental Divorce on
     Courtship."  **Journal of Marriage and the
     Family** 46(1984):85-94.

     Based on sample of 2538 college students,
     this study examines the quality of parent-
     child relations and parental conflict
     before and after the divorce as they relate
     to courtship.  Parental divorce increases
     courtship activity, especially if there was
     great acrimony between parents and a deter-
     ioration of parent-child interaction.
     Little evidence of sex differences.

KEYWORDS: affect, both parents, divorce effects, interaction, perceptions, sex-specification


47. Booth, Alan and David R. Johnson. "Tracking Respondents in a Telephone Interview Panel Selected by Random Digit Dialing." **Sociological Methods and Research** 14(1985):53-64.
Presents results of a three-year panel that used random digit dialing samples. Contends that results can be comparable to traditional sampling methods.

KEYWORDS: longitudinal, methods


48. Boyd, Donald A., Gerald D. Nunn, and Thomas S. Parish. "Effects of Marital Status and Parents' Marital Status on Evaluation of Self and Parents." **The Journal of Social Psychology** 119(1983):229-34.

A survey of 980 college students reveals that children from broken homes rate themselves and both parents less favorably than children from intact homes.

KEYWORDS: affect, both parents, divorce effects, father absence, perceptions, self-esteem


49. Boyd, Donald A., and Thomas Parish. "An Investigation of Father Loss and College Students' Androgyny Scores." **The Journal of Genetic Psychology** 145(1984):279-80.

A survey of 130 college students indicates that males who lost fathers through divorce are more masculine and less feminine than males from either intact families or families in which the father has died.

KEYWORDS: divorce effects, father absence, sex roles

50.  Brofenbrenner, U.  **The Ecology of Human Development.**  Cambridge, Mass:  Harvard University Press, 1976.


51.  Brofenbrenner, U., and A.C. Crouter.  "Work and Family Through Time and Space."  **Families that Work:  Children in a Changing World.**  Edited by S. Kamerman and C. Hayes. Washington, D.C.:  National Academy of Sciences, 1982, pp. 39-83.

     This is a systematic review of the influence of work on family socialization. It deals with the enormous literature on the father's work role and the family as well as the developing literature on the influence of the mother's work role on the family.  It has a substantial bibliography on the relationship between work roles of both parents and child rearing.  Includes many references to work done prior to 1975.

     KEYWORDS:  both parents, child rearing, education, interaction, mother-daughter, review, social class, social structure, status attainment, theory, transmission, values, vocational interest, work


52.  Brook, Judith S., David Brook, Martin Whiteman, and Ann Gordon.  "Depressive Mood in Male College Students:  Father-Son Interactional Patterns."  **Archives of General Psychiatry** 40(1983):665-69.

     Based on a sample of 246 male college students, this paper reports that father's personality attributes and socialization techniques are related to his son's personality, which, in turn, influences his son's depressive mood.

     KEYWORDS:  child rearing, self-esteem, social problems, transmission

53.  Bumpass, L.L., and R.R. Rindfuss.  "Children's
     Experience of Marital Disruption."  **Ameri-
     can Journal of Sociology** 85(1979):46-65.

     Study uses life-table procedures to esti-
     mate the probability that a child will
     experience divorce prior to completing
     adolescence.

     KEYWORDS:  divorce effects, methods


54.  Burgess, Robert L., and Lise M. Youngblade.
     "Social Incompetence and the Intergenera-
     tional Transmission of Abusive Parental
     Practices."  Unpublished manuscript,
     Department of Individual and Family
     Studies, Pennsylvania State University,
     1986.

     This paper examines a process model of how
     child maltreatment will be repeated in one
     generation after another.  It provides an
     extensive literature review.

     KEYWORDS:  affect, child rearing, inter-
     action, parental support, peers vs. par-
     ents, power, review, self-esteem, social
     problems, theory, transmission


55.  Burke, Ronald J., and Tamara Weir.  "Benefits
     to Adolescents of Informal Helping Rela-
     tionships with Parents and Peers."  **Psycho-
     logical Reports** 42(1978):1175-84.

     Data from high school students shows that
     perceptions of support and help from par-
     ents aid the well-being the students re-
     port, controlling for levels of stress
     experienced.

     KEYWORDS:  affect, self-esteem

56.  ———.  "Helping Responses of Parents and
     Peers and Adolescent Well-Being."  **Journal
     of Psychology** 102(1979):49-62.

     Comparison of mothers, fathers, and peers
     on several aspects of well-being among a
     sample of 274 adolescents.  Concludes that
     emotional support by parents is very impor-
     tant to adolescent well-being.

     KEYWORDS:  affect, both parents,
     interaction, peers vs. parents, percep-
     tions, self-esteem


57.  Burlin, Francis-Dee.  "The Relationship of
     Parental Education and Maternal Work and
     Occupational Status to Occupational Aspira-
     tion in Adolescent Females."  **Journal of
     Vocational Behavior** 9(1976):99-104.

     Study of adolescent females finds that
     aspirations for non-traditional occupations
     are associated with father's education and
     mother's occupational status.

     KEYWORDS:  both parents, education, mother-
     daughter, sex roles, status attainment,
     vocational interest, work


58.  Bytheway, Bill.  "Problems of Representation
     in 'The Three Generation Family Study.'"
     **Journal of Marriage and the Family** 39
     (1977):243-50.

     A methodological critique of the
     Minneapolis Three Generation Family Study.
     Focuses on problem of selecting cases.
     Sample used was far more homogeneous than a
     representative sample would be because of
     the way subjects were selected.  This
     criticism applies to the majority of
     studies of parent child influence.

     KEYWORDS:  methods

59.   Cicirelli, Victor G.   "A Comparison of Col-
      lege Women's Feelings Toward Their Siblings
      and Parents."   **Journal of Marriage and the
      Family** 42(1980):111-118.

      A study of 100 college women found them to
      have as strong or stronger feelings for
      siblings as for mother and both mothers and
      siblings were stronger than father.  They
      looked to the mothers for help and advice
      more than to either the fathers or the
      siblings.

      KEYWORDS:  affect, both parents, mother vs.
      father, peer vs. parents

60.   Clausen, John A., Paul H. Mussen, and Joseph
      Kuypers.   "Involvement, Warmth, and Parent-
      Child Resemblances in Three Generations."
      **Present and Past in Middle Life.**   Edited by
      Dorothy H. Eichorn, John A. Clausen, Norma
      Haan, Marjorie P. Honzik, and Paul H.
      Mussen.  New York:  Academic Press, 1981,
      pp. 299-319.

      Comparison of middle-aged children and
      their parents to middle-aged children and
      their own children in terms of similar-
      ities.  Study finds greater personality
      resemblances between adolescents and their
      parents.  Same-sex dyads are more alike
      than opposite sex dyads.  Greater affect
      toward parents and interaction are
      associated with the child's acquisition of
      personality characteristics similar to the
      parent.

      KEYWORDS:  affect, age of parent, both
      parents, generations, interaction, methods,
      same sex parents, transmission, values

61.   Connell, R.W.   "Political Socialization in
      the American Family:  The Evidence Re-
      Examined."  **Public Opinion Quarterly** 36
      (1972):323-33.

One of the major initial attacks on the
argument for substantial correspondence of
political beliefs.  In particular, it is
critical of the classic study by Herbert
Hyman, **Political Socialization** (1959).
Focuses on contrast between cohort and
lineage agreement.
KEYWORDS:  cohort vs. lineage, generations,
methods, political, transmission


62.   Constantinou, S.T., and M.E. Harvey.  "Basic
      Dimensional Structure and Intergenerational
      Differences in Greek American Ethnicity."
      **Sociology and Social Research** 69(1985):234-
      54.
      A study of 44 first generation, 56 second
      generation, and 19 third generation Greek
      Americans shows first generation identifies
      with ancestral land, second generation is
      transitional, and third generation shows
      signs of ethnic revival.

      KEYWORDS:  cross-cultural, ethnicity,
      generations, grandparents, values


63.   Covert, Anita Miller, Joanne Keith, and
      Christine Nelson.  "Parental Expectations
      for Early Adolescence:  Cultural vs. Inter-
      personal."  Paper presented at the Annual
      Meetings of the National Council on Family
      Relations, Minneapolis, 1983.

      Analyzes the perceptions parents have of
      adolescent children.  Shows parental atti-
      tudes toward own children more positive
      than their attitudes toward teenagers in
      general.

      KEYWORDS:  affect, perceptions


64.   Cutler, N.E.  "Toward a Generational Con-
      ception of Political Socialization."  **New
      Directions in Political Socialization.**
      Edited by D.C. Schwartz and S.K. Schwartz.
      New York:  Free Press, 1975, pp. 254-88.

This provides a review of literature and
theories about generational differences and
similarities. A major point is that the
historical context of political socialization is critical. Theories and conceptual
issues are covered.
KEYWORDS: cohort vs. lineage, generations,
historical, perceptions, peers vs. parents,
political, review, social structure,
theory, transmission

65.    ———.   "Generational Approaches to Political Socialization." **Youth and Society** 8
(1976):175-207.

A review of literature on the concept of
generation and political socialization.
Compares cohort and lineage effects.

KEYWORDS: cohort vs. lineage, generations,
historical, political, review, theory,
transmission

66.    ———.   "Political Socialization Research as
Generational Analysis: The Cohort Approach
Versus the Lineage Approach." **Handbook of
Political Socialization: Theory and Re-
search.** Edited by S.A. Renshon. New York:
Free Press, 1977, pp. 294-326.

A theoretical comparison of cohort and
lineage analysis with an emphasis on the
value of cohort analysis. Reviews earlier
research on political socialization and
political alienation.

KEYWORDS: cohort vs. lineage, methods,
political, theory, transmission

67.  Dalton, Russell J.  "Reassessing Parental
Socialization: Indicator Unreliability
Versus Generational Transfer." **American
Political Science Review** 74(1980):421-31.

Based on 1965 Jennings and Niemi survey of
high school seniors and their parents, this
study shows much higher family agreement
than earlier research. Early application
of LISREL to intergenerational influence.

KEYWORDS: blacks, methods, political,
race, transmission

68. ————. "The Pathways of Parental Socialization." **American Politics Quarterly**
10(1982):139-57.
Based on the 1965 Jennings and Niemi survey
of high school seniors and their parents,
this study compares attitude similarity to
the effects of social class and race.
Early application of LISREL to intergenerational influence.

KEYWORDS: blacks, methods, political,
social class, social structure, transmission

69. Douvan, E. "Employment and the Adolescent."
**The Employed Mother in America.** Edited by
F.T Nye and L.W. Hoffman. Chicago: Rand
McNally, 1963, pp. 142-64.

70. ————. **The Adolescent Experience.** New
York: John Wiley and Sons, 1966.

This is a classic study of the effects of
maternal employment on children.

KEYWORDS: mother-daughter, self-esteem,
sex roles, social problems, work

71. Durkheim, Emile. **Moral Education.** New York:
Free Press, 1961.

Classic statement of sociological concern
with the transmission of moral values and
moral beliefs between generations.

KEYWORDS:   generation, transmission, values


72.   Dusek, J.B., and J.F. Flaherty.   1981 "The
      Development of Self-Concept During the
      Adolescent Years." **Monograph Social
      Research Child Development** 46(1981):1-67.


73.   Elder, G.H., Jr.   "Adolescence in the Life
      Cycle:  An Introduction."  **Adolescence in
      the Life Cycle:   Psychological Change in
      Social Context.**   Edited by S.E. Dragastin
      and G.H. Elder, Jr.   Washington:  Hemi-
      sphere Pub. Corp., 1975, pp. 1-22.

      Reviews theory and research dealing with
      adolescence.  Discusses transmission,
      cohort, and relative influence of peers
      versus parents.

      KEYWORDS:  affect, both parents, cohort vs.
      lineage, peers vs. parents, social prob-
      lems, theory, transmission


74.   ————.   "Family and Kinship in Sociological
      Perspective."   **The Family:  NSS Yearbook.**
      Edited by R. Parke.   Chicago:  University of
      Chicago Press, 1977,  pp. 130-59.


75.   Ellis, Godfrey J., G.R. Lee, and L.R. Peter-
      son.   "Supervision and Conformity:   A
      Cross-Cultural Analysis of Parental
      Socialization Values."  **American Journal of
      Sociology** 84(1978):386-403.

      KEYWORDS:  cross-cultural, values


76.   Ellis, Godfrey J., Darwin L. Thomas, and Boyd
      C. Rollins.   "Measuring Parental Support:
      The Interrelationship of Three Measures."
      **Journal of Marriage and the Family** 38
      (1976):713-22.

A methodological analysis of measures of
parental support. Shows that the concept
is multi-dimensional.

KEYWORDS:  methods, parental support


77.   Emmerich, H.  "The Influence of Parents and
      Peers on Choices Made by Adolescents."
      **Journal of Youth and Adolescence** 7(1978):
      175-80.

      KEYWORDS:  peers vs. parents


78.   Farel, A.N.  "Effects of Preferred Maternal
      Roles, Maternal Employment, and Socio-
      economic Status on School Adjustment and
      Competence."  **Child Development** 50(1947):
      159-64.

      KEYWORDS:  education, social class, work


79.   Faris, Robert E.L.  "Interaction of Genera-
      tions and Family Stability."  **American
      Sociological Review** 12(1947):159-64.

      Classic statement of the issues of genera-
      tions and family stability.

      KEYWORDS:  affect, generation, historical,
      transmission, theory


80.   Feather, N.T.  "Generation and Sex Differ-
      ences in Conservatism."  **Australian
      Psychologist** 12(1977):76-82.

      Analyzes sex and generation differences on
      an Australian sample.

      KEYWORDS:  both parents, cohort vs.
      lineage, cross-cultural, generations,
      political

81.    ———.  "Family Resemblances in Conserva-
       tism:  Are Daughters More Similar to Par-
       ents Than Sons Are?"  **Journal of Personal-
       ity** 46(1978):260-78.

       Using an Australian sample, this paper
       argues that there is family similarity in
       conservatism, sons are less similar than
       daughters, there is no evidence supporting
       same-sex modeling, parents are more conser-
       vative than children, and women are more
       conservative than men.

       KEYWORDS:  both parents, cross-cultural,
       political, same sex parents, sex-specifica-
       tion, transmission


82.    Featherman, David L.  "Social Stratification
       and Mobility:  Two Decades of Cumulative
       Social Science."  **American Behavior Science**
       24(1981):364-85.

       This is a brief review of the major re-
       search and issues concerned with social
       stratification and mobility.  It focuses on
       research published since 1960.

       KEYWORDS:  generation, social class, status
       attainment


83.    Filsinger, Erik E., and Leanne Lanke.  "The
       Lineage Transmission of Interpersonal
       Competence."  **Journal of Marriage and the
       Family** 45(1983):75-80.

       Based on 64 father-mother-child triads,
       this study reports on the transmission of
       interpersonal relationship characteristics.
       Father's social self-esteem is signifi-
       cantly related to child's social self-
       esteem.  Lineage transmission of interper-
       sonal competence is related to marital
       stability.

KEYWORDS: affect, both parents, marital
stability, mother vs. father, self-esteem,
transmission


84.    Fischer, L.R.  "Transitions in the Mother-
       Daughter Relationship."  **Journal of Mar-
       riage and the Family** 43(1981):613-22.

       Interviews with 43 daughters and their
       mothers provides information on their
       interaction as the daughters enter mar-
       riage.

       KEYWORDS: mother-daughter, interaction


85.    ————. **Linked Lives: Adult Daughters and
       Their Mothers.** New York: Harper and Row,
       1986.
       KEYWORDS: interaction, mother-daughter,
       transmission


86.    Fox, Greer Litton.  "The Mother-Adolescent
       Daughter Relationship as a Sexual Sociali-
       zation Structure: A Research Review."
       **Family Relations** 29(1980):21-28.

       Review of literature on mother-daughter
       relationship in terms of transmission of
       sexual beliefs and behavior.  Low levels of
       communication are found, but evidence of
       maternal influence is sufficient to warrant
       conclusion that it is under-utilized by
       social service programs.

       KEYWORDS: mother-daughter, review, sex
       roles, sexual beliefs, transmission


87.    ————."Barriers to Parent-Teen Communication
       About Sexuality."  Unpublished Manuscript,
       College of Home Economics, University of
       Tennessee, Knoxville, 1985.

Discusses the role of parents in teenage
sexuality.  Includes such issues as
polarized misattributions.

KEYWORDS:   interaction, perceptions, sexual
beliefs

88.   Fox, Greer Litton and M. Colombo.  "Parental
      Division of Labor in Adolescent Sexual
      Socialization."  Paper Presented at North
      Central Sociological Association Meetings,
      Indianapolis, 1984.

      Qualitative interviews with mothers and
      fathers are used to discuss the role of
      mother and father in sexual socialization.
      Special attention is given to the role of
      the father and to father absence.

      KEYWORDS:   both parents, father absence,
      mother vs. father, sexual beliefs

89.   Fox, Greer Litton and Judith K. Inazu.   "The
      Impact of Mother-Daughter Communication on
      Daughter's Sexual Knowledge, Behavior, and
      Contraceptive Use."  Presented at the
      Annual Meeting of the American Psychologi-
      cal Association, New York, 1979.

      Examines transmission of sexual beliefs and
      behaviors between mothers and adolescent
      daughters based on a sample of 449 dyads.

      KEYWORDS:   mother-daughter, sexual beliefs,
      sex roles, transmission

90.   Gallager, B.J.   "Ascribed and Self-Reported
      Attitude Differences Between Generations."
      **Pacific Sociological Review** 19(1976):317-
      32.

      Survey of 148 college student and same sex
      parent dyads revealed students "overconser-
      vatize" their parents.  At least part of

eneration gap is in the misperceptions of the youth.

KEYWORDS: child-rearing, perceptions, political, religion, same sex parents, sex roles, sexual beliefs

91.  Gecas, Viktor. "Parental Behavior and Dimensions of Adolescent Self-Evaluation." **Sociometry** 34(1971):466-82.
Following a symbolic interactionist perspective, this paper shows that parental support leads to positive self evaluation but that there is no relationship between parental control and self evaluation.

KEYWORDS: affect, parental support, self-esteem

92.  ————. "The Influence of Social Class on Socialization." **Contemporary Theories About the Family**, Vol. 1. Edited by Wesley R. Burr, Reuben Hill, F. Ivan Nye, and Ira L. Reiss. New York: The Free Press, 1979, pp. 365-404.

Review of literature linking social class to socialization practices. Generates a series of propositions.

KEYWORDS: child rearing, self-esteem, social class, social structure, theory, values

93.  Gecas, Viktor and Kay Pasley. "Birth Order and Self-Concept in Adolescence." **Journal of Youth and Adolescence** 12(1983):521-35.

Birth order is related to self-concept and similarity between self-concept of children and their parents. Little support is shown for hypotheses about the relationship between self-concept and birth order.

KEYWORDS: birth order, interaction, self-esteem, transmission

94.  Gecas, Viktor and Michael L. Schwalbe. "Parental Behavior and Adolescent Self-Esteem." **Journal of Marriage and the Family** 48(1986): in press.

Based on 128 mother-father-child triads this paper reports that children between 17 and 19 have self-evaluations that are much more strongly related to their perceptions of parental behavior than to parents' self-reported behavior. In general, perceptions of paternal behavior are somewhat stronger for adolescent self-esteem than are perceptions of maternal behavior.

KEYWORDS: affect, both parents, mother vs. father, parental support, perceptions, self-esteem, sex-specification, theory

95.  Giles-Sims, Jean. "The Stepparent Role: Expectations, Behavior, and Sanctions." **Journal of Family Issues** 5(1984):116-30.

Indicates that less than one third of step parents share equally in decisions regarding children and that sanctions against stepparents who refuse responsibility are not as strong as those against natural parents.

KEYWORDS: divorce effects, father absence, interaction, power

96.  Glass, Jennifer, Vern Bengtson, and Charlotte Dunham. "Attitude Similarity in Three Generation Families: Socialization, Status Inheritance, or Reciprocal Influence?" Unpublished Manuscript. Andrus Gerontology Center, University of Southern California, 1985.

A three generation analysis shows parent-
child convergence is not greater for older
dyads than for parent-youth dyads, parental
attitudes are more important than status
inheritance, and child influence on parental attitudes increases with age.

KEYWORDS:   age of parent, both parents,
methods,   grandparents, political, reciprocal influence, religion, sex roles,
status attainment, transmission

97.  Gold, D., and D. Andres.  "Comparison of
     Adolescent Children with Employed and Non-
     Employed Mothers."  **Merrill Palmer
     Quarterly** 24(1978):243-54.

     Examines surveys from 253 Canadian children
     (14 to 16 years old) and their parents.
     Reports that both sons and daughters of
     working mothers are better adjusted than
     sons and daughters of non-working mothers.

     KEYWORDS:   both parents, cross-cultural,
     education, self-esteem, sex-specification,
     work

98.  Gold, Martin and Denise S. Yanof.  "Mothers,
     Daughters, and Girlfriends."  **Journal of
     Personality and Social Psychology** 49
     (1985):654-59.

     Reports that girls' ratings of their
     mothers as models and affection in their
     mother-daughter relationship is positively
     related with intimacy and identification
     with their girlfriends.  A developmental
     theory is given more support than the
     compensatory theory of parent-child rela-
     tions.

     KEYWORDS:   affect, identification, interac-
     tion, mother-daughter, parental support,
     peers vs. parents, perceptions, same sex
     parents, theory

99.  Goyder, J.C., and J.E. Curtis.  "A Three-
     Generational Approach to Trends in Occupa-
     tional Mobility."  **American Journal of
     Sociology** 81(1975):129-38.

     Secondary analysis of 1947 and 1963 data on
     three-generational occupational mobility
     shows that the congruence between respon-
     dent's and father's occupational status is
     similar to that between father's and pater-
     nal grandfather's.  When farm owners are
     excluded, however, the degree of status
     inheritance is greater between the senior
     pair of generations.

     KEYWORDS:  grandparents, historical, longi-
     tudinal, rural, status attainment, trans-
     mission, work

100. Greenberg, E.F., and W.R. Nay.  "The Inter-
     generational Transmission of Marital
     Instability Reconsidered."  **Journal of
     Marriage and the Family** 44(1982):335-47.

     Survey of 397 college students compares
     intact (happy-unbroken versus unhappy-
     broken), separated/divorced, and parent-
     deceased families.  Those students from
     separated-divorced families espouse the
     most favorable attitude toward divorce.
     This suggests the transmission of a dis-
     inhibitory effect of parental divorce.

     KEYWORDS:  divorce effects, father absence,
     marital stability, transmission, values

101. Greenberg, M.T., J.M. Siegel, and C.J.
     Leitch.  "The Nature and Importance of
     Attachment Relationships to Parents and
     Peers During Adolescence."  **Journal of
     Youth and Adolescence** 12(1983):373-86.

     A sample of 213 adolescents (12-19) demon-
     strates that the quality of their perceived
     attachments to parents and peers predicts
     their feeling of well-being.  Quality of

attachments to parents is most important
and moderates effects of high life stress
on measures of self-esteem

KEYWORDS: interaction, peers vs. parents,
perceptions, self-esteem

102.  Greendorfer, E.M.B., and A.M. Pellegrini.
      "Gender Differences in Brazilian Children's
      Socialization into Sport." Unpublished
      Manuscript, Motor Behavior Laboratory,
      University of Illinois at Urbana-Champaign,
      1986.

      A cross-cultural analysis of sex role
      socialization of children into sports.
      Compares parents, family, peers, oppor-
      tunity set, and teachers as socialization
      agents.
      KEYWORDS: child rearing, cross-cultural,
      education, peers vs. parents, sex roles,
      sex-specification, sports

103.  Greendorfer, Susan L.  "Role of Socializing
      Agents in Female Sport Involvement."
      **Research Quarterly** 48(1977):304-10.

      Survey of 585 college age female athletes
      indicates that family was a strong
      influence only during childhood, while peer
      group was the most consistent influence
      throughout each life cycle stage. Teachers
      and coaches were only influential during
      adolescence, once the women were already
      participating.

      KEYWORDS: mother-daughter, peers vs.
      parents, sports, transmission

104.  ————.  "Differences in Childhood Socializa-
      tion Influences of Women Involved in Sport
      and Women Not Involved in Sport." **The
      Dimensions of Sport Sociology.** Edited by
      M.L. Krotee. West Point, N.Y.: Leisure
      Press, 1979, pp. 59-72.

Discusses research on differences in socialization patterns of women who become athletes and those who do not with an emphasis on the influence of the family.

KEYWORDS:  child rearing, sex roles, sports

105.    ————.  "Gender Differences in Physical Activity."  **Motor Skills:  Theory Into Practice** 4(1980):83-90.
Discusses research on sex typing by parents and how this influences socialization into sport.

KEYWORDS:  child rearing, sex roles, sports.

106.    Greendorfer, Susan L., and J. Lewko.  "Role of Family Members in Sport Socialization of Children."  **Research Quarterly** 49(1978): 146-52.

Compares family members, peers and teachers as significant others in the development of interest in sports.  Neither peers nor teachers serve as significant others.  Among family members, siblings are not important, mothers have a weak effect, and only fathers have a significant effect.  This father effect applies to both boys and girls.

KEYWORDS:  both parents, mother vs. father, peers vs. parents, sex-specification, sports

107.    Grotevant, Harold D.  "The Contribution of the Family to the Facilitation of Identity Formation in Early Adolescence."  **Journal of Early Adolescence** 3(1973):225-37.

Reviews literature and issues dealing with family influence on identity formation.  Argues for greater consideration of gender

differences, domain-specific studies of
identity, and longitudinal studies of
developmental sequences.

KEYWORDS:  child rearing, longitudinal,
methods, sex-specification

108.  ─────.  "Environmental Influences on Vocational Interest Development in Adolescents
from Adoptive and Biological Families."
**Child Development** 50(1979):854-60.
A survey of 844 parents and adolescent
children revealed that parent-child similarity in vocational interest increases
with mother-father agreement.  Comparisons
made between biological and adoptive
families.

KEYWORDS:  both parents, mother-father
agreement, sex-specification, transmission,
vocational interest

109.  Grotevant, Harold D., and Catherine R. Cooper.
"Individuation in Family Relationships:  A
Perspective on Individual Differences in
the Development of Identity and Role Taking
Skill in Adolescence."  **Human Development**
(1986):  in press.

Review of literature and presentation of a
model of individuation.  Discusses
increased symmetry of parent-child
influence during adolescence and identity
formation.

KEYWORDS:  child rearing, interaction,
reciprocal influence

110.  Grotevant, Harold D., and Catherine R. Cooper.
"Patterns of Interaction in Family Rela-
tionships and the Development of Identity
Exploration in Adolescence."  **Child
Development** (1986):  in press.

An experimental analysis of family interaction that discusses how sex-specific
dyadic communication influences identity
exploration.

KEYWORDS:  affect, both parents, experiment, interaction, mother vs. father, same
sex parents, sex-specification

111.  Grotevant, Harold D., S. Scarr, and R.A.
      Weinberg.  "Patterns of Interest Similarity
      in Adoptive and Biological Families."
      **Journal of Personality and Social Psycho-
      logy** 35(1977):667-76.

      Comparison of similarity between children
      and parents in biological families and
      adoptive families.

      KEYWORDS:  both parents, genetics


112.  Grusec, J.E., and L. Kuczynski.  "Direction of
      Effect in Socialization:  A Comparison of
      the Parent's versus the Child's Behavior as
      Determinants of Disciplinary Techniques."
      **Developmental Psychology** 16(1980):1-9.

      KEYWORDS:  reciprocal influence


113.  Gutman, D.  "Parenthood:  Key to the Compara-
      tive Psychology of the Life Cycle."  **Life-
      Span Developmental Psychology.**  Edited by
      N. Datan and L. Ginsberg.  New York:
      Academic Press, 1975.


114.  Hagestad, Gunhild O.  "Lineages as Units of
      Analysis:  New Avenues for the Study of
      Individual and Family Careers."  Paper
      presented at the National Council on Family
      Relations' Theory and Methodology Workshop,
      Portland, Oregon, 1980.

This is a review of literature and
presentation of research approaches for
analyzing lineages.  Theory and methodology
are discussed.

KEYWORDS:  cohort vs. lineage, methods,
review, theory


115.  ————.  "Problems and Promises in the Social
      Psychology of Intergenerational Relations."
      **Stability and Change in the Family.**  Edited
      by R. Fogel, Elaine Hatfield, Sarah
      Kiesler, and J. March.  New York:  Academic
      Press, 1981, pp. 11-47.

      A comprehensive review of theories, litera-
      ture, and research agendas for the study of
      inter-generational relations.

      KEYWORDS:  generations, historical, recip-
      rocal influence, review, theory, transmis-
      sion


116.  ————.  "Parent and Child:  Generations in
      the Family."  **Review of Human Development.**
      Edited by T.M. Field, A. Huston, H.C. Quay,
      L. Troll, and G.E. Finley.  New York:
      Wiley-Interscience, 1982, pp. 485-99.

      Reviews literature and concepts related to
      a multi-generational view of
      intergenerational influence.  Incorporates
      social structure in terms of the impact of
      changes in the demographic conditions of
      family life.  There is a strong emphasis on
      the need for reciprocal influence.

      KEYWORDS:  age of parent, generations,
      grandparents, methods, reciprocal
      influence, review, social structure, trans-
      mission


117.  ————.  "The Continuous Bond:  A Dynamic,
      Multi-generational Perspective on Parent-
      Child Relations Between Adults."  **Parent-**

Child Interaction and Parent-Child
Relations in Child Development, The
Minnesota Symposia on Child Psychology,
Volume 17. Edited by Marion Perlmutter.
Minneapolis: University of Minnesota
Press, 1984, pp. 129-58.

Review of literature of research on intergenerational relations among multi-
generational families. Discusses possible
directions for future research.

KEYWORDS: affect, divorce, generations,
grandparents, reciprocal influence

118. Hagestad, Gunhild O. and M. Kranichfeld.
     "Issues in the Study of Intergenerational
     Continuity." Paper presented at the Annual
     Meetings of the National Council on Family
     Relations, 1982.

     Reviews literature and theory related to a
     three generation approach to intergenera-
     tional continuity.

     KEYWORDS: cohort, reciprocal influence,
     review, theory, transmission

119. Hagestad, Gunhild O., M.A. Smyer, and K.L.
     Stierman. "Parent-Child Relations in
     Adulthood: The Impact of Divorce in Middle
     Age." Parenthood as an Adult Experience.
     Edited by R. Cohen, S. Weissman, and B.
     Cohler. New York: Guilford Press, 1984,
     pp. 247-62.

     Examines the impact of divorce among
     middle-aged people. Parent-child relations
     are discussed in terms of reactions, sup-
     port system, and interaction rates.

     KEYWORDS: affect, age of parent, divorce
     effects, generations, interaction

120.  Hagestad, Gunhild O., and Joan Lisle Speicher.
      "Grandparents and Family Influence:  Views
      of Three Generations."  Presented at the
      Annual Meeting of SRCD, Boston, 1981.

      Study shows sex differences and role of
      middle-aged fathers as mediators between
      grandfathers and grandsons.

      KEYWORDS:  affect, age of parent, grand-
      parents, generations, sex roles, sex-speci-
      fication, transmission


121.  Hareven, T.K.  "Family Time and Historical
      Time."  **Daedalus** 106(1977):57-70.


122.  Hawkes, G.R., N.G. Kutner, M.J. Wells, V.A.
      Christopherson, and E.B. Almirol.
      "Families in Cultural Islands."  **Family in
      Rural Society.** Edited by R.F. Coward and
      W.M. Smith, Jr. Boulder:  Westview Press,
      1981, pp. 87-126.

      KEYWORDS:  rural


123.  Heiss, J.  "On the Transmission of Marital
      Instability in Black Families."  **American
      Sociological Review** 37(1972):82-92.

      KEYWORDS:  divorce effects, marital stabil-
      ity, transmission


124.  Henderson, Ronald W. (ed.).  **Parent-Child
      Interaction:  Theory, Research, and
      Prospects.** New York:  Academic Press,
      1981.

      A collection of papers on parent-child
      interaction.  Includes material on effects
      of divorce, parents vs. peers, measurement
      of interaction, and theoretical perspec-
      tives.

KEYWORDS:  child rearing, divorce effects,
experiment, father absence, interaction,
marital stability, peers vs. parents,
theory, transmission, values, violence

125.  Henry, G.C.  "Generational Transmission of
      Divorce:  Towards an Integrated Model."
      **Family Perspective** 18(1984):53-68.

      A review of literature on generational
      transmission of divorce focusing on
      theoretical and conceptual issues.  Effects
      of divorce when child is an adolescent are
      discussed.
      KEYWORDS:  divorce effects, marital stabil-
      ity, review, theory, transmission

126.  Hess, R.D.  "Social Class and Ethnic
      Influences upon Socialization."
      **Carmichael's Manual of Child Psychology**,
      Vol. 2.  New York:  Wiley, 1970.

      KEYWORDS:  ethnicity, social class

127.  Hetherington, E. Mavis.  "Children and
      Divorce."  **Parent-Child Interaction:
      Theory, Research, and Prospects.**  Edited by
      Ronald W. Henderson.  New York:  Academic
      Press, 1981, pp. 35-58.

      Reviews literature relevant to how divorce
      influences parent-child interaction.

      KEYWORDS:  divorce effects, interaction,
      mother vs. father, sex-specification

128.  Hetherington, E. Mavis, M. Cox, and R. Cox.
      "The Aftermath of Divorce."  **Mother-Child,
      Father-Child Relations.**  Edited by H.
      Stevens, Jr. and M. Matthews.  Washington,
      D.C.:  National Association for the Educa-
      tion of Young Children, 1978.

KEYWORDS:  divorce effects, mother vs.
father, sex-specification


129.  Hill, R., N. Foote, J. Aldous, R. Carlson,
      and R. MacDonald. **Family Development in
      Three Generations.** Cambridge, Mass.:
      Schenkman, 1970.

      KEYWORDS:  both parents, education, genera-
      tion, grandparents, interaction, methods,
      mother vs. father, review, theory, values,
      work


130.  Hoffman, Edward. "Young Adults Relations
      with their Grandparents:  Exploratory
      Study." **International Journal of Aging and
      Human Development** 10(1979-80):299-310.

      Study of 269 undergraduate females indi-
      cates that they are significantly closer to
      their maternal grandparent(s) than to their
      paternal grandparent(s).  They are closest
      to their maternal grandmother.

      KEYWORDS:  affect, grandparents, mother-
      daughter, mother vs. father, sex-specifi-
      cation


131.  Hoffman, L.W.  "Changes in Family Roles,
      Socialization, and Sex Differences."
      **American Psychologist** 32(1979):644-57.

      KEYWORDS:  sex roles


132.  Hoge, D.R., and G.H. Petrillo.  "Determinants
      of Church Participation and Attitudes among
      High School Youth." **Journal for the
      Scientific Study of Religion** 17(1978):359-
      79.

      Survey of 451 tenth graders from three
      denominations finds parental attendance is
      best predictor of church attendance while
      peer pressures are more important predic-

tors of participation of youth in church
youth programs.

KEYWORDS:   interaction, peers vs. parents,
religion


133.   Hoge, D.R., G.H. Petrillo, and E.I. Smith.
       "Transmission of Religious and Social
       Values from Parents to Teenage Children."
       **Journal of Marriage and the Family** 44
       (1982):569-80.

       Survey of 254 mother-father-youth (mean age
       16) triads indicated low levels of value
       transmission.  Younger age of parents,
       parental agreement, and affect enhanced
       religious value transmission.  Religious
       denomination better predictor than parental
       values indicating place of cultural sub-
       group.

       KEYWORDS: affect, age of parent, both
       parents, mother-father agreement, religion,
       sex-specification, social structure,
       transmission, values


134.   Ihinger, Marilyn.  **Attainment Values and
       Parental Value Transmission.**  Unpublished
       Doctoral Dissertation, University of
       Minnesota, 1977.

       KEYWORDS:   transmission, values


135.   ————.   "Family Interaction, Gender, and
       Status Attainment Value."  **Sex Roles**
       8(1982):543-56.

       An experiment based on 79 mother-father-
       child triads shows that interaction styles
       provide much better prediction of attain-
       ment value of adolescent sons than of
       adolescent daughters.

       KEYWORDS: both parents, experiment, inter-
       action, mother vs. father, sex roles, sex

specification, status attainment, vocational interest


136.   Inazu, Judith K. and Greer Litton Fox.
       "Maternal Influence on the Sexual Behavior
       of Teen-Age Daughters:   Direct and Indirect
       Sources."  **Journal of Family Issues**
       1(1980):81-102.

       A sample of 449 mothers and their 14 to 16
       year old daughters indicates that indirect
       forms of sexual socialization have a
       greater impact than direct forms.  This is
       controlling for background factors.

       KEYWORDS:  affect, child rearing, interac-
       tion, mother-daughter, sexual beliefs, sex
       roles, social problems, transmission


137.   Jacobsen, R.B., K.J. Berry, and K.F. Olson.
       "An Empirical Test of the Generation Gap:
       A Comparative Intrafamily Study."  **Journal
       of Marriage and the Family** 37(1975):841-52.

       A survey of 117 college-age adolescent-
       father dyads reveals a lack of significant
       disagreement (mean value of Robinson's A
       about .50).  Misinterprets this as wide-
       spread consensus.  Covers a variety of
       issue areas.

       KEYWORDS:  political, sexual beliefs, sex-
       specification, social class, social
       problems, transmission


138.   Jedlicka, Davor.  "A Test of the
       Psychoanalytic Theory of Mate Selection."
       **Journal of Social Psychology** 112(1980):
       295-99.

       KEYWORDS:  identification

139.  ———. "Indirect Parental Influence on Mate
      Choice:  A Test of the Psychoanalytic
      Theory." **Journal of Marriage and the
      Family** 46(1984):65-70.

      A study of recent brides and grooms of
      mixed parentage in Hawaii indicates mothers
      have more influence on mate selection than
      fathers.  Also, mothers have their greatest
      influence on sons and fathers have their
      greatest influence on daughters.  It is
      argued that this is consistent with psycho-
      analytic theory.

      KEYWORDS:  both parents, ethnicity, identi-
      fication, mother-daughter, mother vs.
      father, same sex parents, sex-specification


140.  Jennings, M. Kent.  "The Variable Nature of
      Generational Conflict:  Some Examples from
      West Germany." **Comparative Political
      Studies** 9(1976):171-88.

      Examines problems studying generational
      conflict as they apply to Germany.

      KEYWORDS:  cohort vs. lineage, cross-
      cultural, education, generations, political


141.  ———. "Analyzing Pairs in Cross-National
      Survey Research." **European Journal of
      Political Research** 5(1977):179-97.

      A methodological discussion of problems
      with studying intergenerational relations.
      Discusses cohort comparisons and lineage
      comparisons as well as the concept of
      generation.

      KEYWORDS:  cohort lineage, cross-cultural,
      generations, methods, political

142.  ————. "The Intergenerational Transfer of
      Political Ideologies in Eight Western
      Nations." **European Journal of Political
      Research** 12(1984):261-76.

      Compares parental attitude, education, and
      religion as predictor of pre-adult child's
      political attitudes. Based on Eight Nation
      data. Shows that parental attitudes are
      better predictors than education or
      religion. Uses only a single parent.
      Compares standardized coefficients (r's and
      beta weights) rather than unstandardized
      coefficients.

      KEYWORDS: education, political, religion,
      social class, social structure, transmis-
      sion


143.  Jennings, M.K., K. Allerbeck, and L.
      Rosenmayr. "Generations and Families:
      General Orientations and Political Satis-
      faction." **Mass Participation in Five
      Western Democracies.** Edited by Samuel
      Barnes and Max Kaase. Beverly Hills:
      Sage, 1979, pp. 279-318.

      KEYWORDS: cross-cultural, generations,
      political, transmission


144.  Jennings, M.K. and P.A. Beck. "Parents as
      'Middlepersons' in Political Socializa-
      tion." **Journal of Politics** 37(1975):83-
      107.

      KEYWORDS: political, social structure,
      transmission


145.  Jennings, M.K. and R. Jansen. "Der Hang der
      Jugendlichen zu Veranderugen und zu
      Meinungsvielfalt in der Politik in
      Deutschland: Der Einfluss von
      Socialstructurefaktoren und der Familie.
      **Politische Vierteljahresschrift** 17(1976):
      317-43.

KEYWORDS:  political, social structure,
transmission


146.   Jennings, M. Kent and Richard G. Niemi.  "The
       Division of Political Labor Between Mothers
       and Fathers."  **American Political Science
       Review** 37(1971):69-82.

       A classic study comparing influence of
       mothers and fathers on adolescent children.
       Concludes that mothers can have significant
       influence depending on their resources
       relative to the resources of their husband.

       KEYWORDS:  both parents, education, mother-
       father agreement, mother vs. father,
       political, power, social class, transmis-
       sion


147.   ———.  **The Political Character of Adoles-
       cence:  The Influence of Families and
       Schools.**  Princeton, N.J.: Princeton
       University Press, 1974.

       The focus of this study is on a national
       sample of high school seniors and the
       components of home and school which have a
       bearing on their political development.

       KEYWORDS:  education, generations, politi-
       cal


148.   ———.  "Continuity and Change in Political
       Orientations:  A Longitudinal Study of Two
       Generations."  **American Political Science
       Review** 64(1975):1316-35.

       KEYWORDS:  longitudinal, political, social
       structure, transmission


149.   ———.  "The Persistence of Political Orien-
       tations:  An Overtime Analysis of Two
       Generations."  **British Journal of Political
       Science** 8(1978):333-63.

KEYWORDS:   historical, longitudinal,
political, social structure, transmission,

150.   ————.   Generations and Politics:   A Panel
Study of Young Adults and Their Parents.
Princeton:   Princeton University Press,
1981.

A massive longitudinal survey (1965 & 1973)
of parents and children.   Monograph
summarizes the results of the survey in
terms of political socialization, cohort
vs. lineage effects, race differences, and
sex-specification.   One of the few longitudinal surveys and data is available from
ICPSR.

KEYWORDS:   cohort vs. lineage, generation,
methods, mother vs. father, political,
race, review, sex-specification, stability,
theory, transmission

151.   Jessop, Dorothy Jones.   The Two Worlds of the
Family:   Agreement in Parent/Adolescent
Responses in a Drug Survey.   Unpublished
Doctoral Dissertation, New York University,
1979.

Analyzes 3988 parent-child dyads for agreement on a variety of drug issues.   Focus is
on how agreement varies across topic and
factors about the dyad that explain the
level of agreement.   Greatest agreement
exists on topics that are objective,
unambiguous and not threatening.   Least
agreement exists on issues involving generational cleavage.

KEYWORDS:   affect, cohort vs. lineage,
generations, mother vs. father, perceptions, sex-specification, social problems,
transmission

152.    ————.  "Family Relationships as Viewed by
        Parents and Adolescents:  A Specification."
        **Journal of Marriage and the Family**
        43(1981):95-107

        Survey of 3,988 high school student-parent
        dyads revealed little agreement on many
        issues and attributions.  Agreement is
        least where there is a threat involved
        (e.g., drug related behavior) and judgments
        about family relations.  Agreement is
        greatest on objective events (e.g.,
        income).  Both parents and youth emphasize
        the areas of power they have in the family.

        KEYWORDS:  attribution, child-rearing,
        interaction, perceptions, power, social
        problems, status attainment, transmission,
        vocational interest


153.    ————.  "Topic Variation in Levels of Agree-
        ment Between Parents and Adolescents."
        **Public Opinion Quarterly** 46(1982):538-59.

        Examines degree of agreement between a
        parent and his/her adolescent child as it
        varies across topics.  Based on survey of
        3,988 parent-child dyads.  Agreement is
        high when topic is objective and
        unambiguous.

        KEYWORDS:  cohort vs. lineage, social
        problems, transmission


154.    Jorgensen, Stephen R., S.L. King, and B.A.
        Torrey.  "Dyadic and Social Network
        Influences on Adolescent Exposure to Preg-
        nancy Risk."  **Journal of Marriage and the
        Family** 42(1980):141-55.


155.    Jorgensen, Stephen R. and Janet S.
        Sonstegard.  "Predicting Adolescent Sexual
        and Contraceptive Behavior:  An Application
        and Test of the Fishbein Model.  **Journal of
        Marriage and the Family** 46(1984):43-55.

A survey of 244 female adolescents ages 13
to 18 shows their attitudes and parental
norms are strongly related to measures of
contraceptive use, but not frequency of
sexual intercourse. Peer norms are only
weakly related to any of the pregnancy-risk
behavior measures.

KEYWORDS: peers vs. parents, perceptions,
sexual beliefs, social problems

156. Kalmus, Debra. "The Intergenerational Transmission of Marital Aggression." **Journal of
Marriage and the Family** 46(1984):11-19.

U.S. survey of 2,143 adults indicates
observing hitting between one's parents is
more strongly related to marital aggression
than is being hit as a teenager by one's
parents. Modeling does not appear to be
sex specific.

KEYWORDS: child rearing, interaction, same
sex parents, sex-specification, transmission, violence

157. Kalter, Neil and James Rembar. "The
Significance of a Child's Age at the Time
of Parental Divorce." **American Journal of
Orthopsychiatry** 51(1981):85-100.

Outpatient evaluations of 144 children of
divorce from 7 to 17 shows divorce timing
was unrelated to overall level of adjustment but was associated with specific
emotional-behavioral difficulties.

KEYWORDS: child rearing, divorce effects,
review

158. Kandel, Denise B., and G.S. Lesser. **Youth in
Two Worlds.** San Francisco: Jossey Bass,
Inc., 1972.

This is a classic statement about the
issues related to the generation gap.

KEYWORDS: generations, methods, review,
theory, transmissions

159.   Keeley, B.J.   "Generations in Tension:
       Intergenerational Differences and Contin-
       uity in Religion and Religion-Related
       Behavior."  **Review of Religious Research** 17
       (1976):221-31.

       Examines areas of continuity and discontin-
       uity between parents and children on a
       range of religious issues and practices.

       KEYWORDS: generations, religion, transmis-
       sion

160.   Kerckhoff, A.C.   "The Status Attainment
       Process."  **Social Forces** 55(1976):368-79.

161.   Kertzer, David I.   "Generation and Age in
       Cross-Cultural Perspective."  **Aging from
       Birth to Death:  Sociotemporal
       Perspectives.**  Edited by Matilda White
       Riley, Ronald P. Abeles, and Michael S.
       Teitelbaum.  Boulder, Colo.:  Westview,
       1982, pp. 27-50.

       A conceptual and cross-cultural analysis of
       the concept of generation.  Compares gener-
       ation to related concepts such as age
       groups.

       KEYWORDS: generation, theory

162.   ————.  "Generation as a Sociological
       Problem."  **Annual Review of Sociology.**
       Edited by Ralph H. Turner and James F.
       Short.  Palo Alto, Calif.: Annual Reviews,
       1983, pp. 125-49.

A systematic review of the concept of
generation and a review of selected literature on socialization. Emphasis is on
theory and need for a more historical
approach to the analysis of generations,
cohorts, and socialization.

KEYWORDS: cohort vs. lineage, cross-
cultural, generations, historical, political, review, status attainment

163. Kidwell, J.S. "Adolescents' Perceptions of
Parental Affect: An Investigation of Only
Children vs. Firstborn and the Effect of
Spacing." **Journal of Population** 1(1978):
148-66.

Only children have greater perceptions of
affect for their parents than do first
born. Results are based on a sample of
adolescents.
KEYWORDS: affect, birth order, number of
children, perceptions

164. ————. "Number of Siblings, Sibling
Spacing, Sex, and Birth Order: Their
Effects on Perceived Parent-Adolescent
Relationships." **Journal of Marriage and
the Family** 43(1981):315-32.

Analysis of 1700 adolescent males indicates
that number of siblings, sibling spacing,
sex, and birth order have small effects on
perceptions of parental power and support.
These small effects are maintained when
controlling for SES, race, and urban/rural
residence.

KEYWORDS: affect, age of parent, birth
order, interaction, number of children,
perceptions, power, rural, social structure, spacing

165.   Klein, David M., S.R. Jorgensen, and B.
       Miller. "Research Methods and Develop-
       mental Reciprocity in Families." **Child
       Influences on Marital and Family Inter-
       action: A Life-Span Perspective.** Edited
       by R.M. Lerner and G.B. Spanier. New York:
       Academic Press, 1978, pp. 107-35.

166.   Kohn, M.L. **Class and Conformity: A Study in
       Values.** 2nd edition. Chicago: University
       of Chicago Press, 1977.

167.   ———. "On the Transmission of Values in
       the Family: A Preliminary Formulation."
       **Research in Sociology of Education and
       Socialization,** Vol. 4. Edited by A.C.
       Kerckhoff. Greenwich, Conn.: JAI Press,
       1983, pp. 1-12.

       A review of selected literature on trans-
       mission with an emphasis on theory and
       methods. Calls for incorporating social
       structural variables into a model of trans-
       mission that includes both parents.

       KEYWORDS: both parents, methods, mother
       vs. father, perceptions, review, social
       structure, theory, transmission

168.   Kohn, Melvin L., Kazimierz M. Slomczynski,
       and Carrie Schoenbach. "Social Stratifica-
       tion and the Transmission of Values in the
       Family: A Cross-National Assessment."
       **Sociological Forum** 7(1986): in press.

       A comparison of results in the U.S. and
       Poland involving the role of the family's
       position in the social structure to
       parental values as influences on the values
       of adolescent offspring. Uses the analysis
       of covariance structures models similar to
       LISREL.

KEYWORDS: both parents, cross-cultural, education, longitudinal, methods, mother-father agreement, mother vs. father, reciprocal influence, social class, social structure, theory, transmission, work

169.   Koziey, P.W., and L. Davies. "Broken Homes: Impact on Adolescents." **The Alberta Journal of Educational Research** 28(1982):95-99.

Based on 54 tenth grade students, the study found no clear-cut patterns linking age of disruption nor sex with scores on the California Personality Inventory. However, adolescents from homes broken by divorce did score lower on self-control, socialization, femininity, and good impression scales.

KEYWORDS: affect, longitudinal, political, transmission

170.   Kraut, R.E., and S.H. Lewis. "Alternate Models of Family Influence on Student Political Ideology." **Journal of Personality and Social Psychology** 31(1975):791-800.

Study uses longitudinal data to show that student political ideology depends on parental ideology and on conflict with parents. The more leftist parents and the greater the conflict with parents the more the student identifies with leftist student ideology.

KEYWORDS: affect, longitudinal, political, transmission

171.   Kriegel, A. "Generational Difference: The History of an Idea." **Daedalus** 107(1978): 23-38.

A review of the concept of generation
including a discussion of its various
meanings.

KEYWORDS:  generations, historical, review,
values

172.  Krishn, Amoorthy, S.  "A Note on the Length
      of Generation."  **Genus** 36(1980):167-71.

      Attempts to develop a mathematical
      definition of generation and ends with (A +
      M)/2 where A is average difference in age
      between mother and daughter and M is aver-
      age difference between daughter and grand-
      daughter.

      KEYWORDS:  generation

173.  Kulka, R.A., and H. Weingarten.  "The Long-
      Term Effects of Parental Divorce in Child-
      hood on Adult Adjustment:  A Twenty Year
      Perspective."  Paper presented at the
      annual meeting of the American Sociological
      Association, Boston, Mass., 1979.

174.  Kurdek, L.A.  "An Integrative Perspective on
      Children's Divorce Adjustment."  **American
      Psychologist** 36(1981):856-66.

      Review of research on divorce effects on
      children, including problems with adoles-
      cent children.

      KEYWORDS:  affect, divorce effects, sex
      roles, sex-specification, stability

175.  Kurdek, L.A., and A.E. Siesky, Jr.  "Child-
      ren's Perceptions of Their Parents'
      Divorce."  **Journal of Divorce** 3(1980):
      339-78.

Study based on 132 children concerning the children's perceptions of their parents divorce.

KEYWORDS: child-rearing, divorce effects, methods, perceptions

176.  Lamb, M.E.  "The Role of the Father:  An Overview."  **The Role the Father in Child Development**.  Edited by M.E. Lamb.  New York:  John Wiley and Sons, 1977, pp. 1-63.

KEYWORDS: affect, child rearing, divorce effects, education, father absence, identification, interaction, mother vs. father, review, sex roles, social problems

177.  Larson, Reed W.  "Adolescents' Daily Experience with Family and Friends:  Contrasting Opportunity System."  **Journal of Marriage and the Family** 45(1983):739-50.

A study of 75 high school students self-reports was used to examine daily interactions with family and friends.  The adolescents report time with friends more enjoyable than time with family.  However, the greater the percentage of their total time was spent with friends the worse they performed at school and the wider their mood variability.

KEYWORDS: affect, education, interaction, peers vs. parents

178.  Lerner, Richard M.  "Adolescent Development: Scientific Study in the 1980s."  **Youth and Society** 12(1981):251-75.

Reviews literature on adolescent development, especially from the life-cycle perspective.  Covers some of the literature on transmission of values.

KEYWORDS: reciprocal influence, review,
theory, transmission, values

179. ———. "Children and Adolescents as Produc-
ers of Their Own Development." **Developmental Review** 2(1982):342-70.

Examines the reasons why there is
substantial reciprocal influence between
parents and children

KEYWORDS: reciprocal influence, transmission

180. Lerner, R.M., M. Karson, M. Meisels, and J.R.
Knapp. "Actual and Perceived Attitudes of
Late Adolescents and Their Parents: The
Phenomenon of the Generation Gap." **The
Journal of Genetic Psychology** 126(1975):
195-207.

Based on a sample of 78 adolescents and 50
of their parents they concluded that
adolescents overestimate number of major
differences while adults underestimate such
differences.

KEYWORDS: both parents, perceptions,
sexual beliefs, social problems, transmission

181. Lerner, R.M., and J.R. Knapp. "Actual and
Perceived Intrafamilial Attitudes of Late
Adolescents and Their Parents." **Journal of
Youth and Adolescence** 4(1975):17-36.

Based on a sample of 184 mother-father-
child triads they conclude that adolescents
overestimate number of major differences
while adults underestimate such differences. They also show that actual
attitudes for parent-child dyads are less
correlated than the actual attitude of the
child and the child's perception of the
parent's attitude.

KEYWORDS: both parents, perceptions,
political, sexual beliefs, social problems,
transmission

182.  Lerner, R.M., and G.B. Spanier (eds.).
      **Adolescent Development: A Life-span Per-
      spective.** New York: McGraw-Hill, 1980.

      A collection of papers dealing with adoles-
      cent development from the life-cycle per-
      spective.

      KEYWORDS: child rearing, historical,
      identification, reciprocal influence,
      theory, transmission, values

183.  Leslie, Leigh A., Ted L. Huston, and Michael
      P. Johnson. "Parental Reactions to Dating
      Relationships: Do They Make a Difference?"
      **Journal of Marriage and the Family** 48
      (1986): in press.

184.  Lewko, J., and S. Greendorfer. "Family
      Influence and Sex Differences in Children's
      Socialization into Sport: A Review."
      **Psychology of Motor Behavior and Sport.**
      Edited by D. Landers and R. Christina.
      Champaign, Ill.: Human Kinetics, 1977, pp.
      434-47.

      Reviews literature on childhood socializa-
      tion into sport. Emphasis is on early
      childhood, but some coverage is given to
      adolescent and young-adult children. Role
      of family compared to peers and school is
      discussed and sex differences are elaborat-
      ed.

      KEYWORDS: child rearing, mother vs.
      father, peers vs. parents, review, sex
      roles, sports, theory

185.   Libby, Roger, Alan C. Acock, and David C.
       Payne.  "Configurational Approach to
       Parental Preferences Concerning Sources of
       Sex Education for Adolescents."  **Adoles-
       cence** 9(1974):73-80.

       Survey of parents of high school students
       concerning the parental influence on sex
       education.

       KEYWORDS:  both parents, education, sexual
       beliefs


186.   Longfellow, C.  "Divorce in Context:  Its
       Impact on Children."  **Divorce and Separa-
       tion:  Context, Causes, and Consequences.**
       Edited by G. Levinger and O.C. Moles.  New
       York:  Basic Books, 1979.

       KEYWORDS:  divorce effects


187.   Looker, E. Dianne and Peter C. Pineo.  "Look-
       ing Forward:  Current Attitudes of Canadian
       Teenagers to Work, Careers, and Marriage."
       **Marriage and Divorce in Canada.**  Edited by
       K. Ishwaran.  New York:  Methuen Press,
       1983, pp. 150-70.

       Surveys attitudes of teenagers including
       discussion of working mothers as well as
       attitudes of both mother and father.

       KEYWORDS:  cross-cultural, mother vs.
       father, sex-specification, social class,
       work


188.   ————.  "Social Psychological Variables and
       Their Relevance to the Status Attainment of
       Teenagers."  **American Journal of Sociology**
       88(1983):1195-219.

       A criticism of the "Wisconsin model" of
       status attainment that contends we need to
       add self concept and parental aspirations
       for youth as intervening social psychologi-

cal variables to the traditional socio-
economic variables that have been utilized.
Based on data from 400 teenagers and their
parents.

KEYWORDS: education, self-esteem, social
class, social structure, status attainment,
transmission

189. Lueptow, Lloyd B. "Parental Status and
Influence and the Achievement Orientations
of High School Seniors." **Sociology of
Education** 48(1975):91-110.

Achievement values of high-school seniors
were related to internal family factors and
external forces. Achievement values higher
among females than males. Male achievement
values more dependent on internal family
factors than is the case for females.
Females may be more dependent on external
factors.

KEYWORDS: education, sex-specification,
status attainment, social class

190. ————. "Social Structure, Social Change and
Parental Influence in Adolescent Sex-Role
Socialization: 1964-1975." **Journal of
Marriage and the Family** 42(1980):93-103.

Examines parental influence on adolescent
sex-roles based on data from 1964 and 1975.
Finds little change in sex roles over
period. Considers affective and cognitive
theories of identification, social learning
theory, and power relationships as well as
social structural variables and same sex
influence. Finds father's influence
related to instrumental orientations among
boys but expressive orientations among
girls.

KEYWORDS: both parents, identification,
longitudinal, mother vs. father, percep-

tions, power, same sex parents, sex roles, sex-specification, social structure, theory

191.   Lueptow, Lloyd B., J. McClendon McKee, and John W. McKeon. "Father's Occupation and Son's Personality: Findings and Questions for the Emerging Linkage Hypotheses." **The Sociological Quarterly** 20(1979):463-75.

A study based on 1750 high school senior males shows that the influence of father's occupational complexity on son's achievement patterns disappears when controlling for family income, father's education, and father's occupational status. This challenges hypotheses about the characteristics of the father's work role influencing his son's achievement orientation.

KEYWORDS: education, social structure, social class, status attainment, transmission, values, work

192.   Mannheim, K. "The Problem of Generations." **Essays on the Sociology of Knowledge.** Edited by Karl Mannheim. London: Routledge and Kegan Press, 1952, pp. 276-322.

This is a classic statement on theories of generations. It covers historical uses of the concept, distinguishes various types of meaning such as cohort. Most of the major issues involving generations are discussed here although there is little attention given to parent-child influence processes.

KEYWORDS: cohort vs. lineage, cross-cultural, generations, genetics, historical, methods, perceptions, political, review, social structure, theory, transmission

193.  Mare, Robert D., and William M. Mason.
      "Children's Reports of Parental Socio-
      economic A Multigroup Measurement Model."
      **Sociological Methods and Research** 9(1980):
      178-98.

      A LISREL analysis of perceptions of
      parental socio-economic characteristics.

      KEYWORDS:  perceptions, social class,
      methods


194.  Margolin, Gayla and Gerald R. Patterson.
      "Differential Consequences Provided by
      Mothers and Fathers for Their Sons and
      Daughters."  **Developmental Psychology** 11
      (1975):537-38.

      Examines interactions between parents and
      children showing some evidence that fathers
      report more positive responding to sons
      than to daughters.  Suggests, but does not
      provide any evidence, that there is trans-
      mission of attitudes and beliefs.

      KEYWORDS:  both parents, child rearing,
      interaction, mother vs. father, same sex,
      sex-specification, transmission


195.  Markides, Kyriakos S.  "Disentangling Genera-
      tional and Life-Cycle Effects on Value
      Differences."  **Social Science Quarterly** 59
      (1978):390-93.

      Critiques paper by Penn for not making a
      clear distinction between a cohort effect
      and a lineage effect when examining the
      study of inter-generational transmission of
      values.  Notes that how cohorts rank order
      values is not direct evidence of lineage
      similarities nor differences.

      KEYWORDS:  cohort vs. lineage, generations,
      life-cycle, methods, transmission, values

196.   Marshall, Victor W., and Vern L. Bengtson.
       "Generations:  Conflict and Cooperation."
       **Aging in the Eighties and Beyond.**  Edited
       by M. Bergener, U. Lehr, E. Lang, and R.
       Schmitz-Scherzer.  New York:  Springer,
       1983, pp. 298-310.

       Reviews research on inter-generational
       solidarity.

       KEYWORDS:  affect, generations, inter-
       action, perception, review


197.   Martin, Barclay.  "Parent-Child Relations."
       **Review of Child Development Research**, Vol.
       4.  Edited by F.D. Horowitz.  Chicago:
       University of Chicago Press, 1975, pp. 463-
       540.

       An extensive review with lengthy references
       to work done prior to 1975.  Emphasis is on
       parent-child relations for infants and
       young children, but covers a wide range of
       issues of relevance to adolescent sociali-
       zation.
       KEYWORDS:  affect, both parents, child
       rearing, review, status attainment, trans-
       mission, values


198.   Matthews, Sarah H., and Jetse Sprey.  "Adoles-
       cents' Relationships with Grandparents:  An
       Empirical Contribution to Conceptual Clari-
       fication."  **Journal of Gerontology**
       40(1985):621-26.

       Late adolescent grandchildren report closer
       ties to maternal than paternal
       grandparents, especially the maternal
       grandmother.  Perceptions of their parents'
       relations with the grandparents are
       important.

       KEYWORDS:  affect, generations, grand-
       parents, perceptions, sex-specification

199.  McBroom, William H.  "The Influence of
      Parental Status Variables on the Status
      Aspirations of Youths."  **Adolescence** 20
      (1985):115-27.

      A large survey of college students shows
      that perceptions of parental status pro-
      vides a better predictor of the status
      aspirations of young adults than does the
      objective status of parents.  It also shows
      that mothers' characteristics are more
      important than those of fathers.

      KEYWORDS:  mother vs. father, perceptions,
      sex-specification, status attainment,
      vocational interests

200.  McBroom, William H., Fred W. Reed, Clarence
      E. Burns, J. Lee Hargraves, and Mary A.
      Trankel.  "Intergenerational Transmission
      of Values:  A Data-Based Reassessment."
      **Social Psychology Quarterly** 48(1985):150-
      63.

      Examines two measures of youth-parent
      agreement.  One is similarity and the other
      is based on directionality.  Youth-parent
      agreement was found to be a predictor of
      youth behavior.  Family structure (democ-
      racy, decision making, intact) variables
      were also found to be important.

      KEYWORDS:  interaction, methods, mother-
      father agreement, perceptions, sexual
      beliefs, social problems, transmission,
      values

201.  McDonald, G.W.  "Parental Identification by
      the Adolescent:  A Social Power Approach."
      **Journal of Marriage and the Family** 39
      (1977):705-19.

      An availability sample of 149 adolescents
      provided evidence to support a social power
      theory of adolescent identification.  Sex-
      specification was not supported.

KEYWORDS: both parents, identification, mother vs. father, perceptions, power, sex-specification

202.  McElroy, M.A.  "Parent-Child Relations and Orientations Toward Sport."  **Sex Roles** 9 (1983):997-1004.

Survey of 898 male and 800 female adolescents from economically disadvantaged backgrounds examined identification with either the mother or the father as a predictor of orientation toward sports.

KEYWORDS: both parents, identification, mother vs. father, perceptions, same sex parents, sex roles, sex-specification, sports, social class, transmission,

203.  Mead, G.H.  **Mind, Self, and Society.** Chicago:  University of Chicago Press, 1934.
Classic statement of symbolic interaction perspective as a theoretical basis for a great deal of inter-generational research.

KEYWORDS: child rearing, interaction, theory

204.  Mead, Margaret.  **Culture and Commitment:  A Study of the Generation Gap.**  New York: Langman, 1970.

Based on fifty years of field work and concern with the cultural aspects of the generation gap, this classic examines generational change and their implications for the world community.

KEYWORDS: cross-cultural, generations, historical, theory, transmission, values

205.  Miller, Karen A., Melvin L. Kohn, and Carmi
      Schooler.  "Educational Self-Direction and
      Cognitive Functioning of Students."  **Social
      Forces** 63(1985):923-44.

      Examines educational self-direction of
      white students in grades seven through
      college.  Includes ideational flexibility
      of both mother and father.  Mother is
      better predictor of student's ideational
      flexibility.

      KEYWORDS:  education, mother vs. father,
      sex-specification, social class, status
      attainment, transmission, values


206.  Montemayor, Raymond.  "Maternal Employment
      and Adolescents' Relations with Parents,
      Siblings, and Peers."  **Journal of Youth and
      Adolescence** 13(1984):543-57.

      Based on a sample of 64 tenth-grade adoles-
      cents, this study concludes males (but not
      females) have more arguments with mothers
      who work.  Both sexes spend less time with
      parents when mothers work.

      KEYWORDS:  affect, interaction, peers vs.
      parents, work


207.  Montemayor, Raymond and Mark D. Clayton.
      "Maternal Employment and Adolescent
      Development."  **Theory Into Practice**  22
      (1983):112-18.

      Reviews research on effects of maternal
      employment on 10 to 17 year olds focusing
      on academic performance, sex-roles, parent
      and peer relations, delinquency and
      psychological adjustment.

      KEYWORDS:  affect, education, interaction,
      peers vs. parents, review, sex roles, sex-
      specification, social problems, values,
      work

208.  Moore, T.W.  "Exclusive Mothering and Its
      Alternatives:  The Outcome to Adolescence."
      **Scandinavian Journal of Psychology** 16
      (1975):255-72.

      KEYWORDS:  cross-cultural


209.  Mortimer, J.T.  "Occupational Value Sociali-
      zation in Business and Professional
      Families."  **Sociology of Work and Occupa-
      tions** 2(1975):29-53.

      Shows that different patterns of occupa-
      tional values (intrinsic and extrinsic) are
      transmitted through close parent-child
      relationships in professional and business
      families.

      KEYWORDS:  affect, interaction, status
      attainment, transmission, values, work


210.  ————.  "Social Class, Work and the Family:
      Some Implications of the Father's Occupa-
      tion for Familial Relationships and Sons'
      Career Decisions."  **Journal of Marriage and
      the Family** 38(1976):241-56.

      Professionals are closer to sons than
      businessmen.  Father's occupation
      influences family relationships largely
      through the income dimension.  Fathers have
      substantial influence on occupational
      values of sons.

      KEYWORDS:  affect, social class, social
      structure, transmission, vocational inter-
      est, work


211.  ————.  "Comment on Kenneth Spenner's
      Occupations, Role Characteristics, and
      Intergenerational Transmission."  **Sociology
      of Work and Occupations** 9(1981):113-17.

      Comments on Spenner's paper discussing
      transmission of work orientations.

KEYWORDS: social class, social structure, transmission, status attainment, vocational interest, work

212.   Mortimer, J.T., and D. Kumka. "A Further Examination of the 'Occupational Linkage Hypotheses'." The Sociological Quarterly 23(1982):3-16.

Finds that the fathers' occupation influences sons' adult occupational destinations as well as their occupational reward values.

KEYWORDS: transmission, values, work

213.   Mortimer, J.T., and J. Lorence. "Self Concept Stability and Change from Late Adolescence to Early Adulthood." Research in Community and Mental Health, Vol. 2. Edited by Roberta G. Simmons. Greenich, Conn.: JAI Press, 1981, pp. 5-42.

Indicates the declining importance of parental support for the child's sense of well-being as the transition is made from late adolescence to early adulthood.

KEYWORDS: parental support, self-esteem, transmission

214.   Moss, N.E., and S.I. Abramowitz. "Beyond Deficit-Filling and Developmental Stakes: Cross-Disciplinary Perspectives on Parental Heritage." Journal of Marriage and the Family 44(1982):357-66.

KEYWORDS: theory, transmission

215.   Mueller, C.W., and H. Pope. "Marital Instability: A Study of its Transmission Between Generations." Journal of Marriage and the Family 39(1977):83-94.

A national sample is used to study the intergenerational transmission of marital instability.

KEYWORDS: divorce effects, marital stability, transmission

216.  Nelsen, H.M.  "Religious Transmission Versus Religious Formation:  Preadolescent-Parent Interaction."  **The Sociological Quarterly** 21(1980):207-18.

Using a sample of 2724 adolescents it is found that both parental religiousness and support are significant predictors of preadolescent religiousness.  Parental · religiousness is the best predictor. Paternal and maternal measures were similar in their abilities to predict religiosity.

KEYWORDS: both parents, mother vs. father, religion, sex-specification, same sex parents, transmission

217.  ————.  "Gender Differences in the Effects of Parental Discord on Preadolescent Religiousness."  **Journal for the Scientific Study of Religion** 20(1981):351-60.

Parental discord does not have a clear effect on the religiosity of girls but does lessen the religiosity of boys.

KEYWORDS: affect, conflict, religion, sex-specification

218.  ————.  "Religious Conformity in an Age of Disbelief:  Contextual Effects of Time, Denomination, and Family Processes upon Church Decline and Apostasy."  **American Sociological Review** 46(1981):632-40.

Examines the role of the family in religious socialization within the context of church and cohort.  Argues for greater conformity among females and firstborn males.

KEYWORDS: birth order, child rearing, religion, sex-specification

219. Nelsen, Hart M. and Alice Kroliczak. "Parental Use of the Threat 'God Will Punish': Replication and Extension." **Journal for the Scientific Study of Religion** 23(1984):267-77.

Using children in grades 4 to 8, they find that parents who used the threat that God will punish them are not just parents who are otherwise powerless. Children whose parents use this threat have greater self-blame and greater feelings that they should be obedient.

KEYWORDS: child rearing, religion, self-esteem, values

220. Nelsen, Hart M. and Arshad Rizvi. "Gender and Religious Socialization: Comparisons from Pakistan and the United States." **Journal of Comparative Family Studies** 15 (1984):281-290.

Provides comparison of religious socialization between Pakistan and the U.S. Examines role of parental support versus parental religiosity as it varies by gender.

KEYWORDS: cross-cultural, parental support, religion

221. Niemi, R.G. **How Family Members Perceive Each Other.** New Haven: Yale University Press, 1974.

A large scale study of political socialization based on a national survey.

KEYWORDS: both parents, methods, mother vs. father, perceptions, political, review, sex-specification

222.  Niemi, R.G. and K. Krehbiel.  "The Quality of Survey Responses about Parents and the Family:  A Longitudinal Analysis."  **Political Methodology** 5(1984):193-209.

A longitudinal study is used to show that adults in their mid-twenties are no better at reporting parental responses to variables than they were as adolescents.

KEYWORDS: age of parent, grandparents, longitudinal, methods, perceptions, political

223.  Niemi, R.G., D. Newman, and D.L. Weiner. "Reassessing the Political Influence of Parents on Children."  **Micropolitics** 2 (1982):203-17.

A reanalysis of the Jennings-Niemi data shows much greater agreement when both parents are used in a regression equation. Parental agreement is shown to be unimportant.

KEYWORDS: both parents, mother-father agreement, mother vs. father, political, sex-specification, transmission

224.  Niemi, Richard G., G. Bigham Powell, Harold W. Stanley, C. Lawrence Evans.  "Testing the Converse Partisanship Model with New Electorates."  **Comparative Political Studies.** (1986):  in press.

The Converse model argues that individual experience and socialization explain strength of partisanship.  This study reports that the Converse model fails to account for the strength of partisanship among new electorates.

KEYWORDS:   cohort vs. lineage, generations,
historical, longitudinal, methods, political, theory, transmission, values

225.  Niemi, R.G., D. Ross, and J. Alexander.  "The
      Similarity of Political Values of Parents
      and College-Age Youths." **Public Opinion
      Quarterly** 42(1978):503-20.

      Interviews with national sample of 17 to 23
      year old children and their parents show
      only moderate association across a variety
      of political and social issues.

      KEYWORDS:  political, religion, social
      problems, transmission

226.  Niemi, R.G. and B. Sobieszek.  "Political
      Socialization." **Annual Review of
      Sociology.** Edited by Alex Ingkeles, James
      Coleman, and Neil Smelser.  Palo Alto,
      Calif.: Annual Reviews, 1977, pp. 209-233.

      Surveys the field of political sociali-
      zation, linking specific research findings
      to classical theoretical and empirical
      research.  Suggests a new emphasis on
      preadult studies.

      KEYWORDS:  political, review, theory,
      transmission

227.  Niemi, Richard G., Harold W. Stanley, C.
      Lawrence Evans.  "Age and Turnout Among the
      Newly Enfranchised:  Life Cycle versus
      Experience Effects." **European Journal of
      Political Research** 12(1984):371-86.

      Challenges importance of pre-adult sociali-
      zation in determining attitudes and activi-
      ties in later years.  Newly enfranchised
      groups cross-culturally, such as women,
      have no pre-adult socialization toward
      political participation.

KEYWORDS:  cross-cultural, cohort vs.
lineage, historical, political, transmission

228.   Nowak, Stefan.   "Values and Attitudes of the
       Polish People."  **Scientific American** 245
       (1981):45-53.

       A comparison of parents and youth is pre-
       sented to explore the generation gap in
       Poland.  A wide variety of issues is cover-
       ed.  Perceptions by students are also
       reviewed.

       KEYWORDS:  cross-cultural, generations,
       historical, perceptions, political,
       religion, sexual beliefs, social problems,
       values, work

229.   Nye, F.I.   "Child Adjustment in Broken and
       Unhappy Unbroken Homes."  **Marriage and
       Family Living** 19(1957):356-60.

       Classic statement of the effects of marital
       instability on offspring.

       KEYWORDS:  affect, both parents, child
       rearing, divorce effects, father absence,
       marital stability

230.   Nye, F.I. and M.B. Lamberts.  **School-age
       Parenthood:  Consequences for Babies,
       Mothers, Fathers, Grandparents, and Others.**
       Extension Bulletin 667, Cooperative Exten-
       sion Service.  Pullman, WA:  Washington
       State University, 1980.

       KEYWORDS:  interaction, sexual beliefs,
       social problems

231.   O'Donnell, William J.   "Adolescent Self-
       Esteem Related to Feelings Toward Parents
       and Peers."  **Journal of Youth and Adoles-
       lence** 5(1976):179-85.

Reports that feelings toward both parents and peers influence self-esteem among eighth and eleventh grade adolescents.

KEYWORDS:   affect, peers vs. parents, self-esteem

232.   Oliver, L.I.   **The Association of Health Attitudes and Perceptions of Youths 12-17 Years of Age with Those of Their Parents. United States, 1966-1970.**   Vital and Health Statistics Series 11, No. 161.  Washington, D.C.:   U.S. Government Printing Office, 1977.

KEYWORDS:   perceptions, transmission

233.   Oliver, L.W.   "The Relationship of Parental Attitudes and Parent Identification to Career and Homemaking Orientation in College Women."   **Journal of Vocational Behavior** 7(1975):1-12.

KEYWORDS:   identification, work

234.   Olsen, N.J.   "The Role of Grandmothers in Taiwanese Family Socialization."   **Journal of Marriage and the Family** 38(1976):363-72.

Reports on role of grandmothers in socialization for 49 three-generation Taiwanese families.

KEYWORDS:   cross-cultural, generations, grandparents, mother-daughter,

235.   Openshaw, D. Kim and Darwin L. Thomas. "Adolescent Self-Esteem in a Family Context."   **Adolescents in Families.**   Edited by Geoffry K. Leigh and Gary W. Peterson. Cincinnati:   South-Western Publishing (1986).   In Press.

KEYWORDS:   self-esteem

236.   Openshaw, D. Kim, Darwin L. Thomas, and Boyd
       C. Rollins.   "Socialization and Adolescent
       Self-Esteem:   Symbolic Interaction and
       Social Learning Explanations."   **Adolescence**
       18(1983):317-29.

       Both symbolic interaction and social
       learning variables are shown to be related
       to adolescent self-esteem.

       KEYWORDS:   interaction, self-esteem, theory

237.   ————.   "Parental Influence of Adolescent
       Self-Esteem."   **Journal of Early Adolescence**
       4(1984):259-74.

       KEYWORDS:   self-esteem

238.   Otto, Luther.   "Family Influences on Youth's
       Occupational Aspirations and Achievements."
       **Adolescents in Families.**   Edited by Geoffry
       K. Leigh and Gary W. Peterson.   Cincinnati:
       South-Western Publishing (1986).   In Press.

       KEYWORDS:   work

239.   Otto, L.B. and A.O. Haller.   "Evidence for a
       Social-Psychological View of the Status
       Attainment Process:   Four Studies Compar-
       ed."   **Social Forces** 57(1979):887-914.

       Study examines longitudinal data to show
       evidence for a social psychological model
       of the status attainment process.

       KEYWORDS:   both parents, education,
       longitudinal, social class, social
       structure, status attainment, transmission

240.   Parish, Thomas S.   "Perceptions of Parents'
       Attitudes and Behaviors as Evidence that

Children Affect Parents." **Psychological Reports** 46(1980):1037-38.

Survey shows that there is a very high correlation (.90) between how college students rate their mother and their father on both permissiveness and warmth.

KEYWORDS: affect, both parents, child rearing, mother-father agreement, parental support, perceptions, sex-specification

241.   ————.  "The Relationship Between Factors Associated with Father Loss and Individuals' Level of Moral Judgment." **Adolescence** 15(1980):535-41.

The longer the father has been gone the less the moral development. Based on an n of 24.

KEYWORDS: father absence, values

242.   ————.  "Young Adults' Evaluations of Themselves and Their Parents as a Function of Family Structure and Disposition." **Journal of Youth and Adolescence** 10(1981):173-78.

Perceptions of self, mother, and father are related to perceptions of family happiness.

KEYWORDS: affect, perceptions, self-esteem

243.   Parish, Thomas S. and Terry F. Copeland. "The Impact of Father Absence on Moral Development in Females." **Sex Roles** 7 (1981):635-36.

A very small convenience sample suggests that the younger the female when the father becomes absent (death or divorce) the less she will advance in terms of moral development.

KEYWORDS: father absence, values

244.    Parish, Thomas S. and Gerald M. Eads. "Col-
        lege Students' Perceptions of Parental
        Restrictiveness/Permissiveness and
        Students' Scores on a Brief Measure of
        Creativity." Psychological Reports 41
        (1977):455-58.

        College students who perceive mothers as
        more permissive in childrearing techniques
        may be more creative.

        KEYWORDS:  child rearing, parental support,
        perceptions


245.    Parish, Thomas S., Darlene M. Hattrup, and
        Ronald Rosenblatt.  "Father Loss and the
        Individual's Subsequent Values Prioritiza-
        tion." Education 200(1980):377-81.

        Compares values of 227 college students
        based on father absence versus intact
        families.

        KEYWORDS:  father absence, values


246.    Parish, Thomas S. and John A. Hortin.  "The
        Impact of Mother Loss on Evaluations of
        Self and Parents." College Student Journal
        17(1983):35-38.

        Evaluations of fathers were enhanced by
        their demise and diminished by divorce.
        Evaluations of mothers dropped drastically
        by their absence.  Self-concepts of males
        higher than females only if they were from
        intact families.

        KEYWORDS:  divorce effects, father absence,
        mother vs. father, perceptions, self-esteem


247.    Parish, Thomas and B. Kappes.  "Impact of
        Father Loss on the Family." Psychology and
        Human Development:  An International Jour-
        nal 8(1980):107-12.

Effect of loss of father on self esteem of children is examined.

KEYWORDS: affect, father absence, marital stability, perceptions, self-esteem

248.  Parish, Thomas S. and Gerald D. Nunn.  "Locus of Control as a Function of Family Type and Age at Onset of Father Absence."  **The Journal of Psychology** 113(1983):187-90. Based on 644 undergraduate students, paper shows relationship between father absence, cause of absence, and age at absence with locus of control.

KEYWORDS: father absence, self-esteem, values

249.  Parish, Thomas S. and Stanley E. Wigle.  "A Longitudinal Study of the Impact of Parental Divorce on Adolescents' Evaluations of Self and Parents."  **Adolescence** 20 (1985):239-44.

A longitudinal study of 639 students examines the impact of divorce on attitudes toward self and both parents.  Children from consistently intact families evaluate themselves and both parents more positively.  Negative effects of divorce are greatest during first year.  Attitude becomes more positive over time but does not reach the level of children from intact homes.

KEYWORDS: affect, both parents, divorce effects, longitudinal, marital stability, mother vs. father, perceptions, self-esteem, social problems

250.  Parsons, T. and R. Bales.  **Family Socialization and Interaction Processes.**  Glencoe, Illinois:  Free Press, 1955.

KEYWORDS: interaction, theory

251.  Penn, J. Roger.  "Measuring Intergenerational
      Value Differences."  **Social Science
      Quarterly** 58(1977):293-301.

           Survey of female college students and their
           parents shows cohort differences in
           terminal values, both in terms of the
           importance of the values and in terms of
           the rank order.  Has lineage data but
           examines it as cohort data.

           KEYWORDS:  cohort vs. lineage, generations,
           social problems, transmission

252.  Percheron, Annick.  "Ideological Proximity
      Among French Children:  Problems of Defi-
      nition and Measurement."  **European Journal
      of Political Research** 5(1977):53-81.

           A methodological examination of the prob-
           lems associated with measuring party
           identification in a sample of children.
           Emphasis is on the special problems doing
           this outside of the United States.

           KEYWORDS:  cross-cultural, generations,
           methods

253.  ————.  "The Influence of Socio-Political
      Context on Political Socialization."
      **European Journal of Political Research** 10
      (1982):53-69.

           KEYWORDS:  political

254.  Percheron, Annick and M. Kent Jennings.
      "Religion, Acculturation, and Political
      Continuities in French Families:  A New
      Perspective on an Old Controversy."
      **Comparative Politics** 13(1981):421-36.

           Examines transmission of political beliefs
           in France.

KEYWORDS:   cross-cultural, generations, political, transmission, values, religion

255.   Perlmutter, Marion (ed.).   "Parent-Child Interaction and Parent-Child Relations in Child Development,"  **The Minnesota Symposia on Child Psychology,** Vol. 17. Minneapolis: University of Minnesota Press, 1984, pp. 221-259.

KEYWORDS:   interaction

256.   Petersen, Larry R., Gary R. Lee, and Godfrey J. Ellis.   "Social Structure, Socialization Values, and Disciplinary Techniques:   A Cross-cultural Analysis."  **Journal of Marriage the Family** 44(1982):131-42.

Using the Standard Cross-cultural Sample and the Human Relations Area Files, this study argues that a cultural emphasis on conformity relative to self-reliance has a substantial and a positive effect on the use of physical punishment.

KEYWORDS:   child rearing, cross-cultural, parental support, social structure, values

257.   Peterson, Gary W.   "Family Conceptual Frameworks and Adolescent Development."  **Adolescents in Families.**   Edited by G.K. Leigh and G.W. Peterson.   Cincinnati:   South-Western Publishing (1986).   In Press.

Compares exchange, symbolic interaction, and systems approaches in terms of parent-adolescent interaction and influence.

KEYWORDS:   interaction, review, theory

258.   Peterson, Gary W., Geoffrey K. Leigh and Randal D. Day.   "Family Stress Theory and the Impact of Divorce on Children."  **Journal of Divorce** 7(1984):1-20.

Reviews literature on family stress and
impact of divorce on children and presents
a theory based on definition of the situation.  Presents, but does not test a series
of hypotheses.

KEYWORDS:  affect, divorce effects, review,
theory

259.    Peterson, Gary W. and Boyd C. Rollins.
        "Parent-Child Socialization:  A Review of
        Research and Applications of Symbolic
        Interaction Concepts."  **Handbook of Mar-
        riage and the Family**.  Edited by Marvin B.
        Sussman and Suzanne K. Steinmetz.  New
        York:  Plenum Press, 1986.  In Press.

        This is an extensive and comprehensive
        review of the literature.  A considerable
        amount of it concerns with younger
        children, but it covers most major issues.
        It is strong on conceptual and theoretical
        issues as well as on methodological con-
        cerns.

        KEYWORDS:  affect, birth order, blacks,
        both parents, child rearing, ethnicity,
        hispanic, parental support, perceptions,
        power, race, reciprocal influence, review,
        social class, theory, transmission

260.    Peterson, Gary W., Boyd C. Rollins, and
        Darwin L. Thomas.  "Parental Influence and
        Adolescent Conformity:  Compliance and
        Internalization."  **Youth and Society**.  16
        (1985):397-420.

        Using both self report and observational
        data, study reports that it is useful to
        distinguish between external compliance and
        internalization of parental views.  These
        are related to parental power and parental
        behavior.

        KEYWORDS:  power, transmission

261.  Peterson, G.W., B.C. Rollins, D.L. Thomas,
      and L. Kay Heaps.  "Social Placement of
      Adolescents:  Sex-Role Influences on Family
      Decisions Regarding the Careers of Youth."
      **Journal of Marriage and the Family** 44
      (1982):647-58.

      A simulation game involving 183 families
      with special attention to 96 of them having
      both a male and female adolescent demon-
      strated that family decisions favored the
      career goals of adolescent males.  Fathers
      favored domestic goals for daughters much
      more than the daughters did.

      KEYWORDS:  both parents, experiment, sex
      roles, sex-specification, status attain-
      ment, transmission, vocational interest

262.  Peterson, Gary W., Lois E. Southworth, and
      David F. Peters.  "Children's Self-Esteem
      and Maternal Behavior in Three Low-Income
      Samples."  **Psychological Reports** 52(1983):
      79-86.

      In a sample of low-income children from
      rural Appalachia, perceptions of maternal
      loving and demanding were positively
      related to the child's self-esteem while
      perceptions of the maternal punishment was
      negatively related.

      KEYWORDS:  affect, child-rearing, parental
      support, rural, self-esteem, social class,
      transmission

263.  Pineo, Peter C. and E. Dianne Looker.  "Class
      and Conformity in the Canadian Setting."
      **Canadian Journal of Sociology** 8(1983):293-
      17.

      Sample of fathers and mothers from Canada
      reported emphasis on self-direction as
      opposed to conformity.  Related to social
      status but less related to work character-

istics than early work by Kohn in the
United States indicated.

KEYWORDS:  child-rearing, cross-cultural,
mother vs. father, social class, transmission, values

264.    Reinhard, D.W.   "The Reaction of Adolescent
        Boys and Girls to the Divorce of Their
        Parents."  **Journal of Clinical Child
        Psychology** 6(1977):15-20.

        Sons and daughters react similarly to
        absence of father.  Reaction to divorce is
        less negative than anticipated.

        KEYWORDS:  divorce effects, marital stabil-
        ity, perceptions, sex roles, sex specifica-
        tion

265.    Renshon, S.A.   "Birth Order and Political
        Socialization."  **New Directions in the
        Study of Political Socialization.**  Edited
        by D.C. Schwartz and S.K. Schwartz.  New
        York:  Free Press, 1975, pp. 39-61.

        This paper argues for the potential
        importance of birth order in political
        socialization.

        KEYWORDS:  birth order, child rearing,
        political, transmission

266.    ————.   "Personality and Family Dynamics in
        the Political Socialization Process."  **Ameri-
        can Journal of Political Science** 19(1975):63-
        80.

        Suggests that family influence involves
        socialization at a more basic level than
        attitudes and influences.  Study emphasizes
        role of interpersonal trust and personal
        control as representing this more basic
        level of transmission.

KEYWORDS:   political, transmission

267.   ————.   Handbook of Political Socialization:
       Theory and Research.   New York:   Free Press,
       1977.

       A collection of papers on political
       socialization which emphasizes theoretical
       issues in the process of acquiring politi-
       cal orientations.

       KEYWORDS:   cohort vs. lineage, generations,
       political, theory, transmission

268.   Ridgeway, Cecilia.   "Parental Identification
       and Patterns of Career Orientation in
       College Women."   Journal of Vocational
       Behavior 12(1978):1-11.

       A sample of 457 college women is used to
       show that parental identification interacts
       with parental characteristics in shaping
       women's career orientations.

       KEYWORDS:   identification, mother-daughter,
       same sex parents, sex-specification, status
       attainment, transmission, vocational inter-
       est, work

269.   Rollins, Boyd C., and Darwin L. Thomas.   "A
       Theory of Parental Power and Child
       Compliance."   Power in Families.   Edited by
       R. Cromwell and D. Olson.   Beverly Hills,
       Calif.:   Sage, 1975, pp. 36-60.

       KEYWORDS:   compliance, parental support,
       power

270.   ————.   "Parental Support, Power, and
       Control Techniques in the Socialization of
       Children."   Contemporary Theories about the
       Family, Vol. 1.   Edited by Wesley Burr,
       Reuben Hill, Ira Reiss, and F. Ivan Nye.

Glencoe, Illinois:   The Free Press, 1979,
pp. 317-364.

This reviews theory and research concerned
with the consequences of parental support,
power, and control techniques.  A number of
propositions are presented based on a
combination of theoretical orientations.

KEYWORDS:  affect, child rearing, identification, interaction, parental support,
power, review, theory

271.   Robertson, J.F.   "Interaction in Three Generation Families, Parents as Mediators:
Toward a Theoretical Perspective."  **International Journal of Aging and Human
Development** 6(1975):103-9.

Develops perspective on role of parents as
mediators in the interactions between
grandparents and grandchildren.

KEYWORDS:  grandparents, interaction

272.   Rosenfeld, Rachel A.   "Women's Intergenerational Occupational Mobility."  **American
Sociological Review** 43(1978):36-46.

Mother's occupation influences her
daughter's occupational destination.
Father's occupation is not sufficient to
account for his daughter's occupational
destination.

KEYWORDS:  generations, mother-daughter,
mother vs. father, sex, roles, status
attainment

273.   Rosow, I.   "What is a Cohort and Why?"  **Human
Development** 21(1978):65-75.

Reviews nature of cohort, indicates that
cohort is an index of specific variables,
analyzes key conceptual and methodological

problems in the use of cohort, and claims
that despite its imprecision, cohort
remains a valuable sensitizing concept.
KEYWORDS: cohort vs. lineage, generations,
historical, methods, theory

274. Ryder, Norman B. "The Cohort as a Concept in
     the Study of Social Change." **American
     Sociological Review** 30(1965):843-61.

     The classic paper on the cohort as a unit
     of analysis in the study of generations.
     Various meanings of the concept of cohort
     are reviewed.

     KEYWORDS: cohort vs. lineage, generation,
     historical, methods, theory

275. Safilios-Rothschild, C. "Family Sociology or
     Wives' Family Sociology: A Cross-Cultural
     Examination of Decision Making." **Journal
     of Marriage and the Family** 31(1969):290-
     301.

     Makes the critically important point that
     much research relied on only interviewing a
     single parent; usually the mother.

     KEYWORDS: cross-cultural, methods, mother-
     father agreement, mother vs. father, sex
     roles, sex-specification

276. Schooler, Carmi. "Psychological Effects of
     Complex Environments During the Life Span:
     A Review and Theory." **Intelligence** 8
     (1984):259-81.

     Reviews evidence about effects of complex
     environments at different stages of life,
     including a section on childhood environ-
     ments. The greater the complexity of the
     environment the more self-directed and the
     higher the IQ of the child as an adult.

     KEYWORDS: child rearing, social structure

277.   Schulenberg, John E., Fred W. Vondracek, and
       Ann C. Crouter. "The Influence of the
       Family on Vocational Development." **Journal
       of Marriage and the Family** 46(1984):129-43.

       A literature review of the effects of
       family variables on vocational development
       of children. Focuses on the influence of
       social structure in the process and
       parental work experience but also reviews a
       variety of related issues.

       KEYWORDS: affect, birth order, blacks,
       child rearing, divorce effects, ethnicity,
       father absence, hispanics, number of child-
       ren, review, sex-specification, social
       class, social structure, spacing, status
       attainment, transmission, values, voca-
       tional interests, work

278.   Schwartz, D.C., and S.K. Schwartz. **New Direc-
       tions in Political Socialization.** New
       York: Free Press, 1975.

       This is a collection of papers on political
       socialization. It deals with a variety of
       topics including theories, cohort-histori-
       cal effects, influence of popular culture,
       and birth order.

       KEYWORDS: birth order, child rearing,
       historical, political, review, theory,

279.   Schwartz, S.K., and D.C. Schwartz. "New
       Directions in Political Socialization."
       **New Directions in Political Socialization.**
       Edited by D.C. Schwartz and S.K. Schwartz.
       New York: Free Press, 1975, pp. 3-25.

       Reviews literature on political socializa-
       tion and argues for a more active role on
       the part of the person being socialized.

       KEYWORDS: child rearing, political,
       reciprocal influence, transmission, values

280.  Sebald, Hans.  "Social Change and Intergener-
      ational Conflict."  **Adolescence;  A Social
      Psychological Analysis.**  Edited by Hans
      Sebald.  Englewood Cliffs, N.J.:  Prentice-
      Hall, 1984, pp. 106-126.

      An integration of major concepts facili-
      tating the understanding of generational
      conflict, including discussions of rapid
      social change, competing authorities:
      parents vs. experts, clash of inferiority
      complexes:  youth vs. adult complexes,
      youth culture in the US, the sexual revolu-
      tion, and parental reaction to modern
      adolescence.

      KEYWORDS:  generations, sexual beliefs,
      social problems, transmission

281.  ————.  "New-Age Romanticism:  The Quest for
      an Alternative Lifestyle as a Force in
      Social Change."  **Humboldt Journal of Social
      Relations.**  11(1984):106-127.

      Discussion of where the counter culture of
      the 1960s and 1970s went and what the
      successor of that movement is:  the New-Age
      movement.  It investigates the setting of
      new norms, values, and Weltanschauung, with
      emphasis on the new religious views that
      try to integrate Eastern and Western
      religious elements.

      KEYWORDS:  cross-cultural, generations,
      religion, values

282.  ————.  "Adolescents' Shifting Emphasis on
      Parent Orientation:  The Curvilinearity of
      the Past Decades."  **Journal of Marriage and
      the Family** 48(1986):  in press.

      Identical questionnaires were administered
      to over 500 teenagers to determine in which
      issues they chose as reference group their
      parents or peers.  This is a longitudinal
      study with inquires in the 1960s, 1970s and

1980s. Comparable samples and questionnaires allow a charting of teenage
attitudes, with disclosing differential
curves for boys and girls.

KEYWORDS: longitudinal, peers vs. parents,
sex-specification

283.  Sebald, Hans and Christine Kraugh. **Ich will
      ja nur Dein Bestes.** Dusseldorf, West
      Germany:  Econ, 1981.

      Focuses on the mother-son relationship and
      how it is characterized by urban-industrial
      lifestyle, especially in situations where a
      mother raises a son without the help of a
      father.  Emphasis is on the outcome of the
      personality formation of the son.

      KEYWORDS:  divorce effects, values

284.  Sebald, Hans and B. White.  "Teenagers'
      Divided Reference Groups:  Uneven Alignment
      with Parents and Peers."  **Adolescence** 15
      (1980):979-84.

      Survey of 100 youths in 1960 and another
      100 in 1976 reveals that:  (a) choice of
      parent or peer as reference group varies
      widely from one issue to another issue and
      (b) there has been an increase in use of
      peers rather than parents as a reference
      group.

      KEYWORDS:  education, longitudinal, peers
      vs. parents, sexual beliefs, status attain-
      ment, vocational interest

285.  Seliktar, O.  "Socialization of National
      Ideology."  **Political Psychology** 2(1980):
      66-94.

      KEYWORDS:  political

286.    Selvin, Kathleen F. and C. Ray Wingrove.
        "Real vs. Perceived Differences in How
        Three Intra-Family Generations of Women
        View their Roles in Society." **Sex Roles** 9
        (1983):609-24.

        Three generation sample of 103 college
        women, 88 mothers, and 30 maternal grand-
        mothers evaluated in terms of sex role
        attitudes.  Major intergenerational differ-
        ences prevailed with younger generations
        being more profeminist.  Labor force
        participation was correlated with liberal
        views.

        KEYWORDS:  generations, grandparents,
        mother-daughter, sex roles, transmission,
        work


287.    Shaffer, D.R., and G.H. Brody.  "Parental and
        Peer Influences on Moral Development."
        **Parent-Child Interaction:  Theory,
        Research, and Prospects.**  Edited by R.W.
        Henderson.  New York:  Academic Press,
        1981, pp. 83-124.

        A review of literature comparing how
        parents and peers influence moral develop-
        ment.  Compares major theoretical
        perspectives and has extensive references
        to empirical research on parental influence
        over a range of moral values and issues.

        KEYWORDS:  child rearing, experiment,
        identification, interaction, methods,
        parental support, peers vs. parents,
        review, social class, theory, transmission,
        values


288.    Sheleff, Leon.  **Generations Apart:  Adult
        Hostility To Youth.**  New York:  McGraw-
        Hill, 1981.

        Book has two themes, adults are hostile
        toward youth and Freud's Oedipus myth is
        one-sided and biased in favor of parents.

KEYWORDS: affect, cross-cultural, generations, historical, identification, interaction


289.    Skvoretz, J.V., and U. Kheoruenromne.   "Some
        Evidence Concerning the Value Hypothesis of
        Intergenerational Status Transmission:   A
        Research Note."  **Social Science Research** 8
        (1979):172-83.

        KEYWORDS:   status attainment


290.    Small, Stephen A.   "Parent-Adolescent Con-
        flict:   Possible Causes and Consequences."
        Paper presented at the Southeastern
        Psychological Association Meetings, New
        Orleans, 1984.

        Examines relationship between parent-child
        conflict, age of child, perceptions of
        parental control, and child's self-esteem.
        Conflict not related to child's self-este-
        em.  The older the child, the less the
        conflict.

        KEYWORDS:   affect, interaction, self-
        esteem, sex-specification


291.    Small, Stephen A., Steven Cornelius, and Gay
        Eastman.   "Parenting Adolescent Children:
        A period of Adult Storm and Stress?"
        Presented at the American Psychological
        Association Meetings.  Anaheim, Calif.:
        August 1983.

        Based on independent measures from parents
        and their children, study finds parental
        stress is greatest during early adolescence
        (13-15).  Higher parental stress associated
        with children who desire more autonomy,
        fail to adhere to parental advice, engage
        in deviant activities, and show little
        affection for parents.

KEYWORDS:   affect, interaction, sex-
specification

292.   Small, Stephen A., and G. Eastman.  "Parental
       Self-Esteem and the Parent-Adolescent
       Relationship."  Paper presented at the
       Annual Meeting of the National Council on
       Family Relations, St. Paul, Minn., 1983.

       A study of the 120 parent-child middle to
       upper middle class dyads reveals that self-
       esteem of mother influences how she inter-
       acts with her child.  Results for fathers
       are far less significant.

       KEYWORDS:   interaction, mothers vs.
       fathers, sex-specification, self-esteem

293.   Smith, M.D., and G.D. Self.  "The Congruence
       Between Mother and Daughters in Sex Role
       Attitude:   A Research Note." **Journal of
       Marriage and the Family** 42(1980):105-9.

       A study of 74 pairs of mothers and
       daughters shows mothers' sex role attitudes
       are better predictors of their daughters'
       attitudes than are social structure
       variables (age, marital status, education,
       and occupational status).  The more
       educated the mother, the greater the
       correspondence whether their attitudes were
       liberal or traditional.

       KEYWORDS:   education, mother-daughter, sex
       roles, social structure, transmission

294.   Smith, T.E.  "Push Versus Pull: Intra-Family
       Versus Peer-Group Variables as Possible
       Determinants of Adolescent Orientations
       Toward Parents."  **Youth and Society** 8
       (1976):5-26.

       Examines the push, pull, and selective
       attachment explanation for why children
       identify with parents or with peers.

KEYWORDS: affect, blacks, birth order, both
parents, peers vs. parents, identification,
number of children, power, sex-specification, stability

295.  ————. "An Empirical Comparison of
Potential Determinants of Parental Authority." **Journal of Marriage and the Family**
39(1977):153-64.

A survey of 3,641 sixth, eighth, tenth, and
twelfth grade students was used to examine
perceptions of parental power and authority. Perceived expertise and benefits
received from parents are key factors in
determining perceptions of authority. The
research supported the importance of
personal parental authority.

KEYWORDS: affect, identification, parental
support, perceptions, power

296.  ————. "Adolescent Agreement with Perceived
Maternal and Paternal Educational Goals."
**Journal of Marriage and the Family** 43
(1981):85-91.

A large sample of students are used to show
that perceived maternal and paternal educational goals are both significant
predictors of the youth's goals. Maternal
goals are more important than paternal.
Perceived parental agreement increases
prediction. Whites agree with perceived
maternal goals slightly more than do
blacks.

KEYWORDS: blacks, both parents, education,
mother-father agreement, mother vs. father,
perceptions, same sex parents, sex-
specification

297.  ————. "The Case for Parental Transmission
of Educational Goals: The Importance of
Accurate Offspring Perceptions." **Journal**

of Marriage and the Family 44(1982):661–74.

With a sample of 206 mother–father–child triads, presents evidence that parental support does not improve parent–offspring concordance on educational goals. Accuracy of offspring perceptions of parents' goals, however, does increase prediction.

KEYWORDS: transmission, education, both parents, perceptions, mother vs. father, sex-specification, mother–father agreement

298.  ———. "Parental Influence: A Review of the Evidence of Influence and a Theoretical Model of the Parental Influence Process." **Research in Sociology of Education and Socialization**, Vol. 4. Edited by Alan C. Kerckhoff. Greenwich, Conn.: JAI Press, 1983, pp. 13–45.

This is a systematic review of theory and research on transmission of values from parents to children. Includes extensive references.

KEYWORDS: affect, child rearing, inter-action, perceptions, power, review, theory, transmission, theory,

299.  ———. "Adolescent Reactions to Attempted Parental Control and Influence Techniques." **Journal of Marriage and the Family** 45 (1983):533–42.

Examines parental control and power as they relate to behavior of sixth, eighth, and tenth grade students. Distinguishes between maternal and paternal behavior.

KEYWORDS: affect, both parents, child rearing, interaction, mother vs. father, parental support, power

300.    ————.   "Sex and Sibling Structure:  Inter-
        action Effects on the Accuracy of Adoles-
        cent Perceptions of Parental Orientations."
        **Journal of Marriage and the Family** 46
        (1984):901-7.

        Uses 291 mother-child and 221 father-child
        dyads to examine effects of birth order and
        sibling sex composition on accuracy with
        which adolescents estimate parental
        attitudes.  Among male adolescents, first-
        borns and lastborns have far more accurate
        perceptions of parents than do middleborns.
        Interprets this and similar findings.

        KEYWORDS:  birth order, identification,
        interaction, perceptions, sex-specification

301.    Smoll, F., R. Schutz, T. Wood, and J.
        Cunningham.  "Parent-Child Relationships
        Regarding Physical Activity Attitudes and
        Behaviors."  **Psychology of Motor Behavior
        and Sport**.  Edited by G. Roberts and N.
        Newel.  Champaign, Ill.:  Human Kinetics,
        1978, pp. 131-43.

        Finds an absence of significant associa-
        tions between parental attitudes toward
        physical activity and children's physical
        activity attitudes, involvement, or
        performance.

        KEYWORDS:  sports

302.    Sorosky, Arthur D.   "The Psychological
        Effects of Divorce on Adolescents."
        **Adolescence** 12(1977):123-36.

        Provides a review of literature on
        psychological effects of divorce on adoles-
        cents.

        KEYWORDS:  divorce effects

303.  Spenner, Kenneth I.   "Occupations, Role
      Characteristics, and Intergenerational
      Transmission."  **Sociology of Work and
      Occupations** 8(1981):89-112.

      Argues that there is modest transmission
      related to occupational roles.

      KEYWORDS:  social class, social structure,
      status attainment, transmission, work,
      vocational interest


304.  Spilka, Bernard, James Addison, Marguerite
      Rosensohn.   "Parents, Self, and God:  A
      Test of Competing Theories of Individual-
      Religion Relationships."  **Review of
      Religious Research** 16(1975):154-65.

      Four theories of the origins of God con-
      cepts (Freudian, Adlerian, Social Learning,
      and Self-Esteem) are compared on a sample
      of 198 Catholic high school students.  The
      Adlerian and Self-Esteem positions have
      more support than the Freudian or Social
      Learning frameworks.

      KEYWORDS:  religion, self-esteem


305.  Stevens, J.H., and M. Mathews (eds.).
      **Mother-Child, Father-Child Relations.**
      Washington:  National Association for the
      Education of Young Children, 1976.

      KEYWORDS:  mother vs. father


306.  Stone, Lorene Hemphil, Alfred C. Miranne, and
      Godfrey J. Ellis.   "Parent-Peer Influence
      as a Predictor of Marijuana Use."  **Adoles-
      cence** 16(1979):109-22.

      Argues that the influence of the most
      salient reference group (either parents or
      peers) is an important predictor of whether
      or not an individual uses marijuana.

KEYWORDS:    peers vs. parents, social
problems


307.    Stryker, S. **Symbolic Interactionism.**   Menlo
        Park:  Benjamin/Cummings, 1980.

        A systematic presentation of Stryker's
        perspective on symbolic interaction.  Does
        not deal directly with socialization of
        adolescents, but provides a theoretical
        perspective that is common to this area of
        research.

        KEYWORDS:    identification, interaction,
        self-esteem, theory


308.    Stryker, S., and R.T. Serpe.   "Toward a Theory
        of Family Influence in the Socialization of
        Children."  **Research in Sociology of Educa-
        tion and Socialization,** Vol. 4.   Edited by
        Alan C. Kerckhoff.  Greenwich, Conn.:   JAI
        Press, 1983, pp. 47-71.

        Compares behavioristic, Freudian,
        structural role theory, and symbolic inter-
        actionism, then introduces an identity
        theory of the role of the family in
        socialization.

        KEYWORDS:    identification, interaction,
        peers vs. parents, reciprocal influence,
        theory, transmission


309.    Tashakkori, A., and A.H. Mehryar.   "The
        Differential Roles of Parents in the
        Family, as Reported by a Group of Iranian
        Adolescents."  **Journal of Marriage and the
        Family** 44(1982):803-9.

        A sample of 473 boys and 574 girls from
        Iran is used to compare perceptions of the
        relative roles of mothers and fathers.
        Mothers have supportive-emotional role and

fathers take responsibility for authorita-
tive-punitive aspects.  Higher SES families
are more egalitarian.

KEYWORDS:  cross-cultural, mothers vs.
fathers, perceptions, sex roles, sex-
specification, social class

310.   Taveggia, Thomas C. and Bruce Ross.  "Genera-
       tional Differences in Work Orientations:
       Fact or Fiction?"  **Pacific Sociological
       Review** 21(1978):331-49.

       Comparison of cohorts of workers which are
       grouped by age shows that there are no
       significant differences in orientations
       toward work.

       KEYWORDS:  generation, status attainment,
       work, vocational interest

311.   Tedin, K.L.  "The Influence of Parents on the
       Political Attitudes of Adolescents."
       **American Political Science Review** 68
       (1974):1579-92.

       Sample of 322 parent-child dyads used to
       test for factors that can enhance inter-
       generational transmission.  Parents have
       potential for transmission if issues are
       salient to parent and adolescent knows
       parents attitude.

       KEYWORDS:  interaction, methods, percep-
       tions, political, social structure, trans-
       mission

312.   ————.  "Assessing Peer with Parent
       Influence on Adolescent Political
       Attitudes."  **American Journal of Political
       Science** 24(1980):136-54.

       A study involving graduating high school
       seniors, their best friend, and one or both
       parents (averaged together) shows that

parents and peers can both have significant
effects. Sometimes the effects are in
different directions. The attitude of the
parent is more correlated with the child
(relative agreement), but the mean of the
child and friend are closer (absolute
agreement). Covers methodological issues,
perceptual accuracy, and salience of the
issue.

KEYWORDS: both parents, cohort vs.
lineage, methods, peers vs. parents,
perceptions, political, theory

313.   Thomas, Darwin L., V. Gecas, A. Weigert, and
       E. Rooney. **Family Socialization and the
       Adolescent.** Lexington, Mass.: Heath
       Lexington, 1974.

       KEYWORDS: social support, transmission,
       values

314.   Thomas, Darwin L., Andrew J. Weigert, and
       Norma Winston. "Adolescent Identification
       with Father and Mother: A Multi-National
       Study." **Acta Paedologica** 1(1985):47-68.

       Argues that greatest parent-child similar-
       ity occurs when parents emphasize support
       rather than control. Uses a purposive
       sample of Catholics from five nations.
       Examines identification, parent- child
       interaction and cross-cultural differences.

       KEYWORDS: cross-cultural, identification,
       interaction, parental support, religion,
       transmission, values

315.   Thompson, L. and G.B. Spanier. "Influence of
       Parents, Peers, and Partners on the Contra-
       ceptive Use of College Men and Women."
       **Journal of Marriage and the Family** 40
       (1978):481-92.

Study of 434 never married, sexually active males and females between 17 and 22 shows parents do not have a significant influence on contraceptive use while sex partner and peers do have.

KEYWORDS: peers vs. parents, sexual beliefs, sex roles, transmission

316.   Thompson, L. and A.J. Walker. "Mothers as Mediators in Grandmother-Granddaughter Relationships." Paper presented at the annual meetings of the National Conference on Family Relations, St. Paul, Minn., 1983.

A survey of 126 triads (granddaughter, mother, and maternal grandmother) evaluates the mediator role of the mother. Grand-mothers love their granddaughters as part of their family. Granddaughters feelings toward grandmothers may be different from general family feelings and contingent on the mother's orientation toward the grand-mother.

KEYWORDS: affect, generations, grand-parents, interaction, mother-daughter

317.   Thornton, Arland. "The Influence of First Generation Fertility and Economic Status on Second Generation Fertility." **Population and Environment** 3(1980):51-72.

Shows impact of parental economic status and family size on the actual and expected fertility of adult children using longitudinal data from two generations based on the Panel Study of Income Dynamics. Ideal family size of the parental family was better predictor of fertility behavior and plans than was the actual family size.

KEYWORDS: longitudinal, number of children, social class

318.    ————.  "Changing Attitudes toward Separa-
        tion and Divorce:   Causes and
        Consequences."  **American Journal of
        Sociology** 90(1985):856-72.

        Based on an intergenerational panel study
        of mothers and their children, it is shown
        that there is a substantial stability in
        attitudes toward divorce over time and
        mothers have an important influence on the
        attitudes of their children.

        KEYWORDS:  divorce effects, father absence,
        longitudinal, mother-daughter religion,
        social structure, values


319.    Thornton, Arland, Duane F. Alwin, and Donald
        Camburn.  "Causes and Consequences of Sex-
        Role Attitudes and Attitude Change."
        **American Sociological Review** 48(1983):211-
        27.

        Based on eighteen year panel study, this
        paper argues that there is a movement
        toward more egalitarian sex roles.   In
        accounting for this change, the paper
        indicates that mothers' sex-role attitudes
        and experiences are especially important.

        KEYWORDS:  education, mother-daughter,
        power, religion, sex roles, transmission,
        work, values


320.    Thornton, Arland and Deborah Freedman.
        "Changing Attitudes Toward Marriage and
        Single Life."  **Family Planning Perspectives**
        14(1982):297-303.

        Reviews research on attitudes toward
        marriage.  Section on mother-child (18
        years old) survey showing marriage more
        important to daughters than to sons and
        parents will provide less pressure to marry
        than they did in the past.

KEYWORDS:   generations, historical, mother-
daughter, sex roles, social problems,
values

321.   Thornton, Arland, Deborah S. Freedman, and
       Donald Camburn.   "Obtaining Respondent
       Cooperation in Family Panel Studies."
       **Sociological Methods and Research** 11
       (1982):33-51.

       This is a methodological piece concerning
       how to minimize loss of respondents in
       panel studies of families.   Was able to
       interview 85% of original sample after six
       waves of the survey ranging from 1962 to
       1980.

       KEYWORDS:   longitudinal, methods

322.   Thornburg, H.D.   "The Amount of Sex Informa-
       tion Learning Obtained During Early Adoles-
       cence."   **Journal of Early Adolescence** 1
       (1981):1971-83.

       KEYWORDS:   sexual beliefs

323.   Troll, L. and V.L. Bengtson.   "Generations in
       the Family."   **Contemporary Theories About
       the Family**, Vol. 1.   Edited by Wesley Burr,
       Reuben Hill, Ira Reiss, and F. Ivan Nye.
       New York:   Free Press, 1979, pp. 127-61.

       A comprehensive review of research and
       theories related to generations and parent-
       child influence among adolescent and post-
       adolescent children.   After extensive
       literature review, the authors develop a
       series of propositions.   A wide variety of
       issues and substantive areas are covered.

       KEYWORDS:   affect, both parents, child
       rearing, cohort vs. lineage, education,
       ethnicity, generations, grandparents,
       historical, interaction, methods, peers vs.

parents, perceptions, political, review,
religion, sex roles, status attainment,
theory, transmission, values, work

324.  Trommsdorff, Gisela.  "Family Roles as
      Perceived by Japanese and German Adoles-
      cents."  Presented at the American
      Sociological Association meetings, San
      Francisco, 1982.

      Demonstrates that attitudes toward family
      roles differ but no difference on perceived
      quality of relation to parents.

      KEYWORDS:  affect, cross-cultural, percep-
      tions, power, same sex parents, sex roles,
      sex-specification, values

325.  ————.  "Future Orientation and Socializa-
      tion."  **International Journal of Psychology**
      18(1983):381-406.

      Examines future orientation and socializa-
      tion with some discussion of role of
      parents and teachers.  Sample is German
      adolescents.

      KEYWORDS:  cross-cultural, transmission,
      values

326.  ————.  "Cross-Cultural Comparison of
      Socialization in the Family:  Japan and
      Germany."  **Zeitschrift für
      Sozialisationsforschung und
      Erziehungssoziologie** 4(1984):97.

      Article in German.

      KEYWORDS:  cross-cultural

327.  Trommsdorff, G., C. Haag, and R. List.
      "Zukunftsorientierung, Belohnungsaufschub
      und Risikobereitschft Bei Weiblichen

Jugendlichen Delinquenten." **Kolner Zeitschrift für Soziologie und Sozialpsychologie** 31(1979):732-45.

Article in German.

KEYWORDS:  cross-cultural


328.  Uddenberg, N.  "Mother-Father and Daughter-Male Relationships:  A Comparison." **Archives of Sexual Behavior** 5(1976):69-79.

KEYWORDS:  sexual beliefs


329.  Wallerstein, J.S., and J. B. Kelly.  "The Effects of Parental Divorce:  The Adolescent Experience." **The Child in His Family: Children as a Psychiatric Risk**, Vol. 3. Edited by E. Anthony and A. Koupernik.  New York:  John Wiley, 1974, pp. 479-505.

This is a small sample study (n = 21) of the impact of divorce on adolescence.

KEYWORDS:  child rearing, divorce effects


330.  ————.  "Effects of Parental Divorce: Experiences of the Child in Later Latency." **American Journal of Orthopsychiatry** 46 (1976):256-69.

KEYWORDS:  divorce effects


331.  ————.  "California's Children of Divorce." **Psychology Today** January (1980):67-76.

KEYWORDS:  divorce effects


332.  Walters, J., and L.H. Walters.  "Parent-Child Relationships:  A Review 1970-79." **Journal of Marriage and the Family** 42 (1980):807-22.

Reviews research done during the 1970s with
an emphasis on early age children. Argues
for reciprocal influence. Covers divorce,
stepparenting, child abuse, adolescent
sexuality, and methodological issues.

KEYWORDS: child rearing, divorce effects,
father absence, interaction, methods,
reciprocal influence, review, sexual
beliefs.

333.   ————. "The Role of the Family in Sex
Education." **Journal of Research and
Development in Education** 16(1983):8-14.

Reviews research pertaining to how parents
can be more effective in the sex education
of their adolescent children.

KEYWORDS: education, interaction, sexual
beliefs

334.   Walters, Lynda Henley, Joe F. Pittman, Jr.
and J. Elizabeth Norrell. "Development of
a Quantitative Measure of a Family from
Self-Reports of Family Members." **Journal
of Family Issues** 5(1984):497-514.

Presents a method for creating a family
score based on responses of individual
family members. Its primary relevance is
in terms of methods of measurement.

KEYWORDS: methods, perceptions

335.   Weiner, Terry S. "Homogeneity of Political
Party Preferences Between Spouses." **Journal of Politics** 40(1978):209-11.

Survey data shows a high degree of homogeneity in party preference of spouses at time
of marriage and that the homogeneity
increases during the years married.

KEYWORDS:   mother-father agreement, political

336.  Weitz, S.  **Sex-Roles: Biological, Psychological, and Social Foundations.** New York: Oxford University Press, 1977.

KEYWORDS:  sex roles

337.  Westholm, Anders.  "Political Heritage, Generational Change and Continuity in the Swedish Electorate." Ph.D. Dissertation, Department of Government, Uppsala University, 1986.

Written in English.  Examines interrelationship between parental influence and generational change using data from Sweden.

KEYWORDS:  cross-cultural, generations, perceptions, political, transmission

338.  Westholm, Anders and Richard G. Niemi. "Partisanship, the Left/Right Dimension and Political Socialization in Sweden:  Variations on a Theme."  Unpublished manuscript. Department of Political Science, University of Rochester, 1985.

Comparing 16 year old youths and their parents in Sweden, this study reports that partisanship as well as position on the left/right spectrum are strongly transmitted.  The fact that both types of orientations are well transmitted distinguishes Sweden from many other Western democracies. Theoretical implications of this finding are discussed and analyzed using data from Sweden as well as other countries.

KEYWORDS:  cross-cultural, generations, perceptions, political, transmission

339.   White, Lynn K., David B. Brinkerhoff, and
       Alan Booth.  "The Effect of Marital Disrup-
       tion on Child's Attachment to Parents."
       **Journal of Family Issues** 6(1985):5-22.

       Study of 2,135 college students shows
       attachment to noncustodial parent is reduc-
       ed. It also analyzes death versus divorce,
       amount of conflict in homes, sex of
       custodial parent, and relationships with
       step-parents.

       KEYWORDS:  affect, both parents, divorce
       effects, father absence, interaction,
       marital stability, sex-specification

340.   Wieder, D. Lawrence and Don H. Zimmerman.
       "Generational Experience and the Develop-
       ment of Freak Culture."  **Journal of Social
       Issues** 30(1974):137-61.

       Compares ethnographic and survey data to
       explain freak culture emerging in middle
       class youth.

       KEYWORDS:  generations, methods

341.   Wietong, S.G.  "An Examination of Intergener-
       ational Patterns of Religious Belief and
       Practice."  **Sociological Analysis** 36
       (1975):137-49.

       KEYWORDS:  religion

342.   Wingrove, C.R. and K.R. Selvin.  "Age
       Differences and Generational Gaps:  College
       Women and Their Mothers' Attitudes Toward
       Female Roles in Society."  **Youth and
       Society** 13(1982):289-301.

       Using a very small sample, authors show the
       generation gap is greater between older

mothers and college daughters than between
younger mothers and college daughters.
Concerns sex role attitudes.

KEYWORDS:   age of parent, mother-daughter,
sex roles, transmission


343.   Wright, James D., and Sonia R. Wright.
       "Social Class and Parental Values for
       Children:  A Partial Replication and Exten-
       sion of Kohn's Thesis." **American
       Sociological Review** 41(1976):527-37.

       A replication of Kohns' Class and Conform-
       ity study using the 1973 NORC General
       Social Survey.  The inclusion of non-class
       variables improves the explanatory power of
       parental values.  Social class effect is
       due more to education attainment than
       occupational prestige.

       KEYWORDS:   education, social class, social
       structure, transmission, values, vocational
       interest, work


344.   Wright, Stuart A. and Elizabeth S. Piper.
       "Families and Cults:  Familial Factors
       Related to Youth Leaving or Remaining in
       Deviant Religious Groups." **Journal of
       Marriage and the Family** 48(1986):   in
       press.

       KEYWORDS:   religion

# CHAPTER THREE:

## FAMILY INFLUENCE ON ADOLESCENTS:

### ETHNICITY

The ethnicity section represents a set of papers
that take in the full range of family influence on
adolescence.  The ethnic families represented in
the research below are the groups of people that
have traditionally been excluded from opportunities, affluence, and security.

The existence of heterogeneous cultures in the
United States is undeniable.  Some argue that this
will continue to be a conglomeration of "unmeltable
ethnics."  Others advocate greater assimilation.
We have attempted to represent the abundant diversity of these views.

A characteristic theme of many of the publications listed below is that we need to give much
more attention to the ethnic family.  The body of
literature on ethnicity as it relates to family
influence on adolescence is limited.  There is
little evidence of a commitment on the part of many
researchers to research which has ethnic minority
groups as a major consideration.  Family scholars
often ignore minority families in their studies.
The explanations frequently note that there are too
few minority families in national surveys so it is
best to limit the analysis to white families.
Alternatively, it is common to lump minority
families in with white families and ignore any
ethnic or racial differences.  The implicit assump-
tion is that there are no differences or that what
differences do exist are inconsequential.

While the preceding chapter noted the lack of
longitudinal data as a major problem in the study
of family influence on adolescents, this is much

more so when studying ethnic families.  Because
much earlier research emphasized assimilation and
the notion of a melting pot, it failed to establish
distinctive baseline data for ethnic and minority
groups.  Thus, the historical database is woefully
deficient.

    The history of ethnic and minority groups in the
United States provides the backdrop that explains
the direction of research.  Consider Native Americans whose land was seized by technologically
advanced Europeans, Blacks who came as slaves,
Asians who came as cheap labor, descendants of the
settlers of the southwest who were colonized and
then annexed, or any of the other histories of
ethnic groups.  All of these histories have the
common denominator of victimization and inequality.
Not surprisingly, such inequities provide the
backdrop for much of the research we inventory in
this section.

    Recent work tends to espouse that on top of all
the struggles of raising children in this world,
ethnic families, especially Blacks and Hispanics,
have magnified problems of preparing a child to
feel proud of his or her ethnic identity.  They
must work as advocates for their children and
families while at the same time attempting to
survive economically.

    Much current attention is paid to developing
conceptual frameworks that provide integration of
the various issues we have mentioned in studying
ethnic families.  Perhaps we are finally moving in
the direction of realizing that socio-economic
oppression is the origin of many problems rather
than an ethnic family deficit.

## Family Structure

    A major question put forth in much of the
research is related to the significant differences
between the socialization experiences of adolescents reared in single and two-parent families.  In
our society the two-parent family is considered the
ideal even as it is becoming less and less the
norm.  There is some evidence that adolescents grow

up with more positive self concepts in two-parent
families.  Much of the literature discusses the
consequences of adolescents being reared in a
single parent household.  Some suggest that father
absence is significantly related to lower self-
concept and lower achievement.  Others argue that
father absence has a greater effect on interpersonal distancing of the ethnic adolescent.

The evidence supporting conclusions about single
parent versus two-parent homes is inconclusive.
Given this, it is safe to say that family structure
alone will not determine the nature of socialization outcomes.  Every family, whether single parent
or two-parent, will develop its own patterns of
interaction.  Therefore, future research should
investigate both family structure and interaction.
A combination of both should prove a better determinant of socialization outcomes than family
structure alone.

## Substantive Content Areas

Within the ethnicity section many areas are
examined extensively.  Specific reference to education appears in over 70 of these publications.
These include references to education in general,
as well as academic achievement, parent education,
and intelligence.

A great deal of work has to do with family
structure.  There are over 70 references related to
this issue such as divorce effects, family cohesion, father absence, marital stability, number of
children, as well as research comparing single
versus two parent families.  Child rearing is also
related to some of this research and is indexed
about 30 times.

The importance of socio-economic issues has been
discussed above and there are many references on
these issues.  Social class and social structure
are umbrella concepts which are catalogued over 50
times.  There are also more than 30 references to
discrimination, economic deprivation, policy,
political, power, prejudice, and racism.

   Not surprisingly, there has been a long standing
interest in parental values from researchers studying socio-economic differences in child rearing
practices and the persistence of social inequality
from generation to generation.  Values is indexed
about 30 times.

   Self-Concept and self-esteem are explicitly
addressed in about 30 articles.  These concepts are
integrally woven into discussions of family
structure and socio-economic issues.

   These are some of the major issues of this body
of literature.  The Subject Index reveals many
more.  Many of the keywords are overlapping in
nature.  However, carefully looking over the index
and references will facilitate the location of
research materials for particular areas of
interest.

345. Aguirre, A. "Language Use in Bilingual Mexican-American Households." **Social Science Quarterly** 65(1984):565.

The results reveal that language choice is closely associated with a person's sex. A pattern of cross-sex language use is present among siblings, and home language use is closely associated with a parent's country of birth.

KEYWORDS: language, male-female, parent-child


346. Alba, R. (Ed.) **Ethnicity and Race in the U.S.A.: Toward the Twenty-First Century.** London, England: Routledge and Kegan Paul, 1985.

This book represents a set of papers that take in the full range of U.S. ethnic and racial experience. The papers assembled by the author are from the Conference on Ethnicity and Race in the Last Quarter of the Twentieth Century, 1984. The focus of the papers are on developments in ethnicity and race.

KEYWORDS: Asians, blacks, cross-cultural, education, family background, Hispanic, historical, language, political, religion, social class, work


347. Allen, W.R. "Race, Family Setting, and Adolescent Achievement Orientation." **Journal of Negro Education** 68(1978):230-43.

An analysis of relationships existing
between adolescent achievement orientation
and family social status, parental aspirations, child-rearing practices and
parent-child relationships.

KEYWORDS: child-rearing, parent-child,
parental aspirations, mobility, self-esteem

348.    ————.   "Race, Income and Family Dynamics:
        A Study of Adolescent Male Socialization
        Processes and Outcomes."  **The Social and
        Affective Development of Black Children.**
        Edited by M. Spencer.  Hillside, New Jersey:
        Lawrence Erlbaum Associates, 1985, pp. 273-
        92.

        The author, being concerned that prior
        conclusions about parent performance, child
        rearing practices and child outcomes in
        black families did not appear correct,
        proposes an alternative ideological
        perspective for the study of black child
        socialization, as well as presenting a
        framework for the assessment of black child
        socialization processes and outcomes.

        KEYWORDS:  child rearing, family back-
        ground, father absence, interaction, intra-
        familial conflict, parent-child, self
        esteem

349.    Allen, W.R., Spencer, M., and G. Brookins.
        "Synthesis:  Black Children Keep on Grow-
        ing."  **The Social and Affective Development
        of Black Children.**  Edited by M. Spencer.
        Hillside, New Jersey:  Lawrence Erlbaum
        Associates, 1985, pp. 301-14.

        The authors purpose is to redefine how
        black children and their families are
        treated in the literature.  They present
        new perspectives on the status of black
        child development in the U.S.A.

KEYWORDS: child rearing, education,
historical, interaction, parent-child, peer
influence, perceptions, self esteem, social
structure, values, work

350.  Alston, D., and N. Williams. "Relationship
      Between Father Absence and Self-Concept of
      Black Adolescent Boys." **Journal of Negro
      Education** 51(1982):134-38.

      The authors find that father absence is
      significantly related to the self-concept
      of black adolescent boys.

      KEYWORDS: academic achievement, father
      absence, father-son, self-concept, single
      parent

351.  Alvirez, D., and F. Bean. "The Mexican-
      American Family" **Ethnic Families in
      America.** Edited by Mendel, C., and R.
      Haberstein. N.Y.: Elsevier, 1981, pp.
      271-92.

      The authors illuminate on how the tradi-
      tional Mexican family structure is being
      influenced by forces of urbanization and
      social mobility.

      KEYWORDS: historical, male-female, social
      class

352.  Alwin, D.F. "Trends in Parental Socializa-
      tion Values: Detroit, 1958-1983." **The
      American Journal of Sociology** 90(1980):
      359-82.

      Using data from sample surveys of the
      Detroit metropolitan area carried out in
      1958, 1971, and 1983, the author examines
      patterns of change in parental socializa-
      tion values over time.

      KEYWORDS: autonomy, child-rearing, educa-
      tion, ethnicity, generations, interaction,

longitudinal, number of children, parental
supervision, social class, religion, work

353.    ————. "Religion and Parental Child-Rearing
        Orientations." Unpublished manuscript,
        Institute for Social Research, University
        of Michigan, Ann Arbor, Michigan, 1985.

        The author focuses on the relationship
        between religion and family life, giving
        particular attention to parental values for
        children and approaches to child-rearing.

        KEYWORDS: child-rearing, ethnicity, genera-
        tions, number of children, parental super-
        vision, religion, social class

354.    Anderson, J., and F. Evans. "Family Sociali-
        zation and Educational Achievement in Two
        Cultures:  Mexican-American and Anglo-
        American."  **Sociometry** 39(1976):209-22.

        Results of this study confirm the findings
        of previous research suggesting that family
        socialization practices strongly influence
        both achievement values and achievement.
        Parental independence training results in
        significant gains in achievement among both
        groups of students by increasing the
        student's confidence in coping with the
        physical and social environment.

        KEYWORDS:  education, parental education,
        self concept

355.    Badaines, Joel.  "Identification, Imitation
        and Sex Role Preference in Father-Present
        and Father-Absent Black and Chicano Boys."
        **The Journal of Psychology** 92(1976):15-24.

        Both boys from father-absent and father-
        present homes imitate the male model more
        than female model but this is not
        correlated with sex role preference.

KEYWORDS: divorce, ethnicity, father
absence, marital stability, sex-roles

356.  Bahr, H.M. **American Ethnicity.** Lexington:
      Heath, 1979.

357.  Banks, J.A.  "Black Youths in Predominately
      White Suburbs: An Exploratory Study of
      Their Attitudes and Self-Concepts." **Jour-
      nal of Negro Education** 53(1984):3-17.

      A study of black family adolescents
      self-concepts and attitudes toward physical
      characteristics, neighborhood, and school.

      KEYWORDS: education, family background,
      residence, self-concept

358.  Barnett, B., I. Robinson, W. Bailey, and J.
      Smith, Jr.  "The Status of Husband/Father
      as Perceived by the Wife/Mother in the
      Intact Lower-Class Urban Black Family."
      **Sociological Spectrum** 4(1984):421-41.

      A sample of black women from intact famil-
      ies living in a predominately low-income
      neighborhood were interviewed concerning
      their general outlook and attitudes about
      family life and future, and their percep-
      tion of the husband/father's roles as
      provider, parent, and decision maker.

      KEYWORDS: both parents, child-rearing,
      economic deprivation, mother-father agree-
      ment, parent-child, parental education,
      parental supervision, residence, social
      class

359.  Bartz, K.W. and E.S. Levine.  "Childrearing
      by Black Parents: A Descriptive and Compar-
      ison to Anglo and Chicano Parents." **Jour-
      nal of Marriage and the Family**
      40(1978):708-19.

Interviews with black, chicano, and anglo parents examined differences in child rearing. All respondents were from a lower working-class neighborhood. Black parents had higher scores on expecting early autonomy, being both high on supportive and high on controlling, valuing strictness, and encouraging egalitarian roles.

KEYWORDS: both parents, child rearing, ethnicity, parental support

360.    Berry, B., and H.L. Tischler. **Race and Ethnic Relations.** Boston: Houghton Mifflin, 1978.

361.    Biddle, E. "The American Catholic Irish Family." **Ethnic Families in America.** Edited by Mendel, C., and R. Haberstein. N.Y.: Elsevier, 1981, pp. 89-123.

The author, a sociologist, applies socio-logical concepts, with personal memories of growing up Irish, and combines both with historical data.

KEYWORDS: education, generations, histori-cal, interaction, parent-child, parental aspirations, religion, social class, social control, work

362.    Blalock, Hubert. **Race and Ethnic Relations.** Englewood Cliffs: Prentice-Hall, 1982.

363.    Blea, Irene. "Nine Ways of Speaking in Mexican American Culture." **Journal of the Association for the Study of Perception** (1986): in press.

The author focuses on the content identifi-cation and direction of the social use of speech, and the proper use of language in the family, between generations.

KEYWORDS: generations, interaction,
language, male-female


364.  Boykin, A., and F. Toms. "Black Child
      Socialization: A Conceptual Framework."
      **Black Children**. Edited by McAdoo, H., and
      J. McAdoo. Beverly Hills, Calif.:  Sage
      Publications, 1985, pp. 33-51.

      The authors feel that a conceptual frame-
      work is needed to provide integration of
      the various issues that must be taken
      simultaneously into consideration when
      studying black family life.  They feel that
      they provide this viable framework for the
      study of black child socialization proces-
      ses.

      KEYWORDS:  child rearing, parent-child,
      social class, theory, urban-rural, values


365.  Brown, J., R. Bakeman, P. Snyder, W.
      Fredrickson, S. Morgan, and R. Helper.
      "Interactions of Black Inner-City Mothers
      with Their Newborn Infants." **Child
      Development** 46(1975):677-86.

      Interactions of 45 black inner-city mothers
      with their healthy full-term newborn
      infants were observed during bottle-feeding
      on the third day after birth.  The infant's
      birth weights, birth order and sex and
      maternal medication were found to affect
      the infant's behaviors and/or the pattern
      of mother-infant interactions.

      KEYWORDS:  birth order, interaction,
      parent-child


366.  Brown, S. "The Commitment and Concerns of
      Black Adolescent Parents." **Social Work
      Research and Abstracts** 19(1983):27-34.

      The author examines black adolescent
      fathers and mothers to assess the quality

of their commitment and concerns as
couples.

KEYWORDS: child rearing, male-female,
mother vs. father

367.   Brunswick, Ann F.  "What Generation Gap?  A
       Comparison of Some Generational Differences
       Among Blacks and Whites."  **Social Problems**
       17(1970):358-71.

       Study uses data from seven national surveys
       to examine age differences in black and
       white populations regarding specific
       attitudes.  The author finds attitudinal
       differences by education as well as by age
       and suggests introducing education as a
       variable in the discussion at generational
       differences.

       KEYWORDS:  blacks, education, generations,
       violence

368.   Buys, C., Fielf, T., and M. Schmidt.
       "Comparison of Low Socioeconomic
       Mexican-American Students and Parents
       Attitudes Toward College Education."
       **Personality and Social Psychology Bulletin**
       2(1976):294-98.

       Students when compared to their parents,
       hold significantly less favorable attitudes
       toward college education.  The authors
       claim the discrepancy between parent-child
       is attributed to generational differences.

       KEYWORDS: education, generations,
       parent-child

369.   Campbell, B., and E. Campbell.  "The Mormon
       Family."  **Ethnic Families in America**.
       Edited by Mendel, C., and R. Haberstein.
       N.Y.:  Elsevier, 1981, pp. 379-412.

The authors present the normative system
promoted by Smith, the founder of the
religion, and examine the developing
patterns of Mormon family life. Special
attention is paid to the consequences of
beliefs for those who adhere to them.

KEYWORDS: divorce effects, historical,
marital stability, parent-child, religion,
sex roles, sexual beliefs

370. Carlson, E. "Family Background, School, and
Early Marriage." **Journal of Marriage and
the Family** 41(1979):341-53.

A longitudinal study examining influence of
family background on high school age
marriages. Compares black girls and white
girls.

KEYWORDS: blacks, divorce effects,
longitudinal, marital stability, social
problems

371. Carlson, J., and J. Iovini. "The Transmission of Racial Attitudes from Fathers to
Sons: A Study of Black and White." **Adolescence** 20(1985):233-37.

The fathers indicated their own racial
attitudes, while sons indicated their
perceptions of their father's racial
attitudes as well as their own.

KEYWORDS: father-son, perceptions, racism

372. Carter, D., and J. Walsh. "Father Absence
and The Black Child: A Multivariate Analysis." **The Journal of Negro Education** 49
(1980):134.

The authors examined the effect of father
absence on black elementary school children. Father absence appears to have a
greater effect on the interpersonal

distancing of the black child than its
effect on achievement or locus of control.

KEYWORDS:  divorce effects, education,
father absence, interaction, parental
discipline, peers vs. parents, religion

373.    Chashmore, E.  **Dictionary of Race and Ethnic
        Relations.**  London, England:  Routledge and
        Kegan Paul, 1984.

The author provides a comprehensive
dictionary with commissioned entries from
leading specialists in the field of race
and ethnic relations.  The scope of the
dictionary is wide which allows the author
to capture a full complexity of the field.

KEYWORDS:  Asians, blacks, Chicanos,
Indians, intelligence, policy, political,
prejudice, race

374.    Cheung, P., and S. Lau.  "Self-Esteem: Its
        Relationship to the Family and School
        Social Environments Among Chinese
        Adolescents."  **Youth and Society** 16 (1985):
        438-56.

The authors argue that they have succeeded
in showing that there is a relationship
between self-esteem and the family and
classroom environment.

KEYWORDS: education, family cohesion,
intra-familial conflict, parental
discipline, religion, self-esteem

375.    Cohen, E., and M. Rosner.  "Relations between
        Generations in the Israeli Kibbutz."  **The
        Sociology of the Kibbutz.**  Edited by E.
        Krausz.  New Brunswick: Transaction Books,
        1983, pp. 291-304.

The authors argue that there are
differences not only between generations

but also between older and younger members
of the second generation, and the third
generation is gradually reaching the age of
membership in the oldest Kibbutzim.

KEYWORDS: both parents, community, education, generations, sex-roles, work

376. Constantinou, S., and M. Harvey. "Dimen-
sional Structure and Intergenerational
Differences in Ethnicity: The Greek Americans." **Sociology and Social Research** 69
(1985):234-54.

The authors identify the basic dimensions
of Greek American ethnicity and examine how
they vary over three generations of Greek
Americans.

KEYWORDS: generations, transmission, values

377. Dancy, B., and P. Handal. "Perceived Family
Climate of Black Adolescents: A Function of
Parental Marital Status or Perceived Conflict?" **Journal of Community Psychology** 8
(1980):208-14.

Real and ideal family climate as perceived
by black lower middle class SES adolescents
from divorced and intact homes was investigated. Adolescents' perception of family
climate, psychological adjustment, and peer
relationships were all significantly
related to level of perceived conflict in
the family.

KEYWORDS: divorce effects, family cohesion,
interaction, intervention, intra-familial
conflict, peer influence, perceptions

378. Dasgupta, S. "The Dynamics of Parent Child
Interactions Within an Indian Immigrant
Family." Paper presented at the Conference
on Family, March, 1984.

The author analyzes parental expectations,
parent-child relations and child socialization within an Indian immigrant family.
The author argues that the Indian immigrant
family, in order to make its young members
fit in the larger society, has changed its
orientation towards its children.  In
relation to parent-child relationships,
control and restrictive norms have been
replaced by discussion and reasoning,
emphasizing the values of open communication and egalitarianism.

KEYWORDS: ethnicity, interaction, parent-
child, punishment, self-esteem, social
control, values

379.   Dashefsky, A., and I. Levine.  "The Jewish
       Family: Continuity and Change." **Families
       and Religions.** Edited by D'Antonio, W.,
       and J. Aldous.  Beverly Hills, Calif.:
       Sage Publications, 1983, pp. 163-190.

380.   de Vaus, D.A.  "The Relative Importance of
       Parents and Peers for Adolescent Religious
       Orientation: An Australian Study." **Adoles-
       cence** 18(1983):147-58.

       The author finds support that parents
       dominate in the areas of transmitting
       values, ideals, and beliefs.

       KEYWORDS: peers vs. parents, religion,
       transmission, values

381.   Devereux, E.C., R. Shouval, U. Bronfenbren-
       ner, R. Rodgers, S. Kav-Venaki, E. Kiely,
       and E. Karson.  "Socialization Practices of
       Parents, Teachers, and Peers in Israel: The
       Kibbutz versus the City." **The Sociology of
       the Kibbutz.** Edited by E. Krausz.  New
       Brunswick: Transaction Books, 1983,
       pp. 305-318.

About 600 Israeli preadolescent, half from
29 Kibbutzim and half from 9 classrooms in
the city of Tel Aviv, were asked to describe the frequency of certain socializing
behaviors of their mothers, fathers,
teachers, peers, and in the Kibbutz care-
givers as well.

KEYWORDS: both parents, education, home
setting, interaction, mother vs. father,
parental support, peers vs. parents

382.  DiCindo, L.  "Race Effects in a Model of
      Parent-Peer Orientation."  **Adolescence**
      18(1983):369-79.

      Race was the strongest predictor of peer
      orientation.  Blacks tended to be more
      parent oriented than whites.  Self-esteem
      was also a strong predictor of parent-peer
      orientation.

      KEYWORDS: male-female, peers vs. parents,
      self-esteem

383.  Dornbusch, S., J. Carlsmith, H. Leiderman, A.
      Hastorf, R. Gross, and P. Ritter.  "Black
      Control of Adolescent Dating."  **Sociologi-
      cal Perspectives** 27(1984):301-23.

      Controlling for social class and area of
      residence, the authors find the impact of
      age norms on dating to be stronger for
      black adolescents, especially black female
      adolescents.

      KEYWORDS: age roles, both parents,
      male-female, parental education, parental
      supervision, residence, social class,
      social control

384.  Dor-Shav, Z.  "Jewish Culture and Sex Differ-
      ences in Psychological Differentiation."
      **The Journal of Social Psychology** 124(1984):
      15-25.

S's were 120 ten-year-old boys and girls
from Jewish population differing in their
fidelity to the cultural patterns of
Eastern-European Jews.

KEYWORDS: male-female, sex roles

385.    Durrett, M., O'Bryant, S., and
        J. Pennebaker.  "Child Rearing Reports of
        White, Black, and Mexican-American
        Families."  **Developmental Psychology** 11
        (1975):871.

Comparisons were made among 29 white, 30
black, and 31 Mexican-American families.
Mothers and fathers were interviewed about
their child rearing orientations and techniques.

KEYWORDS: child rearing, parent-child,
parental education

386.    Eberhardt, C., and T. Schill.  "Differences
        in Sexual Attitudes and Likeness of Sexual
        Behaviors of Black Lower-Socioeconomic
        Father Present Vs. Father Absent Female."
        **Adolescence** 19(1984):99-105.

Father absent subjects were not found to be
more sexually permissive in reported
behavior or attitude than father present
subjects.

KEYWORDS: father absence, father-daughter,
social class, two parent vs. single parent

387.    Edwards, O.  "Family Formation Among Black
        Youth."  **Journal of Negro Education** 51
        (1982):111-21.

The author reviews data concerning marriage
among young blacks and identifies age at
first marriage as a variable deserving
further attention.

KEYWORDS:   age at marriage, divorce
effects, number of children, social class

388.   Elkholy, A.   "The Arab American Family."
       **Ethnic Families in America.**   Edited by
       Mendel, C., and R. Haberstein.   N.Y.:
       Elsevier, 1981, pp. 151-67.

       The author relies on two field studies
       conducted in 1957 and 1972.   The partici-
       pant observation technique is utilized as
       an aid to his interpretation of statistical
       data.

       KEYWORDS:   family structure, historical,
       religion

389.   Fallows, Marjorie.   **Irish Americans.**   Engle-
       wood Cliffs:   Prentice-Hall, 1979.

390.   Farber, D., Mindel, C., and B. Lazerwitz.
       "The Jewish American Family."   **Ethnic
       Families in America.**   Edited by Mindel, C.,
       and R. Haberstein.   N.Y.:   Elsevier, 1981,
       pp. 347-78.

       The author examines the critical question
       of the movement of Jews away from the
       traditions they brought with them from the
       European continent.

       KEYWORDS:   age roles, cross-cultural,
       divorce effects, education, family cohe-
       sion, family structure, generations, sex
       roles, social change, work

391.   Farge, E.J.   "A Review of Findings From
       'Three Generations' of Chicano Health Care
       Behavior."   **Social Science Quarterly** 58
       (1977):407-11.

       Compares health care practices of three
       generations of Chicanos.   SES is a key
       factor in folk medical beliefs.

KEYWORDS: ethnicity, generations, social
class, social structure

392.  Feagin, Joe.  **Racial and Ethnic Relations.**
      Englewood Cliffs:  Prentice-Hall, 1978.

393.  Felice, L.G.  "Black Student Dropout
      Behavior: Disengagement from School Rejec-
      tion and Racial Discrimination."  **Journal
      of Negro Education** 50(1981):415-24.

      The author explores the various reasons
      black students drop out of school when they
      appear to have the ability to do as well as
      anyone else in school.

      KEYWORDS: discrimination, economic depriva-
      tion, education, family background, racism,
      social class

394.  Femminella, F., and J. Quadagno.  "The
      Italian American Family."  **Ethnic Families
      in America.**  Edited by Mindel, C., and R.
      Haberstein.  N.Y.:  Elsevier, 1981, pp. 61-
      88.

      Distinctions are made between old family in
      Italy and the new family in America.

      KEYWORDS:  education, family cohesion,
      generations, male-female, peers vs. parents

395.  Fernandez, J.P.  **Child care and Corporate
      Productivity: Resolving Family/Work
      Conflicts.**  Lexington, Mass.: Lexington
      Books, 1985.

      From data of over 5,000 employees, varying
      in gender, ethnicity, age, managerial
      level, profession, marital status, number
      of children, and ages of children, the
      author found that women primarily bear the
      burden of balancing work and family
      responsibilities, even when they have

husbands who can presumably share the
responsibilities.

KEYWORDS: ethnicity, mother vs. father,
number of children, values, work

396.   Fitzpatrick, J.   "The Puerto Rican Family."
       **Ethnic Families in America.**   Edited by
       Mindel, C., and R. Haberstein.   N.Y.:
       Elsevier, 1981, pp. 192-217.

       The author presents information as Puerto
       Ricans in America and on the island of
       Puerto Rico.

       KEYWORDS: historical, values

397.   Fox, G.L., and J.K. Inazu.   "Patterns and
       Outcomes of Mother-Daughter Communication
       About Sexuality."   **Journal of Social Issues**
       36(1980):7-29.

       Drawing on data from 449 black and white
       mother-daughter dyads, this study examines
       direct verbal communication about sex
       between the mother and her daughter.   Finds
       frequent discussions, but considerable role
       discomfort.

       KEYWORDS: affect, blacks, interaction,
       mother-daughter, sexual beliefs, sex roles

398.   ————.   "The Influence of Mother's Marital
       History on the Mother-Daughter Relationship
       in Black and White Households."   **Journal of
       Marriage and the Family** 44(1982):142-53.

       Survey of 449 black and white mothers and
       teenage daughters revealed little
       difference in interaction patterns between
       black and white families and between
       maritally nonintact and intact homes.

KEYWORDS: both parents, interaction, marital stability, mother-daughter, single parent, social class

399.  Fox, Greer Litton and Christine Medlin. "Teenage Daughters and Single Mothers: Patterns of Sexual Socialization." Paper presented at the American Sociological Association Meetings, Washington, D.C., 1985.

Based on 97 qualitative interviews with black and white families. Focuses on single mother household with daughters who have been successful in some way (sports, school, church, etc.).

KEYWORDS: blacks, divorce effects, father absence, mother-daughter, sexual beliefs, transmission

400.  Frank, D.B. **Deep Black Funk and Other Stories: Portraits of Teenage Parents.** Chicago: University of Chicago Press, 1983.

Interviews and stories of teenage parents and expectant parents from predominately lower-class black families.

KEYWORDS: mother-father agreement, single parent vs. two-parent, social class

401.  Franklin, A., and N. Body-Franklin. "A Psychoeducational Perspective on Black Parenting." **Black Children.** Edited by McAdoo, H., and J. McAdoo. Beverly Hills, Calif.: Sage Publications, 1985, pp. 194-210.

The author concludes that the struggle to raise children in this world is magnified when a parent and child are black. On top of all the other jobs of a black parent is the task of preparing a child to feel proud

of his or her racial identity in a racist
world.

KEYWORDS:  child rearing, education,
environment, historical, mother-son,
religion, self concept, single vs. two
parent

402.    French, L.  "The Franco American Working
        Class Family."  **Ethnic Families in America**.
        Edited by Mindel, C., and R. Haberstein.
        N.Y.:  Elsevier, 1981, pp. 323-346.

        The author provides a critical sociological
        analysis of the French Canadian Family in
        America.

        KEYWORDS:  birth order, both parents,
        education, family structure, mother-father
        agreement, generations, historical,
        religion, sex roles, subculture, work

403.    Fusfeld, D., and T. Bates.  **The Political
        Economy of the Urban Ghetto**.  Carbondale:
        Southern Illinois University Press, 1984.

        The author examines the origins and
        development of the economies of the urban
        ghetto and contends that American elite
        need and benefit from an economically
        deprived underclass.

        KEYWORDS: blacks, economic deprivation,
        education, political, social class, work

404.    Gabriel, A., and E. McAnarney.  "Parenthood
        in Two Subcultures:  White, Middle Class
        Couples, and Black, Low Income Adolescents
        in Rochester, N.Y."  **Adolescence** 19(1984):
        595-604.

        Socio-cultural observation and analysis
        shows that the decision to become parents
        was related to different subcultural
        values.  In contrast to whites, black

adolescents did not see marriage as a
prerequisite for motherhood, nor did they
view completion of schooling and economic
independence as phases of maturation preceding parenthood.

KEYWORDS: social class, subculture, values

405.   Gecas, V.   "Family and Social Structure
       Influences on the Career Orientations of
       Rural Mexican-American Youth." **Rural
       Sociology** 45(1982):272-89.

       The focus of the study is on family
       environment regarding parental aspirations
       and emphasis on education and structural
       and situational obstacles stemming from
       cultural and economic circumstances.

       KEYWORDS: interaction, male-female,
       parental aspirations, values

406.   Gibbs, J.   "Black Adolescents and Youth: An
       Endangered Species." **American Journal of
       Orthopsychiatry** 54(1984):6-21.

       The author analyzes major social indicators
       showing that black youth are in relatively
       poorer condition in the 80's than they were
       in the 60's.

       KEYWORDS: community, family background,
       prevention, work

407.   Griswold del Castillo, R.   **La Familia:
       Chicano Families in the Urban Southwest,
       1848 to the Present.**   Notre Dame: Univer-
       sity of Notre Dame Press, 1984.

       The author suggests that in the past 150
       years there has been a conflict between
       values held by Mexican-Americans regarding
       conducive living conditions within families
       and the economic pressures of American
       capitalism.

KEYWORDS: child-rearing, family cohesion,
intermarriage

408.  Gustavus Philliber, S. and E.H. Grahman.
      "The Impact of Age of Mother on Mother-
      Child Interaction Patterns." **Journal of
      Marriage and the Family** 43(1981):109-15.

      Examines 282 black and hispanic women
      finding no independent effect of age of
      mother on mother-child interaction.

      KEYWORDS: age of parent, black, hispanic,
      interaction, mother-daughter

409.  Gutman, H.G. **The Black Family in Slavery and
      Freedom:  1750-1925.** New York:  Random
      House, 1976.

      A systematic review of family experience of
      blacks.  While this does not focus on
      parent-child influence, it provides
      pertinent background for studying ethnicity
      and race as they relate to intergener-
      ational influence.

      KEYWORDS:  blacks, child rearing, gener-
      ations, historical, review, social
      structure

410.  Hainline, Louise and Ekkeb Feig.  "The Corre-
      lates of Childhood Father Absence in
      College-Aged Women."  **Child Development** 49
      (1978):37-42.

      Father-absent females, interviewed when in
      college, are not different in heterosexual
      behaviors.  Primary factors appear to be
      age at interview, SES, race, ethnicity,
      education.

      KEYWORDS:  child rearing, education,
      ethnicity, father absence, race, sex roles,
      social class

411.   Halpin, G., Halpin, G., and T. Whiddon.  "The
       Relationship of Percieved Parental
       Behaviors to Locus of Control and Self
       Esteem Among American-Indian and White
       Children."  **Journal of Social Psychology**
       11(1980):189.

412.   Hamilton, D., and G. Bishop.  "Attitudinal
       and Behavioral Effects of Initial Integra-
       tion of White Suburban Neighborhoods."
       **Journal of Social Issues** 32(1976):47-68.

       Results show a marked difference in how
       black and white families are received by
       white residents and also reveal patterns of
       change over time which reflect the
       processes inherent in the integration
       experience.

       KEYWORDS: blacks, integration, residence

413.   Hanson, W.  "The Urban Indian Woman and Her
       Family."  **Social Casework** 61(1980):476-83.

       The author presents case illustrations to
       provide a profile of Indian Women who
       successfully face new challenges in a
       changing world.  The emerging Indian Woman
       personality is portrayed as a woman pur-
       suing a career in social work, law or poli-
       tics, and a woman who teaches her children
       the cultural heritage while serving as a
       role model for her children and other
       women.

       KEYWORDS:  genetics, historical, parental
       education, parental modeling, work

414.   Harrison, A.  "The Black Family's Socializing
       Environment:  Self-Esteem and Ethnic
       Attitude Among Black Children."  **Black
       Children.**  Edited by McAdoo, H., and J.
       McAdoo.  Beverly Hills, Calif.:  Sage
       Publications, 1985, pp. 175-93.

This article is a review of the self-esteem and ethnic attitudes and black family environment. The author focuses on conceptual issues, methodological issues, and a description of the family socializing environment.

KEYWORDS: environment, peer influence, self-concept, self esteem, social class

415.  Hendricks, L.  "Black Unwed Adolescents."
      **Urban Research Review** 6(1980):7-9.

      The author profiles a selected sample of black, unmarried, adolescent fathers, their problems and possible sources of help.

      KEYWORDS: education, family background, male-female, number of children

416.  Hendricks, L., and T. Montgomery.  "Educa-
      tional Achievement and Locus of Control Among Black Adolescent Fathers." **Journal of Negro Education** 53(1984):182-88.

      The authors find that unmarried black adolescent fathers are more likely than unmarried black adolescent non-fathers to be school dropouts.

      KEYWORDS: academic achievement, single parent

417.  Hendericks, L., Robinson, D., and L. Gary.
      "Religiousity and Unmarried Black Adoles-
      cent Fatherhood." **Adolescence** 19(1984): 417-34.

      Results indicate that the fathers did not differ so much from the nonfathers in the degree that they are religiously oriented but in the manner that they give expression to their religious movement.

KEYWORDS: education, religion, single
parent

418.   Hernandez, Norma.  "Variables Affecting
       Achievement of Middle School
       Mexican-American Students."  **Review of
       Educational Research** 43(1973):1-39.

       The author points out that unless all
       factors that contribute to a person's sense
       of well-being are attended to, the results
       of educational efforts will continue to be
       highly ineffective, uneconomical, and
       meager.

       KEYWORDS: academic achievement, education,
       family background, intelligence, language,
       self-esteem, social class, values

419.   Himmilfarb, H.  "The Interaction Effects of
       Parents, Spouse and Schooling:  Comparing
       the Impact of Jewish and Catholic
       Schools."  **Sociological Quarterly** 18(1977):
       464-77.

420.   Hirata, L.  "Youth, Parents, and Teachers in
       Chinatown: A Triadic Framework of Minority
       Socialization." **Urban Edition** 10(1975):
       279-96.

421.   Hraba, J.  **American Ethnicity**.  Itasca, Ill.:
       F.E. Peacock Publishers, 1979.

       A well read book on American Ethnicity.
       The author surveys sociological and psycho-
       logical perspectives on race and ethnic
       relations in the U.S.A. and examines the
       sociological lore on ethnic evolution and
       societal change, which includes theories of
       assimilation, ethnic pluralism, and ethnic
       conflict.  The psychology of prejudice and
       discrimination is also analyzed, as well as
       capital and the ethnic subeconomy for
       minority groups.

KEYWORDS: Asians, blacks, education,
Hispanics, historical, Indians, political,
prejudice, social change, subculture, work

422. Hraba, J., and P. Yarbrough. "Gender
Consciousness and Class Action for Women: A
Comparison of Black and White Female
Adolescents." **Youth and Society** 15 (1983):
115-31.

The authors research objective is to compare black and white female adolescents in
their development of a commitment to femin-
ist class action.

KEYWORDS: economic deprivation, family
cohesion, social class

423. Huang, L. "The Chinese American Family."
**Ethnic Families in America.** Edited by
Mindel, C., and R. Haberstein. N.Y.:
Elsevier, 1981, pp. 124-47.

The author argues for the Chinese American
Family as a neglected minority group.
Exploitation, violence, ghettoization, and
the development of values for survival are
characteristic of the Chinese American
experience.

KEYWORDS: community, discrimination,
divorce effects, education, parent-child

424. Hunt, L.L. and J.G. Hunt. "Race and
Father-Son Connection: the Conditional
Relevance of Father Absence for the Orien-
tations and Identities of Adolescent
Boys." **Social Problems** 33(1975):35-52.

Study of a sample of black and white children shows that father absence has damaging
effects only among white boys. Study
raises questions about the role of the
black family in sustaining intergenerational patterns of racial inequality.

KEYWORDS: blacks, father absence,
self-esteem, sex-roles, status attainment,
values

425.   Huntington, G.   "The Amish Family."   **Ethnic
       Families in America.**   Edited by Mindel, C.,
       and R. Haberstein.   N.Y.:   Elsevier, 1981,
       pp. 295-327.

       The author points out that this growing
       population has managed to resist the
       onslaught of modern technology and major
       social change.

       KEYWORDS:   age roles, education, family
       structure, religion, social change, social
       class, social structure

426.   Jacobson, Cardell.   "Separation, Integration-
       ism, and Avoidance among Black, White, and
       Latin Adolescents."   **Social Forces**
       55(1977):1011-27.

427.   ———.   "School Racial Position Effects on
       Avoidance, Separatism, and Integrationist
       Attitudes of Adolescents."   **Sociological
       Quarterly** 20(1979):223-35.

428.   Jensen, G., White, C., and J. Galliher.
       "Ethnic Status and Adolescent
       Self-Evaluations: An Extension of Research
       on Minority Self-Esteem."   **Social Problems**
       30(1982):226-39.

       An examination of the impact of racial
       consonance and dissonance of percieved
       racial mistreatment and self-esteem among
       black, Chicano, and white adolescents.

       KEYWORDS: black, Hispanic, self-esteem

429.    Johnson, C.  "Sibling Solidarity:  Its Origin
        and Functioning in Italian-American
        Families."  **Journal of Marriage and the
        Family** 44(1982):155-67.


430.    Jordan, T.J.  "Self-Concepts, Motivation, and
        Academic Achievement of Black
        Adolescents."  **Journal of Educational
        Psychology** 73(1981):509-17.

        The author investigates the unique and
        common contributions of global self-
        concept, academic self-concept, and the
        need for academic competence to the vari-
        ance in academic achievement of inner-city,
        black adolescents.

        KEYWORDS:  academic achievement,
        male-female, self-concept


431.    Kahane, R.  "The Committed:  Preliminary
        Reflections on the Impact of the Kibbutz
        Socialization Pattern on Adolescents."  **The
        Sociology of the Kibbutz.**  Edited by
        E. Krausz.  New Brunswick:  Transaction
        Books, 1983, pp. 319-29.

        The author suggests that by means of this
        research, one may be able to discern to
        what extent an educational system may
        succeed in transmitting value commitment
        and responsible behavior while at the same
        time increasing innovative capacity as a
        response to cultural pluralism and rapid
        social change.

        KEYWORDS: education, generations, social
        change, transmission, values


432.    Kaplan, H. (Ed.).  **American Minorities and
        Economic Opportunity.**  Itasca, Ill.:   F.E.
        Peacock Publishers, 1977.

        The author states that this book presents
        evidence of the value and meaning of work

to groups of people who traditionally have
been excluded from the opportunities,
affluence, and security of upward mobility
in our past and present society.  Familism
and family planning are also discussed.

KEYWORDS:  Asians, blacks, education,
family background, hispanics, social class,
work

433.   Kellam, S., R. Adams, C. Brown, C. Hendricks,
and M. Ensminger.  "The Long Term Evolution
of the Family Structure of Teenage and
Older Mothers."  **Journal of Marriage and
the Family** 44(1982):539-54.

Results indicate that teenage mothers
frequently begin child rearing as the only
adult at home and are also at risk of
becoming the only adult and remaining so
for as long as 15 years after child birth.
This tendency toward what the authors refer
to as mother aloneness is associated with
less help in child rearing and less participation in voluntary associations.

KEYWORDS:  blacks, child rearing, family
structure, longitudinal, single vs. two
parent families

434.   Kellam, S., Ensminger, M., and J. Turner.
"Family Structure and the Mental Health of
Children."  **Archives of General Psychiatry**
34(1977):1012-22.

The authors provide a map of variations of
families and some of the care relationships
between types of family and the mental
health of children.

KEYWORDS:  blacks, both parents, child
rearing, economic deprivation, education,
father absence, grandparents, social
structure

435.  Kitano, H., and A. Kikumura.  "The Japanese
      American Family."  **Ethnic Families in
      America.**  Edited by Mindel, C., and R.
      Haberstein.  N.Y.:  Elsevier, 1981, pp. 41-
      60.

      The authors present the distinctive
      cultural elements of Japanese culture that
      play themselves out through the mediation
      of the family and discuss the impact of
      modern life on the present day Japanese
      American family.

      KEYWORDS:  discrimination, family
      structure, historical


436.  Kourvetaris, G.  "The Greek American Family."
      **Ethnic Families in America.**  Edited by
      Mindel, C., and R. Haberstein.  N.Y.:
      Elsevier, 1981, pp. 168-91.

      The author discusses the Greek American
      family in terms of an ethnic generational
      frame of reference, covering three genera-
      tions.

      KEYWORDS:  generations, historical, number
      of children


437.  Krause, N.  "Interracial Contact in Schools
      and Black Children's Self Esteem."  **Black
      Children.**  Edited by McAdoo, H., and J.
      McAdoo.  Beverly Hills, Calif.:  Sage
      Publications, 1985, pp. 257-69.

      The purpose of this study was to assess the
      insulation hypothesis by examining the
      effects of racial contact on black self-
      esteem.  Little support was found for the
      hypothesis that increased contact with
      whites lowers the self-esteem of black
      school children.

      KEYWORDS:  education, family cohesion,
      parental education, self-esteem, work

438.   Krausz, E. (ed.).   **The Sociology of the
       Kibbutz.**   New Brunswick:   Transaction
       Books, 1983.

       This book is a collection of papers brought
       together to represent an example of the
       social research undertaken on the Kibbutz
       movement over the past thirty years.

       KEYWORDS: community, historical, social
       change, social structure, values


439.   Kushnir, T.   "Israeli Parents' Role in
       Emergencies."   **The Journal of Social Psych-
       ology**  125(1985):75-79.

       This study involved views of parents con-
       cerning whose role it was to take a sick
       child to the emergency department and their
       attributions of causes for the absence of a
       parent in such cases.

       KEYWORDS: father-mother, sex roles, work


440.   Lamb, M., A.M. Frodi, C.P. Hwang, and M.
       Frodi.   "Mother and Father-Infant Inter-
       action Involving Play and Holding in Tradi-
       tional and Nontraditional Swedish
       Families."   **Family Studies Review Yearbook,**
       Vol. 2.   Edited by Olson, D., and B.
       Miller.   Beverly Hills: Sage Publications,
       1984, pp. 171-214.

       The authors present their findings from
       observations of 51 firstborn
       eight-month-olds interacting with their
       parents in unstructured home settings.

       KEYWORDS: interaction, mother-father agree-
       ment, parent-child


441.   Laosa, L.   "Billingualism in Three United
       States Hispanic Groups:   Contextual Use of
       Language by Children and Adults in Their

Families." **Journal of Educational Psychology** 67(1975):617-27.

The author studied the use of language pattern among Central Texas Mexican-Americans, Miami Cuban-Americans and New York Puerto Rican Children and adults in their families. There were significant adult-child differences in language use among the Mexican-American and Cuban-American families.

KEYWORDS: education, interaction, language, parent-child

442.   Lee, C.  "Successful Rural Black Adoles-cents: A Psychosocial Profile."  **Adoles-cence** 20(1985):129-42.

The author examines the psychosocial vari-ables related to academic and social success among southern rural black adoles-cents. The profile was developed from personal interviews with 68 black students identified by teachers as successful, often despite social and economic hardship.

KEYWORDS: academic achievement, community, education, environment, interaction, parental modeling, parental supervision, policy, self-concept, values

443.   LeCorgne, L.L. and L.M. Laosa.  "Father Absence in Low-Income Mexican-American Families:  Children's Social Adjustment and Conceptual Differentiation of Sex-Role Attributes."  **Developmental Psychology** 12 (1976):470-71.

Examines effects of father absence on cognitive and emotional development of Mexican-American families. Emphasis is on sex role characteristics.

KEYWORDS: divorce effects, marital stabil-ity, sex-roles

444.  LeVine, E., and K. Bartz.  "Comparative
      Child-Rearing Attitudes Among Chicano,
      Anglo, and Black Parents."  **Hispanic Jour-
      nal of Behavioral Sciences** 1(1979):165-78.

      The authors state that Chicanos are
      characterized as emphasizing early assump-
      tion of responsibility.  In contrast to
      Blacks, less support and control attitudes
      are expressed.  Chicanos ascribe to more
      permissiveness than Anglos and are less
      equalitarian in child-rearing attitudes
      than are either Anglos or Blacks.  The
      authors argue that even though attitudes of
      Chicano mothers and fathers were not
      significantly different from one another,
      cross-ethnic differences are more
      attributable to Chicano fathers than
      Chicano mothers.

      KEYWORDS:  autonomy, child rearing, parent-
      child, parental control, parental disci-
      pline


445.  Lopata, H.  "The Polish American Family."
      **Ethnic Families in America.**  Edited by
      Mindel, C., and R. Haberstein.  N.Y.:
      Elsevier, 1981, pp. 15-40.

      The author focuses upon the Polish American
      family as it exists within the developing
      and changing Polish ethnic community.
      Background characteristics of Old World
      Polish culture are presented.

      KEYWORDS:  community, education, histori-
      cal, interaction, parent-child


446.  Luhman, R., and S. Gilman.  **Race and Ethnic
      Relations.**  Belmont:  Wadsworth, 1980.


447.  Lyman, Stanford.  **The Asian in North America.**
      New York:  Clio Press, 1977.

This book contains two essays of relevance
to adolescence and family factors.  The
essays are entitled "Red Guard on Grant
Avenue:  The Rise of Youthful Rebellion in
Chinatown" and "Generation and Character:
The Case of the Japanese Americans."

KEYWORDS:  ethnicity, family background,
gangs, generations, values

448.  Marden, C., and G. Meyer.  **Minorities in
      American Society.**  N.Y.:  Van Nostrand,
      1978.

449.  Marjoribanks, K.  "Sibling and Family
      Environment Correlates of Children's
      Achievement:  Ethnic Group Differences."
      **Journal of Biosocial Science** 14(1982):99–
      107.

450.  Markides, K., and T. Cole.  "Change and
      Continuity in Mexican-American Religious
      Behavior: A Three Generation Study." **Social
      Science Quarterly** 65(1984):618.

      Results show that little change in
      religious affiliation took place from
      generation to generation.

      KEYWORDS: generations, religion, transmis-
      sion, values

451.  Markides, K., and S. Vernon.  "Aging,
      Sex-Role Orientation, and Adjustment: A
      Three Generations Study of
      Mexican-Americans."  **Journal of Gerontology**
      39(1984):586–91.

      There is little evidence to support the
      hypothesis that less traditional sex-role
      attitudes make adjustment easier in old
      age.

      KEYWORDS: generations, sex-roles

452. Mason, W.M., R.M. Hauser, A.C. Kerckhoff,
     S.S. Poss, and K. Manton. "Models of
     Response Error in Student Reports of Paren-
     tal Socioeconomic Characteristics."
     **Schooling and Achievement in American
     Society.** Edited by W.H. Sewell, R.M.
     Hauser, and D.L. Featherman. New York:
     Academic Press, 1976, pp. 443-94.

     Various statistical models of response
     error are examined in the ability of
     students to gauge their parents' socio-
     economic characteristics. It is an early
     application of LISREL to research involving
     family socialization variables.

     KEYWORDS: attainment, attribution, blacks,
     ethnicity, methods, perceptions, social
     class, status attainment

453. McAdoo, H. (Ed.). **Black Families.** Beverly
     Hills, Calif.: Sage Publications, 1981.

     The author put together articles from some
     of the best thinkers on the American black
     families. Black families tie the male and
     female together into the family unit as
     they attempt to survive economically,
     procreate and raise their children, and act
     as advocates for their children and
     families.

     KEYWORDS: child rearing, economics, educa-
     tion, family structure, historical,
     methods, policy, social class, theory,
     values, work

454. ————. "Racial Attitude and Self Concept of
     Young Black Children Over Time." **Black
     Children.** Edited by McAdoo, H., and J.
     McAdoo. Beverly Hills, Calif.: Sage Pub-
     lications, 1985, pp. 213-42.

     Findings show that black children develop
     more positive attitudes toward their own
     group over time. More supportive environ-

mental changes increase the developmental
changes and result in children being able
to place a positive evaluation on their own
ethnic group.

KEYWORDS: education, environment, longitudinal, peer influence, self concept, single
vs. two parents

455. McAdoo, H., and J. McAdoo. **Black Children:
Social, Educational, and Parental Environments.** Beverly Hills, Calif.: Sage Publications, 1985.

This book is a collection of articles that
explore the unique experiences and situa-
tions that are common to black children and
their parents. The volume was developed
within the framework that all children,
regardless of characteristics, must
complete similiar developmental tasks in
route to becoming adults.

KEYWORDS: community, economic deprivation,
education, environment, interaction, self
esteem, social class, theory, values

456. McAdoo, J. "Involvement of Fathers in the
Socialization of Black Children." **Black
Families.** Edited by H. McAdoo. Beverly
Hills, Calif.: Sage Publications, 1981,
pp. 225-37.

The author notes that when economic
sufficiency rises within black families, an
increase in the active participation of the
black fathers in socialization of his
children was observed. A call for future
research to move beyond the ethnocentric
studies of the past is put forth.

KEYWORDS: child rearing, father-daughter,
father-son, interaction, mother-child,
parent-child, self-esteem

457.   McGoldrich, M., Pearce, J., and J. Giordano.
       **Ethnic and Family Therapy**. New York:   The
       Guilford Press, 1982.

458.   McLanahan, Sara.   "Family Structure and the
       Reproduction of Poverty."  **American Journal
       of Sociology** 90(1985):873-91.

       Using a longitudinal analysis of the Income
       Dynamics Data, this paper argues that
       growing up in a female headed household
       increases the risk of poverty, but not
       because of father absence.  Among whites,
       economic deprivation and stress associated
       with family disruption accounts for nearly
       all negative effects, however, the results
       for blacks are more mixed.

       KEYWORDS:  blacks, divorce effects, father
       absence, longitudinal, marital stability,
       social class, social structure, social
       problems, status attainment, work

459.   McLemore, S.  **Racial and Ethnic Relations in
       America**.  Boston:  Allyn and Bacon, 1980.

460.   McRoy, R., and L. Zurcher.  **Transracial and
       Inracial Adoptees:  The Adolescent Years**.
       Springfield, Ill.: Charles C. Thomas,
       1983.

       The authors present the experiences of
       black adolescents who were adopted either
       transracially (by white families) or intra-
       racially (black families).

       KEYWORDS: biological vs. adoptive parents,
       peers vs. parents, self-concept

461.   Miller, M.  "Mexican Americans, Chicanos, and
       Others:  Ethnic Self-Identification and
       Selected Social Attributes of Rural Texas
       Youth."  **Rural Sociology** 41(1976):235-47.

The author attempts to delineate primary
terms for ethnic self-identification; to
test the generalizability of past findings;
and to examine several factors not
considered in previous research (sex, farm
labor, force participation, and language
use).

KEYWORDS: ethnicity, language, residence,
social class, work

462.  Milner, D. **Children and Race.** Beverly
      Hills, Calif.: Sage Publications, 1983.

      The author provides an insightful account
      of racial attitude development in young
      children and describes some of the effects
      of racism on the development of black
      children, while making note of recent
      developments in research and in the wider
      society.

      KEYWORDS: blacks, child rearing, educa-
      tion, family background, historical, intel-
      ligence, racism, social class, values

463.  Mindel, C., and R. Haberstein (Eds.).
      **Ethnic Families in America:  Patterns and
      Variations.** New York:  Elsevier, 1981.

      One of the most well read books on ethnic
      families.  Most major American ethnic
      groups are represented.

      KEYWORDS: ethnicity

464.  Mirande, A.  "The Chicano Family:  A Reanaly-
      sis of Conflicting Views." **Journal of
      Marriage and Family** 39(1977):747-56.

      The author dispels what he claims are
      erroneous negative stereotypes about the
      Chicano family.  In doing so he puts forth
      a positive set of stereotypes and offers an
      alternative view of the Chicano family.

KEYWORDS: historical, mother versus
father, parent-child, stereotypes, values

465.   Montero, D.  "The Japanese Americans:
       Changing Patterns of Assimilation Over
       Three Generations."  **American Sociological
       Review** 46(1981):829-39.

       The higher the socioeconomic achievement of
       three generations of Japanese Americans,
       the greater the assimilation.  A
       socio-historical model explains the
       assimilation process.

       KEYWORDS: cross-cultural, education, gener-
       ations, historical, longitudinal, social
       class, social structure, status attainment,
       work

466.   Montero, D., and R. Tsukashima.  "Assimila-
       tion and Educational Achievement:  The Case
       of the Second Generation Japanese Ameri-
       can." **The Sociological Quarterly** 18(1977):
       490-503.

467.   Morgan, D.H.J.  **The Family:  Politics and
       Social Theory.**  London, England: Routledge
       and Kegan Paul, 1985.

       The author explores and clarifies major
       issues and developments within 'family
       theorizing'.  The author discusses a var-
       iety of approaches to the family over the
       past decade, with special attention to the
       impact of feminism and the professional and
       state intervention into the family through
       marital and family therapy.

       KEYWORDS: divorce effects, ethnicity,
       generations, historical, policy, theory,
       values, work

468.   Morgan, S.P., and K. Hirosima.  "The Persis-
       tence of Extended Family Residence in

Japan: Anachronism or Alternative
Strategy?" **American Sociological Review** 48
(1983):269-81.

1978 data from a study of wives with
preschool-age children. The authors suggest that extended residence offers
tangible benefits to modern Japanese
families and society.

KEYWORDS: generations, interaction, residence, work

469. Morgan, W.R., D.F. Alwin, and L.J. Griffin.
"Social Origins, Parental Values, and the
Transmission of Inequality." **American
Journal of Sociology** 85(1979):156-66.

Analysis of school children shows only
limited support for hypothesized link
between parental social position, parental
values, and the adolescent schooling experience.

KEYWORDS: blacks, child rearing, social
class, social structure, status attainment

470. Munroe, R.H., and R.L. Munroe. "Birth Order
and Intellectual Performance in Three East
African Societies." **The Journal of Social
Psychology** 123(1984):273-74.

A study of Abaluyia males in Western
Kenya. Later status in birth order and
larger family size were associated with
lower school grades.

KEYWORDS: academic achievement, birth
order, number of children

471. Munsinger, H. "Children's Resemblance to
Their Biological and Adopting Parents in
Two Ethnic Groups." **Behavior Genetics** 5
(1975):239-54.

472.  Nolle, David B.  "Changes in Black Sons and
      Daughters:  A Panel Analysis of Black
      Adolescents' Orientations Toward Their
      Parents."  **Journal of Marriage and the
      Family** 34(1972):443-47.

      Survey of 278 Southern black adolescents
      reports stability in affect, respect, and
      openness toward parents.

      KEYWORDS:  affect, blacks, longitudinal,
      sex-specification


473.  Nowak, S.  "Values and Attitudes of the
      Polish People."  **Scientific American** 245
      (1981):45-53.

      A comparison of parents and youth is
      presented to explore the generation gap in
      Poland.  A wide variety of issues are
      covered.  Perceptions by students are also
      reviewed.

      KEYWORDS:  cross-cultural, generations,
      historical, perceptions, political,
      religion, sexual beliefs, social problems,
      values, work


474.  O'Connor, J.  **Tradition and Change in Three
      Generations of Japanese Americans.**
      Chicago:  Nelson-Hall, 1977.


475.  Orive, R.  "Social Contact of Minority Parents
      and Their Children's Acceptance by Class-
      mates."  **Sociometry** 38(1975):518-24.


476.  Osako, M.  "Intergenerational Relations as an
      Aspect of Assimilation:  The Case of Japan-
      ese Americans."  **Sociological Inquiry** 46
      (1976):67-72.

      The author examines the intergenerational
      living arrangements, interactions and
      economic assistance of Japanese-Americans.

Both first and second generation Japanese-
Americans have a stronger desire to be in
close geographic proximity and be emotionally attached to each other.

KEYWORDS:  generations, interaction, values

477.  Owuamanam, D.  "Peer and Parental Influence
on Sexual Activities of School Going
Adolescents in Nigeria."  **Adolescence** 18
(1983):169-79.

Peer-oriented adolescents differed significantly from parent-oriented adolescents in
their degree of indulgence in sexual
activities.  Peers were also found to be
more engaged in imparting sexual information to adolescents than were parents.

KEYWORDS: child rearing, parent-child,
peers vs. parents

478.  Paul, M., and J. Fisher.  "Correlates of
Self-Concept among Black Early Adolescents."  **Journal of Youth and Adolescence** 9
(1980):163-73.

The authors examine the self-concepts of
black eight-grade students from the Midwest
in relation to black acceptance, social
intimacy, locus of control, and sex-role
types.

KEYWORDS: self-concept, sex-roles, values

479.  Peters, M.  "Parenting in Black Families with
Young Children:  A Historical Perspective."
**Black Families.**  Edited by H. McAdoo.
Beverly Hills, Calif.:  Sage Publications,
1981, pp. 211-24.

The author describes the child rearing
patterns and socialization practices of
black parents from the perspective of their
effectiveness as relevant, supportive, or

practical strategies appropriate to the
social realities black people face.

KEYWORDS: child rearing, ecological,
economic deprivation, historical, intervention, parent-child, parental discipline,
values

480.    ————.  "Racial Socialization of Young Black
        Children."  **Black Children.**  Edited by
        McAdoo, H., and J. McAdoo.  Beverly Hills,
        Calif.:  Sage Publications, 1985, pp. 159-
        73.

        Three propositions were supported in this
        study:  racism acts as an intervening
        variable in the socialization process;
        socio-cultural/racial environments and
        experiences of mothers influence their
        perception of social reality, and this
        perception of social reality and adapta-
        tions parents make affect their child
        rearing values and behavioral strategies.

        KEYWORDS: child rearing, education,
        environment, parent-child, perceptions,
        self-concept, values

481.    Peterson, G.W., and David F. Peters.  "The
        Socialization Values of Low-Income White
        and Rural Black Mothers:  A Comparative
        Study."  **Journal of Comparative Family
        Studies** 26(1985):75-91.

        A study of low income black and white
        mothers reveals that both groups prepare
        young people to live in their socioeconomic
        setting and marginally within the larger
        society.  Rural black mothers also show
        adjustment to the power structure of the
        rural South which combines conformity and
        obedience with private alienation from a
        white-dominated social context.

        KEYWORDS: blacks, ethnicity, rural, social
        class, social structure, values

482.  Peterson, G.W., M.E. Stivers, and D.F.
      Peters.  "Career Decisions:  Family Versus
      Nonfamily Significant Others of Low Income
      Youth."  **Family Relations** 35(1986):  in
      press.

      Survey of 302 white Appalachian and 117
      rural black youths shows parents are the
      most frequently chosen significant others
      by adolescents making decisions about
      occupations.  A "deficit" interpretation of
      the black family is not supported.

      KEYWORDS:  blacks, ethnicity, perceptions,
      rural, social class, status attainment,
      vocational interest, work

483.  Pope, H.W., and C. W. Mueller.  "The Inter-
      generational Transmission of Marital Insta-
      bility:  Comparisons by Race and Sex."
      **Journal of Social Issues** 32(1976):49-66.

      Using five surveys, the authors argue that
      there is transmission of the tendency to
      divorce or separate for whites, blacks,
      females, and males.

      KEYWORDS: blacks, divorce effects, father
      absence, sex-roles

484.  Price, J.  "North American Indian Families."
      Edited by Mindell, C., and R. Haberstein.
      **Ethnic Families in America.**  N.Y.:
      Elsevier, 1981, pp. 248-70.

      The similarities of family life styles are
      presented through the experience of the
      American Indian since the European
      settlers.

      KEYWORDS:  cross-cultural, historical

485.  Proudian, A.  "Perceived Parental Power and
      Parental Identification Among Armenian-

American Adolescents." **Psychological Reports** 53(1983):1101.

486.  Quarter, J.  "The Development of Political Reasoning on the Israeli Kibbutz." **Adolescence** 19(1984):569-93.

Through using a cross-sectional design, with subjects ages 7, 11, 16, and over 20 drawn from five Kibbutzim, subject's reasoning about kibbutz socio-political norms and outside political issues are analyzed inductively.

KEYWORDS: male-female, mother-daughter, political, values, work

487.  Richardson, B.  "Racism and Child-Rearing:  A Study of Black Mothers." **Dissertation Abstracts** 42(1981):125.

488.  Robinson, I., Bailey, W., and J. Smith, Jr. "Self-Perception of the Husband/Father in the Intact Lower Class Black Family." **Phylon** 46(1985):136-47.

The authors attempt to determine whether the husband/father perceives a father position in the family as an action-oriented position and whether he fulfills selected roles commonly associated in the larger society with his position in the family.

KEYWORDS: child-rearing, education, mother-father agreement, parent-child, residence, social class

489.  Rutledge, Essie.  "Socialization and Aspirations of Black College Females." **Conference on Empirical Research in Black Psychology** New York: Ford Foundation, 1981, pp. 59-72.

The author concludes that early childhood
socialization appears to be a positive
experience, providing the skills and knowledge as well as the psychological insula-
tion for coping in a competitive, racist
society.

KEYWORDS: both parents, interaction, mother
vs. father, parental education, two-parent
vs. single parent

490.    ————.    "Socialization Experiences by Family
        Structure."   Paper presented at the Annual
        Meeting of the Association of Black
        Sociologists, Detroit, Michigan, 1983.

        The author's purpose in this paper is to
        determine whether socialization experiences
        differ by family structure; in other words,
        are there significant differences between
        the socialization experiences of those
        reared in one and two-parent families.

        KEYWORDS: blacks, interaction, mother
        vs. father, sex-roles, two-parent
        vs. single parent

491.    Scanzoni, J.   "Black Parental Values and
        Expectations of Children's Occupational and
        Educational Success."   **Black Children.**
        Edited by McAdoo, H., and J. McAdoo.
        Beverly Hills, Calif.:  Sage Publications,
        1985, pp. 113-22.

        The author argues that as many blacks
        continue to have less access to resources
        than whites, their capabilities of prepar-
        ing their children to participate
        effectively in the world of work is reduc-
        ed.

        KEYWORDS:  education, generations, parent-
        child, parental education, parental
        modeling, social class

492.  Schaefer, Richard.  **Racial and Ethnic Groups.**
      Boston:  Little, Brown, 1979.


493.  Scheinfeld, D.  "Family Relationships and
      School Achievement Among Boys of
      Lower-Income Urban Black Families."  **Jour-
      nal of Orthopsychiatry** 53(1983):127-43.

      This is a study of poor, black, urban
      families relating mothers' views of the
      ideal relationship between their sons and
      the world to the sons' academic
      achievement.

      KEYWORDS: academic achievement, inter-
      action, mother-son


494.  Schmidt, A.  "Grandparent-Grandchild Inter-
      action in a Mexican-American Group."
      **Hispanic Journal of Behavioral Sciences** 5
      (1983):181.


495.  Scott, W.J., and H.G. Grasmick.  "Generations
      and Group Consciousness:  A Quantification
      of Mannheim's Analogy."  **Youth and Society**
      11(1979):191-213.

      Compares levels of generational, class, and
      racial consciousness in a community survey
      of 221 respondents.

      KEYWORDS:  ethnicity, generations, social
      class


496.  Serrano, R.  "Mexican-American Adolescent
      Self-Disclosure in Friendship Formation."
      **Adolescence** 19(1984):539-55.

      Differences in self-disclosure between
      anglo-american and mexican-american
      students were noted in several areas,
      including mother and best friend as favor-
      ite disclosure targets.

KEYWORDS: male-female, parent-child, peers vs. parents

497.  Shepherd, J., and L. Tiger. "Kibbutz and Parental Investment" **The Sociology of the Kibbutz.** Edited by E. Krausz. New Brunswick: Transaction Books, 1983, pp. 279-90.

The authors argue that the double phenomenon of polarization of sexual division of labor and familization are parallel processes. In fact, they argue that the two phenomena are different facets of the same process, namely, the reindividualization of parental investment.

KEYWORDS: environment, genetics, mother vs. father, parental investment, sex-roles, work

498.  Sidanuis, J., Ekehammar, B., and J. Lukowsky. "Social Status and Sociopolitical Ideology among Swedish Youth." **Youth and Society** 14(1983):395-415.

The authors report that Swedish working-class adolescents appear to be more socially conservative than middle-class adolescents.

KEYWORDS: values, work

499.  Smith, T.E. "Parental Social Power: Race and Sex Differences and Similarities." **Youth and Society** 11(1979):215-36.

Examines social power, race and sex as they relate to how much parents influence the educational goals of their offspring. Parental unity increases transmission. Socioeconomic power is very important. Referent power and legitimate power are also supported.

KEYWORDS: blacks, both parents, education,
identification, mother-father agreement,
power, sex-specification, social class,
status attainment, transmission

500.   ———.   "Adolescent Agreement with Perceived Maternal and Parental Educational
Goals." **Journal of Marriage and the Family**
43(1981):85-91.

A large sample of students is used to show
that perceived maternal and parental educational goals are both significant predictors of the youth's goals.  Maternal
goals are more important than paternal.
Perceived paternal agreement increases
prediction.  Whites agree with perceived
maternal goals slightly more than do
blacks.

KEYWORDS: blacks, both parents, education,
mother vs. father, mother-father agreement,
perceptions, same sex parents,
sex-specification, transmission

501.   Spiro, M.E.   "Is the Family Universal?-The
Israeli Case."  **The Sociology of the
Kibbutz**.  Edited by E. Krausz.  New
Brunswick:  Transaction Books, 1983,
pp. 239-50.

This paper represents a case study of a
kibbutz community which has evolved a
social structure which does not include the
family.

KEYWORDS: both parents, child-rearing,
community, education, interaction

502.   Spivey, G.   "The Health of American-Indian
Children in Multi-Problem Families."
**Social Science and Medicine** 11(1977):357-
59.

The author compared health histories of
American-Indian Children from families with
multiple psychosocial problems to children
with adequately functioning families living
under similar conditions on reservations.
Children of multi-problem families were
found to have more illness than children of
control families.

KEYWORDS: environment, health, parental
mental health

503.   Stack, C.B.   "Black Kindreds: Parenthood and
       Personal Kindreds Among Urban Blacks."
       **Journal of Comparative Family Studies** 3
       (1972):194-206.

       KEYWORDS: blacks, urban

504.   Staples, Robert.  "The Black American
       Family."    **Ethnic Families in America.**
       Edited by Mindel, C., and R. Haberstein.
       N.Y.: Elsevier, 1981, pp. 221-47.

       The author offers a new perspective on
       black families while concentrating on the
       strengths of black families. Emphasis is
       on the historical importance of family and
       kinship among black people through African
       society, in slavery, and in their current
       situation.

       KEYWORDS: historical, social class, social
       structure

505.   Staples, Robert and Alfredo Mirande.   "Racial
       and Cultural Variations Among American
       Families: A Decade Review of the
       Literature on Minority Families." **Journal
       of Marriage and the Family** 42(1980):887-
       903.

       Review of Literature from 1970's dealing
       with Asian-American, Black, Chicano, and
       Native American families.  Relevant to

intergenerational relations insofar as it
describes family relations for these
different ethnic groups. Little research
on Asian-American and Native American
families is reported.

KEYWORDS: blacks, child rearing,
hispanics, review, values

506.   Steelman, L., and J. Doby. "Family Size and
       Birth Order as Factors on the IQ Perfor-
       mance of Black and White Children."
       **Sociology of Education** 56(1983):101-9.

       Birth order is unrelated to the verbal and
       nonverbal IQ of black or white children.
       Family size is inversely related to verbal
       IQ but not nonverbal IQ for both blacks and
       whites. The inverse impact of family size
       on verbal ability does not differ by race.

       KEYWORDS: birth order, intelligence,
       number of children

507.   Sudarkasa, N. "African and Afro-American
       Family Structure." **The Black Scholar** 11
       (1980):37-59.

508.   Sundberg, N.D., and L. Tyler. "Adolescents'
       Perceptions of Family Decision-Making and
       Autonomy in India, Australia, and the
       United States." **Journal of Comparative
       Family Studies** 13(1983):349-58.

       Groups of high school boys and girls in
       small towns from the title countries indi-
       cated whether a variety of decisions about
       their plans and actions were primarily made
       by their mother, father, another family
       member, someone outside the family, or
       themselves.

       KEYWORDS: autonomy, both parents,
       father-son, male-female, mother-daughter,
       peers vs. parents

509.  Talmon-Garber, Y.  "The Family in a Revolu-
      tionary Movement: The Case of the Kibbutz
      in Israel."  **The Sociology of the Kibbutz.**
      Edited by E. Krausz.  New Brunswick:
      Transaction Books, 1983, pp. 251-78.

      The purpose of this study is to analyze the
      interrelation between changes in communal
      structure and modification of family organ-
      ization in a revolutionary and collectivist
      movement.

      KEYWORDS: both parents, child-rearing,
      community, interaction, mother vs. father,
      sexual beliefs, social structure

510.  Tashakkori, A. and A.H. Mehryar.  "The
      Differential Roles of Parents in the
      Family:  As Reported by a Group of Iranian
      Adolescents."  **Journal of Marriage and the
      Family** 44(1982):803-9.

      A sample of 473 boys and 574 girls from
      Iran is used to compare perceptions of the
      relative roles of mothers and fathers.
      Mothers have supportive-emotional role and
      fathers take responsibility for
      authoritative-punitive aspects.  Higher SES
      families are more egalitarian.

      KEYWORDS: cross-cultural, mother
      vs. father, perceptions, sex-roles,
      sex-specification, social class

511.  Teyber, E.  "Effects of Parental Coalition on
      Adolescent Emancipation from the Family."
      **Journal of Marital and Family Therapy** 9
      (1983):305-10.

      The authors examine the relationship
      between late adolescents' perceptions of
      their parents marital coalition and
      academic success as a college freshman.

      KEYWORDS: academic achievement, both
      parents, ethnicity, interaction

512.   Thernstrom, S. (Ed.). **The Harvard
       Encyclopedia of American Ethnic Groups.**
       Cambridge:  Harvard University Press, 1980.


513.   Thomas, W.I., and F. Znanicki.  **The Polish
       Peasant in Europe and America.**  New York:
       Octagon Books, 1974.


514.   Thornton, A., Ming-Cheng, C. and S. Te-Hsiung
       "Social and Economic Change, Inter-
       generational Relationships, and Family
       Formation in Taiwan."  **Demography** 21(1984):
       475-99.

       As the authors expected, their analysis
       shows that social change has been
       accompanied by rapid changes in family
       structure and relationships.  Also
       experiences early in the life course are
       shown to have important ramifications for
       later behavior and transitions.

       KEYWORDS: age at marriage, generations,
       interaction, parental education, work


515.   Touliatos, J.  "Behavioral Disturbance in
       Children of Native Born and Immigrant
       Parents."  **Journal of Community Psychology**
       8(1980):28-33.

       The mental health status of children whose
       parents were foreign-born was examined.
       Incidence of behavioral disturbance were
       compared among white native-born children
       and children with immigrant parents.
       Results show that subjects of Chinese,
       Japanese or Southeast descent display
       significantly fewer disorders than children
       of native born.

       KEYWORDS:  child mental health, cross-
       cultural

516.  Tuma, N., and M. Hallinan.  "The Effects of
      Sex, Race, and Achievement on School Child-
      ren's Friendships."  **Social Forces**
      57(1979):1265-85.

      Characteristics of children appear to
      affect friendship changes because children
      tend to favor those similiar to themselves.
      Children's race does not significantly
      influences changes in friendship choices
      when their achievement is controlled.

      KEYWORDS:  achievement, social class

517.  Valencia, R., Henderson, R., and R. Rankin.
      "Family Status, Family Constellation, and
      Home Environmental Variables as Predictors
      of Cognitive Performance of Mexican Ameri-
      can Children."  **Journal of Educational
      Psychology** 77(1985):323-31.

      The authors examine the relative contribu-
      tions of family status variables, such as,
      child and parental language, parental
      schooling attainment and location, socio-
      economic status, a family constellation
      variable, specifically, family size and the
      Henderson Environmental Learning Process
      Scale to prediction of cognitive perfor-
      mance among 140 Mexican American preschool
      children from low-income neighborhoods.

      KEYWORDS:  education, language, number of
      children, parental education, social class

518.  Weissberg, R. and R. Joslyn.  "Methodological
      Appropriateness in Political Socialization
      Research."  **Handbook of Political Socializ-
      ation.**  Edited by S.A. Renshon.  New York:
      Free Press, 1977, pp. 45-84.

      An excellent review of the literature on
      political socialization which addresses a
      broad range of methodological issues.
      Useful to anybody with methodological
      concerns.  Criticizes frequently used

measures of influence and transmission as
well as explores measurement problems.

KEYWORDS: blacks, ethnicity, methods,
political, review, theory, transmission

519.   Williams, T., and W. Kornblum. **Growing Up
       Poor**. Lexington: Lexington Books, 1985.

       This book is about what the authors call
       the "generation of shrinking horizons."
       The experiences and outlooks of American
       teenagers who are growing up under
       extremely difficult economic and social
       conditions is studied.

       KEYWORDS: blacks, community, economic
       deprivation, education, family background,
       generations, hispanics, parental support,
       peers vs. parents, social class, transmis-
       sion, values, work

520.   Wilson, M.  "Mothers' and Grandmothers'
       Perceptions of Parental Behavior in
       Three-Generational Black Families."  **Child
       Development** 55(1984):1333-39.

       The author suggests that black family
       patterns are more complicated than previous
       research has assumed.

       KEYWORDS: child-rearing, generations,
       interaction, parental support, two-parent
       vs. single-parent

521.   Woehrer, Carol E.  "Cultural Pluralism in
       American Families:  The Influence of
       Ethnicity on Social Aspects of Aging."  **The
       Family Coordinator** 27(1978):329-39.

       The author examines ethnic variations in
       the structure of the nuclear family, inter-
       dependence between generations, and the
       relationship between the family and wider
       society.

KEYWORDS: age roles, generations, interaction, parent-child, sex-roles

522.    ———.  "The Influence of Ethnic Families on
        Intergenerational Relationships and Later
        Life Transitions."  **ANNALS,AAPSS** 464(1982):
        65-78.

        The author argues that the foundation for
        intergenerational relationships is laid
        early in the family life cycle as children
        are growing up and ethnic family structure
        and socialization of children are closely
        related to intergenerational interaction in
        adulthood.

        KEYWORDS: child-rearing, generations,
        interaction, parent-child, parental super-
        vision, subculture

523.    ———.  "Expanding the Circumplex Model of
        Family Systems by Studying Ethnic
        Families."  Paper presented at the National
        Council on Family Relations Theory-Methods
        Workshop, Dallas, TX, November, 1985.

        The author analyzes American ethnic
        families, their strengths, and their
        problems from  the perspective of the
        Circumplex Model.  Questions addressed
        include:  why doesn't the circumplex model
        apply to families valuing togetherness?  To
        what range of cultures does the Circumplex
        Model apply?  And, how might the hypotheses
        of the Circumplex Model be revised or
        expanded to include families with a wider
        range of norms or expectations?

        KEYWORDS: communication, family adaptabil-
        ity, family cohesion, methods, theory

524.    Wyatt, G.  "Studying The Black Mother-Child
        Interaction."  **Young Children** 33(1977):16-
        22.

525.  Yinger, J.  "Ethnicity."  **Annual Review of
      Sociology** 11(1985):151-80.

      The demography of ethnic groups, the
      sources of ethnic survival and revival, and
      the major themes in the literature on
      ethnicity are examined.

      KEYWORDS: cross-cultural, discrimination,
      methods, political, theory, values

# CHAPTER FOUR:

## DELINQUENCY AND THE FAMILY

Interest in the family's role in delinquency is not a recent development. In fact, Rodman and Grams (1967) gathered some 250 research articles prior to 1967 while we have uncovered an additional 271 for the period of 1975 to 1986.

The research literature provided here is representative of a diversity of causal images in search of an understanding of juvenile delinquency. While the focus of this collection centers around the role of the family, the reader will realize that the importance of education, peer influence, and social conditions accompanied by economic deprivation cannot be overlooked. We make this statement even though we realize it is theoretically difficult to distinguish between such factors as an adolescent's place of residence, family resources, and the practices and values of their family members.

The family is an appropriate focus of attempts to understand juvenile delinquency. Because an effective socialization process is believed to inhibit delinquent behavior, delinquent activity is often attributed to an ineffective socialization process. And it is because the family is a major socializing agency for the adolescent, that it may be effective in building social controls that prevent delinquent behavior.

Still, we must realize that even where the family is a strong force for communicating norms to, and soliciting conformity from adolescents, it is itself not sufficiently involved, but is often locked into other conflict-generating relationships that are conducive to delinquent activity.

There seems no doubt that the nature of the parent-child tie plays a causal role in explaining delinquency. We remind the reader, however, that there is a big difference between demonstrating co-variation and showing a causal relationship.

## Parental Supervision

Family life and the lives of adolescents have been described as undergoing change over past decades. Concern with juvenile delinquency has escalated in recent years along with additional attention directed toward changes taking place in contemporary family living. Some argue that the family is a declining institution. This debate need not concern us here. But, many of the changes in the family are targeted as causing much of the juvenile delinquency going on today. These changes involve the high divorce rate, complications associated with single parent families, and the number of employed mothers.

The causal images are varied. Most people's notion of juvenile delinquency is linked to parental supervision. Parental supervision is a family factor that is consistently linked with juvenile crime. Some researchers refer to this as parental discipline, or parental control. Regardless of classification some parents are seen as too permissive or lax, while others are seen as indifferent. Many parents are perceived as overly constraining, while many more are portrayed as inconsistent and erratic.

While many parents may be unsure about the extent of their involvement in intervening in the child's life, there seems to be a firm public opinion that lack of parental supervision over children is a primary cause of delinquency. And while the family is often viewed as the single most important determinant of juvenile delinquency, researchers disagree on the significance of parental supervision, with results that are contradictory and inconclusive.

## Parental Criminal Record

Another issue regarding parental influences on delinquency revolves around the question of the effects of parental criminal record. Some researchers predict deviant parents tend to socialize and reinforce deviance in their offspring. Thus, an affective tie to a parent with a criminal record can lead to a child's adoption of the parent's dysfunctional behavioral patterns. Many provide support for this thesis and state that delinquency increases with parental criminality.

Conclusions seem to center around the argument that in order for parental ties to perpetuate consistent conformity, both parents must adhere to conventional norms or at least represent conformity in the eyes of their children. In light of these conclusions we must also be aware that even parents who claim to support and expect conformity may at the same time be projecting and modeling all kinds of non-conventional behavior in the presence of their impressionable adolescents.

## Age Roles and Peer Influence

Research indicates that the family's role in delinquency may be overemphasized. Values do not merely stem from intergenerational transmission. Covington (1982) argues that values arise from the common experiences and roles specific to certain age groups. Moreover, Agnew (1984) suggests that no matter how strongly the family is in communicating norms and values, adolescence leads to an increased need for autonomy. Thus, it appears that delinquency may be explained in terms of a break with parental sponsored values and a substitution of new age-based values that can arise as an adaptation to age-related role change, or perhaps even social change.

This is possibly the source of peer influence. Peers with common social experiences and roles may assume a crucial role in socializing adolescents. While the results of much research on the relationship between peer influence and attachment is often contradictory it is clear that peer

influence cannot be ignored when considering causal
factors of juvenile delinquency.

## Methods

Past methods have tended to perpetuate an
ethnocentric orientation, associating the phenomena
of juvenile delinquency with the lower class.
These studies measured delinquency utilizing
official records as an indicator of juvenile
delinquency.  As can be seen in the subject index,
many more recent studies tend to employ a self-
report method.

The self-report method has its share of
problems.  Many appear concerned about the validity
of self-reported behavior compared to overt
behavior.  Our purpose is not to add to the debate
here.  Suffice it to say, that critics of the self-
report technique can no longer ignore the
inadequacies of earlier methods.

Certainly the critics deserve attention to their
claims of distorted data generated from the self-
report method.  Nonetheless, there is evidence that
the self-report method is becoming increasingly
popular, and through refinement, a highly valid
instrument.

## Substantive Content Areas

There are various content areas within the
delinquency literature that are amenable to
grouping and highly represented in the research
itemize below.  Much attention is paid to parent-
child interactions.  Parent-child interaction and
issues relevant to interactional patterns are
indexed over 110 times.  Keywords relevant to
parent-child interactions include parental
attachment, control, deprivation, discipline,
involvement, modeling, rejection, supervision, and
support.  Other factors discuss influence of
parental background characteristics such as;
criminal record, drug use, education, and mental
health.  These factors are discussed in over 30 of
the references.

Family structure is also a highly represented area. There are over 100 references on issues from family cohesion and marital stability to divorce effects, father absence, and intra-familial conflict. There is also work on restructured families, family size and comparisons of single and two parent families.

Social control and policy issues are extensively examined, being indexed about 100 times. Most of the policy work focuses on prevention, punishment, recidivism and rehabilitation.

Socio-economic factors also receive a lot of attention being discussed in nearly 100 of the references. Economic deprivation, labeling effects, social class, and social structure are used as parameters for the discussion.

As in the two preceding sections, education is highly represented being a concern of about 75 papers. Discussions center around general educational issues as well as intelligence and school performance.

A considerable portion of the delinquency literature deals with comparisons of populations. Delinquent populations are compared to non-delinquent populations in 36 of the studies. Males are compared to females in 28 studies. About 25 of the studies compare peer influence to parental influence.

## Future Investigations

The analysis of family interaction and family communication patterns is of utmost importance to the research in all sections of this book. The dynamic nature of the family as a potential deterrent as well as a labeler needs to continue to receive attention in the literature as well as the effects of deviance on family interaction.

Research on value differences within the family structure and family process both require investigation so that the effects of family interaction on adolescent development and social behavior can be

evaluated.  These studies should focus on parental
supervision, parental attachment, parental support,
parental deprivation, parental control, parental
rejection, parental involvement, and parental
modeling.  Items of family structure that should be
addressed include: family size, social class,
intra-familial conflict, father absence, family
cohesion, marital stability, and education.
Intersubjective information about the family
structure and situation should continue to receive
attention, while perceived impressions should also
be examined.

Finally, the family needs to be related to the
macro-context of the particular social environment
in which it is located.  This strategy will help
avoid enclosing the family from society as a
separate entity.  This strategy will also allow us
to realize that the family is influenced by the
socio-cultural and economic forces operating within
our society.

## REFERENCES:  DELINQUENCY

526.  Acock, A., Wright, C., and K. McKenzie.
      "Traditional Religious Beliefs and the
      Transmission of Intolerance Toward
      Deviance." **Deviant Behavior** 3(1981):65-
      84.

      Traditional religious beliefs are described
      as a mechanism for transmitting intolerance
      of deviance between generations.

      KEYWORDS: both parents, methods, religion,
      transmission

527.  Adler, P., Ovando, C., and D. Hocevar.
      "Family Correlates of Gang Membership:  An
      Exploratory Study of Mexican American
      Youth." **Hispanic Journal of Behavioral
      Sciences** 6(1984):65.

528.  Agnew, Robert.  "Physical Punishment and
      Delinquency." **Youth and Society** 15(1983):
      225-36.

      The author concludes that when parents make
      inconsistent demands on their children, the
      use of physical punishment promotes
      delinquency.  However, when parents make
      consistent demands physical punishment does
      not promote delinquency and may even reduce
      it.

      KEYWORDS: parent-child, parental disci-
      pline, punishment

529.  ————.  "Autonomy and Delinquency."
      **Sociological Perspectives** 22(1984):219-40.

The author tests the theory that
delinquency stems from the adolescent's
need for autonomy.  Data support this
theory.

KEYWORDS:  autonomy, family background,
role strain, social class, social control,
status attainment, work

530.     ————.  "A Revised Strain Theory of Delin-
         quency."  **Sociological Inquiry** 64(1985):
         151-67.

The author points to another major source
of frustration and delinquency, the
blockage of pain avoidance behavior.  He
states that adolescents are compelled to
remain in certain environments, such as
family and school.  If these environments
are painful or aversive, there is little
that adolescents can do legally to escape.

KEYWORDS:  education, environment, parent-
child, parental discipline, social control,
subculture, theory

531.    Akers, R., M. Krohn, L. Lanza-Kadnce, and M.
        Radosevich.  "Social Learning and Deviant
        Behavior:  A Specific Test of General
        Theory."  **American Sociological Review**
        44(1979):636-55.

The authors test a social learning theory
of deviant behavior with survey data on
adolescent drinking and drug behavior.  The
theory is supported and major explanatory
variables such as differential association,
differential reinforcement, definitions,
and imitation combined to account for 68%
of the variance in marijuana use (39% of
abuse) and 55% of alcohol use (32% of
abuse).

KEYWORDS:  deterrence, drug use, parental
discipline, peer influence, punishment

532.  Alexander, J.  "Systems Behavioral Interven-
      tion with Families of Delinquents:  Thera-
      pist Characteristics, Family Behavior, and
      Outcome."  **Journal of Consulting and
      Clinical Psychology** 44(1976):656-64.


533.  Anolik, S.  "The Family Perceptions of
      Delinquents, High School Students, and
      Freshman College Students."  **Adolescence** 15
      (1980):903-11.

      Data were gathered on the subjects percept-
      ions of his or her rebelliousness toward
      parents.  Data show that delinquents and
      non-delinquents tend to have similar
      negative family perceptions when they
      perceive themselves as rebellious and their
      parents as unhappy.

      KEYWORDS:  delinquent vs. non-delinquent,
      intra-familial conflict, marital stability,
      parental discipline, perceptions


534.  ————.  "Family Influences Upon Delinquency:
      Biosocial and Psychosocial Perspectives."
      **Adolescence** 18(1983):489-98.

      Theories and research are reviewed and it
      is concluded that biosocial and psycho-
      social theories of delinquency must be
      considered before a full understanding of
      delinquent behavior can be reached.

      KEYWORDS:  family background, heredity,
      parental discipline, theory


535.  Austin, R.L.  "Race, Father-Absence, and
      Female Delinquency."  **Criminology:  An
      Interdisciplinary Journal** 15(1978):487-95.

      Father absence was shown to have a
      detrimental effect on white females.  Lack
      of parental control was also shown to be
      correlated to delinquency for both black
      and white females.

KEYWORDS:   autonomy, economic deprivation,
ethnicity, father absence, parental
control, parental discipline, work

536.   Bahr, S.   "Family Determinants and Effects of
       Deviance."  **Contemporary Theories About the
       Family.**  Edited by W. Burr, R. Hill, F. I.
       Nye, and I. L. Reiss.  New York:   The Free
       Press, 1979, pp. 615-43.

       The author identifies, evaluates, and
       refines existing theories of deviant
       behavior and determines the role of the
       family in each theory.  The theoretical
       orientations examined include:   anomie,
       deterrence, differential association,
       labeling, psychoanalytic, and social
       control.

       KEYWORDS:   ethnicity, family cohesion,
       parental attachment, parental control,
       parental discipline, parental support,
       peers vs. parents, punishment, self esteem,
       social class, social control, theory,
       values

537.   Bainbridge, W., and R. Crutchfield.   "Sex
       Role Ideology and Delinquency."  **Sociologi-
       cal Perspectives** 26(1983):253-74.

       The authors suggest that "sex role" refers
       to a cluster of phenomena, rather than
       being a unitary concept.  Social bonds or
       organizations' influence is required to
       render any part of it salient for crime and
       delinquent behavior.

       KEYWORDS:   drug use, male-female, religion,
       self-reported delinquency, sex roles,
       values

538.   Baldwin, John.   "Ecological and Areal Studies
       in Great Britain and the United States."
       **Criminal Justice:   An Annual Review of
       Research.**  Edited by Morris, N., and M.

Tonny. Chicago: University of Chicago
Press, 1979, pp. 19-66.

This article is a critical assessment of
the ecological approach to deviance and its
contribution to our understanding of
delinquency.

KEYWORDS: anomie, divorce effects,
environment, generations, self-reported
delinquency, transmission

539. Balkan, S., Berger, R., and J. Schmidt.
     **Crime and Deviance in America.** Belmont,
     Calif.: Wadsworth Publishing, 1980.

     A critical text on the different forms of
     crime and deviance, highlighting their
     historical and political economic context,
     with attention paid to the family.

     KEYWORDS: economic deprivation, ethnicity,
     family background, historical, intra-
     familial conflict, social class, theory,
     work

540. Bank, B., B. Biddle, D. Anderson, R. Hauge,
     D. Keats, J. Keats, M. Marlin, and S.
     Valantin. "Comparative Research on the
     Social Determinants of Adolescent Drink-
     ing." **Social Psychology Quarterly** 48
     (1985):164-77.

     In this study, interviews conducted in
     Australia, France, Norway, and the U.S.
     provide data to examine alcohol use by
     adolescents. Peer modeling has a signifi-
     cant effect on adolescent drinking in all
     four countries. Parental norms are related
     to adolescent drinking in Australia and the
     U.S., but not in France and Norway.

     KEYWORDS: cross-cultural, parent-child,
     peer influence, peers vs. parents, values

541.   Baumrind, D.   "Familial Antecedents of
       Adolescent Drug Use:   A Developmental
       Perspective."   **Etiology of Drug Abuse:
       Implications for Prevention.**   Edited by
       Jones, C., and R. Bates.   NIDA Research
       Monograph No. 56; DHHS Publication No. 85-
       1335.   Rockville:   National Institute on
       Drug Abuse, 1985, pp. 13-44.

       The author considers the impact of early
       childhood and preadolescent socialization
       experiences on adolescent drug use from a
       developmental perspective.   Preliminary
       analyses do not support the proposition
       that adolescent drug use arises from
       pathological personal characteristics,
       pathogenic socialization characteristics,
       or pathogenic socialization practices, nor
       that use of such illegal substances as
       marijuana is deviant behavior for adoles-
       cents.

       KEYWORDS:   child rearing, drug use,
       education, parental discipline, parental
       support, self-esteem

542.   Bell, D.S., and R. Champion.   "Deviancy,
       Delinquency and Drug Use."   **British Journal
       of Psychiatry** 134(1979):269-76.

       A system for monitoring drug use was based
       on data from annual surveys of two contras-
       ting population groups, a general cross-
       section of young people and a cross-
       section of antisocial deviants.

       KEYWORDS:   delinquent vs. non-delinquent,
       divorce effects, drug use, intervention,
       intra-familial conflict, parental
       rejection, parental mental health, school
       performance

543.   Belson, W.   **Juvenile Theft:   The Causal
       Factors.**   London:   Harper, 1975.

A British study finding that boys who admitted the most stealing were poorly supervised by their parents and had parents who argued frequently but had not experienced erratic parental punishment or parental separation. The author also reported that self-reported stealing increased with decreasing socioeconomic status of the family.

KEYWORDS: intra-familial conflict, parental discipline, parental supervision, self-reported delinquency

544. Beschner, G., and A. Friedman. **Teen Drug Use.** Lexington, Mass.: Lexington Books, 1985.

This book discusses the stress and frustration parents feel when they learn their child is using drugs. It illustrates different types of reactions, effective and ineffective, and suggests where and whom to turn for help.

KEYWORDS: both parents, drug use, education, family background, peers vs. parents, social control

545. Biles, D., and D. Challinger. "Family Size and Birth Order of Young Offenders." **International Journal of Offender Therapy and Comparative Criminology** 25(1981):60-66.

The authors find that both birth order and family size are related to delinquency-proneness. The authors suggest that middle born children may be significantly more apt to deviate because they always have a higher number of siblings at home than the first and last born.

KEYWORDS: birth order, number of children

546. Biron, L., and M. LaBlanc. "Family Component and Home Based Delinquency." **The British Journal of Criminology** 17(1977):157-68.

The results reveal that the structure of the family and the identification process have indirect effects on home-based delinquency. Supervision and communication have a more immediate impact on home-based delinquency.

KEYWORDS: interaction, parental supervision

547. Blos, P. **The Adolescent Passage: Developmental Issues.** New York: International Universities Press, 1979.

The author deals with questions concerning the differences between male and female adolescent development. He examines delinquency and preoedipal factors in female delinquency.

KEYWORDS: age roles, male-female, parental mental health

548. Blumstein, A., Farrington, D.P., and S. Moitra. "Delinquency and Careers: Innocents, Desisters, and Persisters." **Crime and Justice, Volume 6.** Edited by Tonny, M., and N. Morris. Chicago: University of Chicago Press, 1985, pp. 187-219.

Findings are based on four longitudinal delinquency studies-from London; Racine, Wisconsin; Marion, Oregon; and Philadelphia. The prediction results closely match the results of predictions based on a theoretical model that uses aggregate recidivism data to partition a cohort into the above three groups: innocents, who have no offending record, desisters, who have a low recidivism probability, and

persisters, who have a high recidivism
probability.

KEYWORDS: delinquent vs. non-delinquent,
discrimination, family background, intelligence, longitudinal, parental criminal
record, recidivism, sibling criminal
record, social class

549.  Brennan, T., Huizinga, D., and D.S. Elliot.
      **The Social Psychology of Runaways.**
      Lexington:  Lexington Books, 1978.

      The author's primary objectives are to
      focus upon descriptive, taxonomic, and
      etiological issues regarding runaway youth
      and their families.

      KEYWORDS:  education, family background,
      peers vs. parents, social control

550.  Broder, P.K.  "Further Observations on the
      Link Between Learning Disabilities and
      Juvenile Delinquency."  **Journal   of
      Educational Psychology** 73(1981):838-50.

      A sample of 1,617 boys was classified with
      respect to the presence or absence of
      learning disabilities and were interviewed
      concerning family background, school
      attitude, and self-reported delinquency.

      KEYWORDS:  delinquent vs. non-delinquent,
      family background, self-reported
      delinquency

551.  Brook, Judith S., M. Whiteman, D. Brook, and
      A. Gordon.  "Paternal Determinants of Male
      Adolescent Marijuana Use."  **Development
      Psychology** 17(1981):841-47.

      This study was designed to examine the
      interconnection of sets of parental person-
      ality attributes, parental socialization
      techniques, and adolescent personality

factors with adolescent sons' marijuana
use.

KEYWORDS:  drug use, father-son,
interaction


552.   ————.  "Parental and Peer Characteristics:
Interactions and Association with Male
College Students' Marijuana Use."  **Psycho-
logical Reports** 51(1982):1319-30.

Paternal absence is associated with higher
reported drug use than when the father is
present in the home.  Provides information
about differences in socialization practices of father absent from father present
homes.

KEYWORDS:  both parents, father absence,
parental support, peers vs. parents, social
problems


553.   Brook, Judith S., M. Whiteman, A. Gordon, and
D. Brook.  "Fathers and Sons:  Their Rela-
tionship and Personality Characteristics
Associated with the Son's Smoking
Behavior."  **Journal of Genetic Psychology**
142(1983):271-81.

Father personality attributes, father
socialization techniques, and adolescent
personality attributes are all predictors
of a son's use of tobacco.

KEYWORDS:  affect, child rearing, identification, parental support, same sex parents,
social problems


554.   ————.  "Identification With Paternal
Attributes and its Relationship to the
Son's Personality and Drug Use."  **Develop-
mental Psychology** 20(1984):1111-19.

The purpose of this study was to examine
the main and interactional effects of

parental identification on a son's personality and drug use.

KEYWORDS: drug use, father-son, interaction

555.  ———.  "Paternal Determinants of Female
      Adolescent's Marijuana Use."  **Developmental**
      **Psychology** 20(1984):1032-43.

      The purpose of this study was to examine
      the interrelationship of sets of parental
      personality attributes, parental-daughter
      relationship variables and adolescent
      personality factors with adolescent
      daughter's use of marijuana.

      KEYWORDS: drug use, father-daughter,
      interaction

556.  Brown, S.  "The Class-Delinquency Hypothesis
      and Juvenile Justice System Bias."
      **Sociological Quarterly** 55(1985):212-23.

      The author finds that only offenses against
      persons consistently correlates negatively
      with measures of social class.  Analysis of
      self-reported contacts with police and
      courts suggests the presence of social
      class biases in the juvenile justice
      process.

      KEYWORDS: parental education, self-
      reported delinquency, social class, work

557.  Brown, W.  "Black Gangs as Family Exten-
      sions."  **International Journal of Offender**
      **Therapy and Comparative Criminology**
      22(1978):39-45.

      The author presents the dynamics of lower-
      class black family life in order to
      understand the context of black gang
      delinquency.  Strategies for survival, and
      strong themes in lower-class existence are

presented as well as peer group relationships and the influences of older gang
members.

KEYWORDS: father-son, gangs, interaction,
parental supervision, peer influence,
subculture

558.    ———. "A Case Study of Delinquency Devolu-
tion." **Criminal Justice and Behavior**
8(1981):425-38.

The author examines the life experiences of
one former juvenile delinquent to identify
the inception, development, and end of
anti-social behavior.

KEYWORDS: family background, self-reported
delinquency

559.    Bruhn, A. "Earliest Memories and the
Dynamics of Delinquency." **Journal of
Personality Assessment** 47(1983):476-82.

Data from the first two childhood memories
was used to distinguish 15 delinquent from
18 non-delinquent controls. Subjects were
middle class males, 15-17 years of age, and
equated for verbal IQ.

KEYWORDS: delinquent vs. non-delinquent,
intelligence, parent-child

560.    Brutz, Judith L., and Bron B. Ingoldsby.
"Conflict Resolution in Quaker Families."
**Journal of Marriage and the Family**
46(1984):21-33.

A convenience survey of 288 Quakers reveals
patterns of family violence similar to
those for general population, except more
Quaker fathers are violent toward their
children than fathers nationally. Quaker
siblings are also more violent toward each
other.

KEYWORDS: interaction, religion, sex-
specification, social problems, violence

561. Burgess, R.L. "Family Violence: Some
     Implications from Evolutionary Biology."
     **Understanding Crime: Current Theory and
     Research.** Edited by T. Hirschi and M.
     Gottfredson. Beverly Hills, Calif.: Sage,
     1980, pp. 91-99.

     KEYWORDS: child rearing, genetics, power,
     review, transmission, violence

562. Burgess, R.L., and R.D. Conger. "Family
     Interaction in Abusive, Neglectful, and
     Normal Families." **Child Development**
     49(1978):1163-73.

     This study represents an attempt to
     discover whether there are distinctive
     patterns of day-to-day interactions that
     distinguish neglectful families from
     families with no known history of abusing
     or neglecting their children.

     KEYWORDS: family background, interaction,
     mother vs. father, mother-father agreement

563. Burgess, R.L., J. Garbarino, and B. Gilstrap.
     "What Comes Naturally? An Evolutionary
     Perspective on Child Abuse." **The Dark Side
     of Families: Current Family Violence
     Research.** Edited by D. Finkelhor, R.J.
     Gelles, G.T. Hotaling, and M.A. Strauss.
     Beverly Hills, Calif.: Sage, 1983, pp. 88-
     101.

     KEYWORDS: child rearing, genetics, power,
     review, transmission, violence

564. Bursik, R.J., Jr., and J. Webb. "Community
     Change and Patterns of Delinquency."
     **American Journal of Sociology** 88(1982):24-
     42.

The authors re-examine the important Shaw
and McKay research finding that the
distribution pattern of delinquency
remained relatively stable over time
despite processes of ethnic and racial
invasion and succession.

KEYWORDS: community, ecological,
ethnicity, historical, methods

565.   Byles, J.A.   "Adolescent Girls in Need of
       Protection."   **American Journal of Ortho-
       psychiatry** 50(1980):264-278.

       Describes 120 girls taken into care under
       the Child Welfare Act (Ontario) as in need
       of protection.  No significant differences
       in behaviors were noted between girls from
       chaotic families and girls reacting to
       traumatic experience.

       KEYWORDS: family background, parental
       deprivation, parental support

566.   Byles, J.A., and A. Maurice.   "The Juvenile
       Services Project:  An Experiment in
       Delinquency Control."   **Canadian Journal of
       Criminology** 20(1978):155-65.

       The authors question the relevance of
       efforts by the Canadian administration with
       the execution of programs aimed at the
       control or prevention of juvenile
       delinquent behavior in the community.

       KEYWORDS: both parents, community,
       intervention, parental support, sibling
       criminal record, single parent, social
       control

567.   Campbell, A.   **Girl Delinquents.**   New York:
       St. Martin's Press, 1981.

The author examines why girls are delinquent and if female delinquency is different from male delinquency.

KEYWORDS: education, family background, male-female, peers vs. parents

568.   Canter, R.J.   "Family Correlates of Male and Female Delinquency."   **Criminology** 20 (1982):149-67.

The authors examine sex differences in family bonds as a possible explanation of sex differences in self-reported delinquent behavior. They did not support their hypothesis that girls would show stronger family bonds and lower delinquency than boys.

KEYWORDS: family cohesion, male-female, methods, parental supervision, single parent

569.   Capuzzi, D., and L. LeCog.   "Social and Personal Determinants of Adolescent Use and Abuse of Alcohol and Marijuana."   **Personal and Guidance Journal** 62(1983):199-205.

The authors found that peer group support influenced the use and abuse of alcohol and marijuana while parental use and abuse is most predictive of adolescent initiation to alcohol and illicit drugs other than marijuana.

KEYWORDS: drug use, peers vs. parents

570.   Carter, T.J.   "Juvenile Court Disposition."   **Criminology** 17(1979):341-60.

571.   Chassin, L., Eason, B., and R. Young.   "Identifying with a Deviant Label:   The Validation of a Methodology."   **Social Psychology Quarterly** 44(1981):31-36.

The authors evaluate the validity of using
Burke and Tully's technique to measure the
role/identities of deviant individuals.
Self-concepts of incarcerated delinquents
were assessed in relation to three social
role labels (popular teenager, juvenile
delinquent, and emotionally disturbed
teenager).

KEYWORDS:   methods, self concept

572.   Christiansen, K.   "A Preliminary Study of
       Criminality Among Twins."   **Biosoial Bases
       of Criminal Behavior.**   Edited by Mednick,
       S., and K. Christiansen.   New York:
       Gardner Press, 1977.

573.   Clair, J.M.   "Black Juvenile Gangs."
       Unpublished manuscript, Department of
       Sociology, Louisiana State University,
       1986.

       An overview of black street gangs in
       California based on interviews with black
       gang leaders.   Special attention is paid to
       gang dynamics and the kinetic element in
       black gang idiom.

       KEYWORDS:   family background, gangs,
       language, subculture

574.   Clarke, R.V.G., and P. Softley.   "The Male:
       Female Ratio Among the Siblings of Delin-
       quents."   **British Journal of Psychiatry**
       126(1975):249-51.

       This research attempts to close a small gap
       in the literature about the families of
       delinquents and it provides a further
       example (ratio of brothers to sisters) of
       the dangers of drawing conclusions about
       delinquents in general from the study of
       administrating defined categories of
       offenders.

KEYWORDS:   both parents, family background,
number of children

575.   Coates, R., Miller, A., and L. Ohlin.
       **Diversity in a Youth Correctional System:**
       **Handling Delinquents in Massachusetts.**
       Cambridge, Mass.: Ballinger, 1978.

       The authors examine the short- and long-run
       impacts of such programs as foster care,
       forestry, group home, and forms of incar-
       ceration from boarding schools to adult
       jails.

       KEYWORDS:   community, rehabilitation,
       residence

576.   Cogner, R.  "Social Control and Social
       Learning Models of Delinquent Behavior."
       **Criminology** 14(1976):17-40.

577.   Colvin, M., and J. Pauly.  "A Critique of
       Criminology:   Toward and Integrated
       Structural-Marxist Theory of Delinquency
       Production."  **American Journal of Sociology**
       89(1983):513-51.

       A review and a critique of the major
       theoretical perspectives in criminology are
       presented.  Then a new integrated theory of
       delinquency, grounded in Marxist insights
       on the productive relations-social
       relationships, is developed and supported
       with empirical evidence from research
       representing a variety of theoretical
       perspectives.

       KEYWORDS:   child rearing, education,
       interaction, labeling, parent-child, peer
       influence, social control, theory, values,
       work

578.   Covington, Jeanette.   "Adolescent Deviation
       and Age."   **Journal of Youth and Adolescence**
       11(1982):329-44.

       In this study, an age-based theory of
       delinquency causation is developed.   This
       theory draws upon the assumption that
       socialization is recurrent, in contrast to
       the premises regarding socialization which
       underlie traditional theories of adolescent
       deviance.

       KEYWORDS:   age-roles, anomie, both parents,
       generations, peers vs. parents, role
       strain, transmission, values

579.   Cruichshank, W., Morse, W., and J. Johns.
       **Learning Disabilities:  The Struggle From
       Adolescence Toward Adulthood.**   Syracuse,
       New York:  Syracuse University Press, 1980.

       The authors explore the question "are
       learning disabled children prone to
       delinquency, or do the studies begin with
       the delinquent youth who are, after the
       fact, determined by some ill-defined
       definition to be learning disabled?"

       KEYWORDS:   age roles, education, learning
       disabilities

580.   Dannefer, D., and R. Schutt.   "Race and
       Juvenile Justice Processing in Court and
       Police Agencies."   **American Journal of
       Sociology** 87(1982):1113-32.

       The authors develop and test hypotheses
       that affect the likelihood of race bias in
       the juvenile justice system:  the charac-
       teristics and procedural constraints of
       processing agencies and the characteristics
       of their social environments.   They control
       for the influence of prior record, type of
       allegation, family structure, sex, race,
       and county.

KEYWORDS: ethnicity, single vs. two
parents, social structure, urban-rural

581.  Datesman, S., and F. Scarpitti.  "Female
      Delinquency and Broken Homes." **Criminology**
      13(1975):33-56.

      The authors show that the relationship
      between broken homes varies between sexes
      depending on the type of delinquent offense
      with which the juvenile is charged.  Female
      delinquents who appear in family court are
      more likely to be from broken homes than
      males if they have been charged with a
      family related delinquency.  Male and
      female delinquents who are charged with
      property crimes, however, are equally
      likely to come from broken homes.

      KEYWORDS: autonomy, divorce effects,
      family cohesion, parental control

582.  Daum, J., and V. Bieliauskas.  "Fathers-
      Absence and Moral Development of Male
      Delinquents." **Psychological Reports** 53
      (1983):223-28.

      40 urban delinquent adolescent males were
      randomly selected from a Juvenile Court
      Population.  20 of them came from families
      in which the father was absent and 20 lived
      with father present.  Comparisons of the
      mean moral maturity suggests that male
      delinquents whose father was absent scored
      lower on moral maturity.

      KEYWORDS: aggression, ethnicity, father
      absence, intelligence, values

583.  Davis, P. **Suicidal Adolescents.** Spring-
      field, Ill.:  Charles C. Thomas, 1983.

      The author examines the motivations and
      causes underlying suicidal behavior.

Prevention, intervention and postvention
are also discussed.

KEYWORDS: both parents, intervention,
parental modeling, prevention

584.    Dawkins, R. "Alcohol Use and Delinquency
        Among Black, White, and Hispanic Adolescent
        Offenders." **Adolescence** 18(1983):799-809.

        Findings show that drinking is the strong-
        est single predictor of juvenile offenses
        among blacks with less importance for
        whites and little importance for hispanics.

        KEYWORDS: drug use, ethnicity

585.    Delfini, L., Bernal, M., and P. Rosen.
        "Comparison of Deviant and Normal Boys in
        Home Settings." **Behavior Modification and
        Families.** Edited by E. Mash. New York:
        Brunner & Mazel Publishers, 1976, pp. 228-
        48.

        The purpose of this paper is to compare the
        behavior of primary grade boys who were
        identified by their parents as presenting
        behavior problems at home with boys
        identified by their parents as being no
        more disruptive than the average boy.

        KEYWORDS: compliance, delinquent vs. non-
        delinquent, number of children, residence,
        social class, two-parent vs. single parent

586.    DeMotte, C. "Conflicting Worlds of Meaning:
        Juvenile Delinquency in 19th Century
        Manchester." **Deviant Behavior** 5(1984):
        193-215.

        The author contends that a closer and more
        skilled reading of the evidence suggests
        that juveniles fluctuate between normative
        values and those of subculture of delin-
        quency.

KEYWORDS:  gangs, history, theory, values


587.  Denga, D.  "Juvenile Delinquency Among
      Polygynous Families in Nigeria."  **The
      Journal of Social Psychology** 112(1981):3-7.

      100 Nigerian families were investigated to
      test if the incidence of delinquency is
      greater among polygynous vs. monogynous
      families.

      KEYWORDS:  cross-cultural, interaction,
      mother vs. father, parent-child


588.  Denno, Deborah.  "Sociological and Human
      Developmental Explanations of Crime:
      Conflict or Consonance?"  **Criminology**
      (1986):  in press.

      Structural equation models are applied to
      assess biological, psychological, and
      environmental variables collected from
      birth through age 17 on a sample of 800
      black children at high risk for learning
      and behavioral disorders.  Results show
      that for both males and females aggression
      and disciplinary problems in school during
      adolescence are the strongest predictors of
      repeat offense behavior.

      KEYWORDS:  age roles, aggression, educa-
      tion, family cohesion, genetics, male-
      female, social class, social structure


589.  Dinitz, S., and B. Pfau-Vincent.  "Self-
      Concept and Juvenile Delinquency:  An
      Update."  **Youth and Society** 14(1982):133-
      58.

      The authors review and update the "soft"
      theoretical perspectives (containment
      theory, differential association, moral
      development stages, and personality
      theories) and the research flowing from
      them, and attempt to determine the

contributions and limits of these perspectives, in particular, the relationship
between self-concept and delinquency.

KEYWORDS: delinquent vs. non-delinquent,
education, family background, prevention,
self-concept, social control, religion

590. Dishion, T. "Skill Deficits and Male
Adolescent Delinquency." **Journal of
Abnormal Child Psychology** 12(1984):37-54.

The general findings strongly suggest that
multiple skill deficits often accompany a
patterned participation in delinquent
behavior, and not exclusively official
detection for anti-social behavior.

KEYWORDS: academic achievement, child
rearing, delinquent vs. non-delinquent,
drug use, intelligence, intervention,
parental criminal record, peer influence

591. Duke, M., and E. Fenhagen. "Self Parental
Alienation and Locus of Control in Delin-
quent Girls." **The Journal of Genetic
Psychology** 127(1975):103-7.

Delinquent girls were, as predicted, more
external and showed greater distancing of
parental figures than non-delinquents. The
authors state that belief in external locus
of control is related to degree of social
maladjustment.

KEYWORDS: academic achievement, delinquent
vs. non-delinquent, ethnicity, rehabilitation

592. Duntstan, J., and S. Roberts. "Ecology,
Delinquency and Socioeconomic Status." **The
British Journal of Criminology** 20(1980):
329-34.

593.   Elliott, D., and S. Ageton.   "Reconciling
       Race and Class Differences in Self-Reported
       and Official Estimates of Delinquency."
       **American Sociological Review** 45(1980):95-
       110.

       This paper addresses the general question
       of whether or not the satisfactory resolu-
       tion of the methodological criticisms of
       self-report research will result in greater
       consistency between self-reported and
       official data with respect to race and
       class distributions of delinquent behavior.

       KEYWORDS:  ethnicity, methods, social class

594.   Elliot, D., Ageton, S., and R. Canter.   "An
       Integrated Theoretical Perspective on
       Delinquent Behavior."  **Crime and
       Delinquency** 16(1979):3-27.

595.   Elliot, D., Huizinga, D., and S. Ageton.
       **Explaining Delinquency and Drug Use.**
       Boulder, Col.:  Behavioral Research Insti-
       tute, 1982.

       The book reports on follow-up data of 1725
       adolescents (out of a nationally repre-
       sentative sample of 2360) aged 11-17 years
       in 1976, interviewing them every year up to
       1981.

       KEYWORDS:  education, family background,
       methods, peer influence, theory, work

596.   Ellis, Godfrey J. and Lorene H. Stone.
       "Marijuana Use in College:  An Evaluation
       of a Modeling Explanation."  **Youth and
       Society** 10(1979):323-34.

       Shows that college students model their
       parents less than they do their peers and
       this is especially true for male college
       students.

KEYWORDS:  both parents, peers vs. parents,
perceptions, sex-specification, social
problems, transmission

597.    Emshoff, J., and C. Blakely.  "The Diversion
of Delinquent Youth:  Family Focused
Intervention."  **Children and Youth Services
Review** 5(1983):343-56.

This paper describes the practices of the
Adolescent Diversion Project and presents
data evaluating the program's effectiveness.  The 73 youth involved in the project
had a mean age of 14.5.  Two-thirds were
male and white.

KEYWORDS:  education, ethnicity, family
background, intervention

598.    Ensminger, M., Brown, C.H., and S. Kellam.
"Sex Differences in Antecedents of Subs-
tance Use Among Adolescents."  **Journal of
Social Issues** 38(1982):25-42.

This research focuses on sex differences in
teenage marijuana, alcohol and cigarette
use.  The population consisted for the 705
first-graders in 1966-67 and reassessed ten
years later.

KEYWORDS:  drug use, education, male-
female, peers vs. parents, social control,
theory

599.    Ensminger, M., Kellam, S., and B. Rubin.
"School and Family Origins of Delinquency:
Comparisons by Sex."  **Prospective Studies
of Crime and Delinquency.**  Edited by Van
Dusen, K., and S. Mednick.  Boston:
Kluwer-Nijhoff Publishing Co., 1983, pp.
73-97.

The authors focus on early social adaptation and family antecedents of teenage
delinquent behavior in a population of

first graders whom were reassessed ten
years later as teenagers. Paths, whether
different or similiar, leading to
delinquency for males and females are
explored in order to develop more complete
explanations of delinquency.

KEYWORDS: aggression, child rearing, drug
use, education, family background, male-
female, parent-child, social structure

600.   Farnworth, M.  "Male-Female Differences in
       Delinquency in a Minority Group Sample."
       **Research in Crime and Delinquency** 21
       (1984):191-212.

       The author finds that the sex effect and
       the manner in which sex operates to affect
       delinquency depends upon the type of
       delinquent outcome under investigation.

       KEYWORDS: blacks, family background, male-
       female

601.   Farrington, D.P.  "The Effects of Public
       Labelling."  **British Journal of Criminology**
       17(1977):112-25.

       The aim of this paper is to move one step
       towards a scientific labelling theory, by
       proposing and testing a hypothesis about
       deviance amplification.

       KEYWORDS: labelling, self-reported
       delinquency, social class

602.   ————.  "The Family Backgrounds of Aggres-
       sive Youths."  **Aggressive and Antisocial
       Behavior in Childhood and Adolescence.**
       Edited by L. Hersove.  Oxford:  Pergamon,
       1978.

603.   ————.  "Environmental Stress, Delinquent
       Behavior, and Convictions."  **Stress and**

Anxiety, Volume 6. Edited by Sarason, I.,
and C. Spielberger. Washington, D.C.:
Hemisphere, 1979, pp. 93-107.

This research forms part of the Cambridge
Study in Delinquent Development, which is a
prospective longitudinal survey of a sample
of 411 males. The presented results
suggest that most aspects of a stressful
family environment produce convictions
rather than delinquent behavior.

KEYWORDS: child rearing, delinquent vs.
non-delinquent, intelligence, methods,
number of children, parental criminal
record, parental supervision, sibling
criminal record, social class, work

604.    ———. "Truancy, Delinquency, the Home and
the School." **Out of School: Modern
Perspectives in Truancy and School Refusal.**
Edited by Berg, I., and L. Hersov.
Chichester: Wiley, 1980.

605.    ———. "Delinquency Prevention in the
1980's." **Journal of Adolescence** 8(1985):
3-16.

It is argued in this paper that it is just
as plausible to locate the causes of
delinquency in the individual as in the
environment, and that there is good reason
to expect delinquency prevention efforts
targeted toward individuals to be successful.

KEYWORDS: delinquent vs. non-delinquent,
education, environment, intervention,
methods, prevention

606.    Farrington, D.P., Gundry, G., and D.J. West.
"The Familial Transmission of Criminality."
**Medicine, Science, and Law** 15(1975):177-
86.

This investigation is based on 394 young
males whose names, together with those of
their parents, brothers and sisters, were
searched for repeatedly in the Criminal
Record Office as part of a delinquency
project known as the Cambridge Study in
Delinquent Development.

KEYWORDS:  family background, genetics,
heredity, parental criminal record, sibling
criminal record, transmission

607.   Feather, N.T., and D.G. Cross.  "Value Systems
       and Delinquency:  Parental and Generational
       Discrepancies in Value Systems for Delin-
       quent and Non-Delinquent Boys."  **British
       Journal of Social and Clinical Psychology**
       14(1975):117-29.

       A sample of 82 delinquent boys in two
       institutions and a matched sample of 82
       non-delinquent boys from three secondary
       schools ranked values from the Rokeach
       Value Survey in their order of importance
       for self, mother and father.

       KEYWORDS:  both parents, delinquent vs.
       non-delinquent, generations, mother vs.
       father, values

608.   Feldman, R.  "Juvenile Offending:  Behavioral
       Approaches to Prevention and Intervention."
       **Child and Family Behavior Therapy** 5(1983):
       37.

609.   Feldman, R., Caplinger, T., and J. Wodarski.
       **The St. Louis Conundrum:  The Effective
       Treatment of Antisocial Youths.**  Englewood
       Cliffs:  Prentice-Hall, 1983.

610.   Feldman, R., and A. Stiffmann.  **Advances in
       Adolescent Mental Health.  Volume 1:
       Mental Health Disorders in Adolescence.**
       Greenwich, Conn.:  JAI Press, 1986.

611.    Feldman, R., Stiffman, A., and K. Jung. **In
        The Webb of Mental Illness: Victims,
        Vulnerables and Invincibles.** New York:
        Rutgers University Press, 1986.

612.    Ferracuti, F., and E. Acosta de Brenes.
        **Delinquents and Non-delinquents in the
        Puerto Rican Slum Culture.** Columbus: Ohio
        State University, 1975.

        Utilizing a modified version of the
        methodology employed by the classic Gluecks
        study the author matched 101 delinquent
        males with 101 non-delinquents by social
        history, psychiatric examination, psycho-
        logical test battery, physical exam,
        neurological exam, and electroencephalo-
        gram.

        KEYWORDS: delinquent vs. non-delinquent,
        economic deprivation, education, family
        background, gangs, parental mental health,
        self-concept

613.    Fischer, D. "Parental Supervision and
        Delinquency." **Perceptual and Motor Skills**
        56(1983):635-40.

614.    ————. "Family Size and Delinquency."
        **Perceptual and Motor Skills** 58(1984):527-
        34.

        A review of the literature shows large
        family size is related to greater
        delinquency. The author suggests that the
        relationship remains when a number of
        f=variables such as, income, SES, parental
        criminality, and family composition are
        controlled.

        KEYWORDS: birth order, interaction, number
        of children, parent-child, parental
        criminal record, parental supervision,
        sibling criminal record, social class

615.   Frazier, Charles.  "Evaluation of Youth
       Services Programs:  Problems and Prospects
       from a Case Study."  **Youth and Society** 14
       (1983):335-62.

       This article is an examination of one
       program's efforts to curb recidivism and it
       is a critique of the state of the art of
       delinquency programs and evaluation
       research.

       KEYWORDS:  labeling, methods, recidivism,
       rehabilitation


616.   Frease, Dean E.  "Delinquency, Social Class,
       and the Schools."  **Sociology and Social
       Research** 57(1973):443-59.

       The authors report findings showing no
       relationship between social class and
       juvenile delinquency.

       KEYWORDS:  delinquent vs. non-delinquent,
       social class, white collar vs. blue collar


617.   Friday, Paul.  "International Review of Youth
       Crime and Delinquency."  **Delinquency and
       Crime:  Comparative Perspectives.**  Edited
       by Graeme Newman.  Beverly Hills:  Sage,
       1981, pp. 100-29.

       The author concludes that criminality is
       not reduced simply by the formation of
       attachments to a given set of relation-
       ships, but by a function of the interaction
       of attachment and control by the overlap of
       groups themselves (family, community,
       school).

       KEYWORDS:  age roles, community, cross
       cultural, economic deprivation, education,
       parental criminal record, parental disci-
       pline, recidivism, religion, social
       control, social structure, theory, trans-
       mission, two parent vs. single parent,
       values, work

618.    ———.  "Patterns of Role Relationships and
        Crime."  **The Many Faces of Crime and
        Deviance.**  Edited by S. Giora Shoham.  New
        York:  Sheridan House, 1981, pp. 61-80.

        The author puts forth the argument that
        many youths are unable to develop conform-
        ing, responsible, meaningful social roles
        due to technological and socio-economic
        development.  Roles are generated through
        structural conditions and modified by
        institutional arrangements, thus, creating
        for individuals variable role repertoires.

        KEYWORDS:  age roles, economic deprivation,
        policy, role strain, technology, theory,
        social class, social structure

619.    ———.  "Delinquency Prevention and Social
        Policy."  **Providing Criminal Justice for
        Children.**  Edited by Paul Friday.  London:
        Edward Arnold, 1983, pp. 36-51.

        The author's major conclusion is that crime
        prevention requires radical social
        structural change that will redefine the
        economic order with an emphasis on property
        as the primary source of status and
        rewards.

        KEYWORDS:  age roles, community, economic
        deprivation, education, parental attach-
        ment, peers vs. parents, policy, preven-
        tion, social control, social structure,
        theory

620.    Furtek, J.  "Juvenile Delinquency:  Histori-
        cal Theories and Their Impact."  **New
        Designs for Youth Development** 3(1982):17-
        20.

        The author writes that the 20th century
        concept of juvenile delinquency and
        treatment of offenders reflects the 19th
        century in that the public still views
        juvenile delinquency as an inherited social

problem from the family's inability to deal
with children.

KEYWORDS:  family background, historical

621.  Ghosian, B.  "A Longitudinal Study of
      Maternal Depression and Child Behavior
      Problems."  **Journal of Child Psychology and
      Psychiatry and Applied Disciplines**
      25(1984):91-109.

      Child problems at 14 months were unrelated
      to present and past maternal depression.
      Child problems at 27 and 42 months were
      related.  There was little indication of
      behavioral problems preceding maternal
      depression.

      KEYWORDS:  parent-child, parental mental
      health

622.  Giallombardo, R. (ed.).  **Juvenile
      Delinquency:  A Book of Readings, 4th
      Edition.**  New York:  John Wiley and Sons,
      1982.

      A collection of papers on various juvenile
      delinquent issues.

      KEYWORDS:  community, education, ethnicity,
      labeling, male-female, methods, single
      parent, social class, social control,
      subculture

623.  Glueck, S., and E. Glueck.  **Unraveling
      Juvenile Delinquency.**  Cambridge:  Harvard
      University Press, 1950.

      A classic U.S. study of convicted juvenile
      delinquents.  Results show that the
      delinquents' social environments were
      characterized by poverty; slum housing;
      large families; the absence of one or both
      natural parents; parents in marital
      conflict; poor parental supervision;

parents with rejecting attitudes, and
criminal parents and siblings.

KEYWORDS: economic deprivation, intra-
familial conflict, number of children,
parental criminal record, parental discipline, parental rejection, parental
supervision, sibling criminal record, two
parent vs. single parent

624.  Greenberg, David F.  "Delinquency and the Age
      Structure of Society."  **Contemporary Crises**
      1(1977):189-93.

      The author presents a theoretical analysis
      of the age distribution of criminal
      involvement.  In particular, he attempts to
      show that there is an increasingly dispro-
      portionate involvement of juveniles in
      major crime categories.

      KEYWORDS: age roles, both parents,
      education, ethnicity, genetics,
      historical, social class, social structure,
      status attainment, values, work

625.  Grinnell, R., Jr., and C. Chambers.  "Broken
      Homes and Middle Class Delinquency."
      **Criminology** 17(1979):395-400.

626.  Gunn, J., and D.P. Farrington (eds.).
      **Abnormal Offenders, Delinquency and the
      Criminal Justice System, Volume 1.**  New
      York:  John Wiley, 1982.

      Reviews and presents research concerned
      with juvenile crime and punishment.

      KEYWORDS: both parents, cross-cultural,
      environment, family background, father
      absence, longitudinal, male-female,
      parental criminal record, prevention

627.  Hagan, J.  "The Class Structure of Gender and
      Delinquency:  Toward a Power-Control Theory
      of Common Delinquent Behavior."  **American
      Journal of Sociology** May(1985).


628.  Hagan, J., and J. Leon.  "Rediscovering
      Delinquency:  Social History, Political
      Ideology and the Sociology of Law."
      **American Sociological Review** 42(1977):
      587-98.

      Using Canadian delinquency legislation as
      a historical example, the authors find a
      Marxian perspective assumes a great deal
      that is unconfirmed.  One finding worth
      noting is that although this legislation
      substantially changed the operations of the
      juvenile and criminal courts, the overall
      effect was not to intensify a formal and
      explicit system of coercion, but rather to
      reinforce and intervene in informal systems
      of social control, particularly the family.

      KEYWORDS:  historical, policy, social
      class, social control, theory


629.  Hanson, C., S. Henggeler, W. Haefele, and J.
      Rodic.  "Demographic, Individual, and
      Family Relationship Correlates of Serious
      and Repeated Crime Among Adolescents and
      their Siblings."  **Journal of Consulting and
      Clinical Psychology** 52(1984):528-37.


630.  Hardt, R.H., and S. Peterson-Hardt.  "On
      Determining the Quality of the Delinquency
      Self-Report Method."  **Journal of Research
      in Crime and Delinquency** 13-14(1977):247-
      61.

      Using data from a self-report study of
      adolescents, the validity of the results of
      using this technique is appraised.

KEYWORDS: education, ethnicity, methods,
school performance, self-report
delinquency, social class

631.    Harrell, K.F.   "Juvenile Gangs."   Public
        Administration Series P-1233.   Monticello,
        Ill.:   Vance Bibliographies, 1983.

632.    Hartjen, C.   "Delinquency, Development, and
        Social Integration in India."   **Social
        Problems** 29(1982):464-73.

        The author argues that unlike the U.S.A.,
        delinquency in India is not considered to
        be a major problem, and delinquency rates
        remain low.   Several socio-economic
        features of Indian society are put forth as
        deterrents for the development of an
        adolescent subculture, more specifically,
        interpersonal ties of family and the social
        requirements of an agrarian - scarcity,
        economy

        KEYWORDS: age roles, cross cultural,
        family background, parental support,
        political, power, social class, work

633.    Haskell, M.R., and L. Yablonsky.   **Juvenile
        Delinquency**.   Boston:   Houghton Mifflin,
        1982.

        A widely used book with more than average
        attention examining parent-child, adult-
        youth interaction and conflict.

        KEYWORDS: age roles, autonomy, both
        parents, delinquent vs. non-delinquent,
        parent-child, social control, values

634.    Hassin, Yael.   "Raising the Age of Criminal
        Responsibility in Israel."   **Israel Law
        Review** 16(1981):225-49.

The author deals with three questions which
have been debated since the passing of
Penal Law (the Yitzhaki Law) in 1978;
first, is the age 13 in fact the appropriate age to impose criminal responsibility
on juveniles; second, has the change in the
law given rise to an increase in delinquent
behavior, recidivism and severity; and
third, do these juvenile suspects receive
the correct care and supervision, in
conformity of the law.

KEYWORDS:  education, ethnicity, parental
involvement, recidivism

635.    ————.  "Presence of Parents During Inter-
rogation of their Children."  **Juvenile and
Family Court Journal** 19(1981):33-42.

The author examines several aspects of
police interrogations of minors.  The
author looks at a number of negative
effects of the encounter between police and
minors as it occurs today, and concentrates
primarily on those arguments supporting the
rights of parents to be present when their
children are being questioned by the
police.

KEYWORDS:  family background, intervention,
labeling, self-esteem, social control

636.    ————.  "Juvenile Delinquency in Israel
1948-1977:  Patterns and Trends."  **Research
in Law, Deviance and Social Control**
5(1983):25-50.

The author discusses the extent of juvenile
delinquency; the types of offenses involved
in juvenile delinquency; and the connection
between country of origin and juvenile
delinquency utilizing official criminal
statistics in Israel from 1948 to 1977.

KEYWORDS:  cross cultural, drug use,
ethnicity, family background, recidivism

637.    Henderson, Ronald.    "Effects of Ethnicity and
        Child's Age on Maternal Judgments of
        Children's Transgressions Against Persons
        and Property."    **The Journal of Genetic
        Psychology** 140(1982):253-63.

        The authors present results based on 256
        mothers of four different cultural groups
        judging the culpability of children whose
        actions are described depicting commission
        of harm under various conditions:  Child's
        age, harm to persons vs. material objects,
        intentions, and amount of harm are
        systematically varied.

        KEYWORDS:  child-rearing, ethnicity


638.    Henggeler, S.W. (ed.).    **Delinquency and
        Adolescent Psychopathology:  A Family-
        Ecological System Approach.**  Boston:  John
        Wright, 1982.

        Readings from the family-ecological systems
        perspective viewing the adolescent as
        embedded in the family system with sub-
        systems such as parents, siblings, and the
        extended family.

        KEYWORDS:  both parents, interaction,
        parent-child


639.    Hennessy, M., Richards, P., and R. Berk.
        "Broken Homes and Middle-Class
        Delinquency."    **Criminology** 15(1978):505-
        28.

        The authors find family structure to
        account for only a small part of
        delinquency.  They also address
        methodological problems in other research.

        KEYWORDS:  delinquent vs. non-delinquent,
        family background, parent-child, parental
        control, social class, social control, two
        parents vs. single parent

640.  Hindelang, M., Hirschi, T., and J. Weis.
      **Measuring Delinquency.** Beverly Hills:
      Sage, 1981.

      The authors explore theories of measurement
      and statistics for the study of delin-
      quency.

      KEYWORDS: ethnicity, male-female, methods,
      social class

641.  Hirschi, Travis. **Causes of Delinquency.**
      Berkeley: University of California Press,
      1969.

      A classic text, cross-sectional in design,
      involving retrospective information about
      family background gathered from children
      rather than their parents. The author
      found that high self-reported delinquents
      tended to come from large families, to have
      unemployed fathers, to have stepfathers,
      and to be exposed to poor parental super-
      vision.

      KEYWORDS: biological vs. adopted parents,
      methods, number of children, parental
      supervision, self-reported delinquency,
      work

642.  ————. "Families and Crime." **The Wilson
      Quarterly** 7(1983):132-39.

      A report of the Oregon Social Learning
      Center in Eugene, which employed a treat-
      ment method to train problem children by
      rewarding good actions and ignoring bad
      ones.

      KEYWORDS: both parents, methods, parental
      supervision, single parent, social control

643.  Hirschi, Travis., and M. Gottfredson. "Age
      and the Explanation of Crime." **American
      Journal of Sociology** 89(1983):553-84.

The authors state that although correlated
with crime, age is not useful in predicting
involvement in crime over the life course
of offenders.  They also argue that the
traditional discussion of the etiological
problem into juvenile and adult segments is
unlikely to be useful.

KEYWORDS:  age roles, ethnicity, social
control, theory

644.    Hirschi, Travis, and M. Hindelang.   "Intelli-
        gence and Delinquency:   A Revisionist
        Review."  **American Sociological Review**
        42(1977):571-87.

        In an analysis of the history of the
        research in the IQ-delinquency relation,
        the authors trace the developments leading
        to the current textbook position that IQ is
        not an important factor in delinquency.
        The authors show that IQ has an effect on
        delinquency independent of class and race,
        and they argue that this effect is mediated
        through a host of school variables.

        KEYWORDS:  education, ethnicity, intelli-
        gence, social class

645.    Hraba, J., Miller, M., and V. Webb.
        "Mutability and Delinquency:   The Relative
        Effects of Structural, Associational, and
        Attitudinal Variables on Juvenile
        Delinquency."  **Criminal Justice and
        Behavior** 2(1975):408-20.

        Data are analyzed to illustrate that by
        making the issue of mutability manifest in
        research, findings from research would have
        more practical import.

        KEYWORDS:  anomie, birth order, both
        parents, divorce effects, education,
        ethnicity, methods, number of children,
        prevention, religion, social class, theory

646.  Hraba, J., D. Specht, R. Warren, and M.
      Miller. "A Demographic Diagnosis of
      Delinquency." **Criminal Justice Review**
      (1977):133-43.

      The authors propose a demographic diagnosis
      of self-reported delinquency and examine
      its utility. They support their hypothesis
      that some delinquency correlates operate
      differently in demographic categories of
      youth.

      KEYWORDS: both parents, ethnicity, male-
      female, number of children, two parents vs.
      single parent, work

647.  Humm-Delgado, D.,and M. Delgado. "Hispanic
      Adolescents and Substance Abuse:   Issues
      for the 1980's." **Child and Youth Services**
      6(1983):71-87.

      The authors present the state of the art
      literature on substance abuse among
      hispanic youth, and identify policy issues
      in the decade ahead.

      KEYWORDS: drug use, policy, subculture

648.  Hutchings, B., and S. Mednick. "Criminality
      in Adoptees and Their Adoptive and Biologi-
      cal Parents: A Pilot Study." **Biosocial
      Bases of Criminal Behavior**. Edited by
      Mednick, S., and K. Christiansen. New
      York: Gardner Press, 1977, pp. 127-45.

      The authors argue that there appears to be
      a correlation between criminality in
      adoptees and criminality in their biologi-
      cal parents.

      KEYWORDS: biological vs. adoptive parents,
      both parents, genetics, heredity, methods,
      social class

649.    Imperio, A.   "Male Delinquents Perceptions of
        Their Parents:   A Factor Analysis."
        **Perception and Motor Skills** 51(1980):829-
        30.

650.    Inverarity, J., Lauderdale, P., and B. Feld.
        **Law and Society:   Sociological Perspectives
        on Criminal Law.**   Boston:   Little, Brown
        and Company, 1983.

        Many parts of this book focus on the
        control of youth and the juvenile justice
        system.   This work focuses on the political
        economy.   The family system is also given
        attention and some discussion focuses on
        how the family system has been altered to
        devote more attention to the socialization
        of children.

        KEYWORDS:   family background, historical,
        rehabilitation, social control, theory

651.    The Jack Roller and J. Snodgrass.   **The Jack
        Roller at Seventy:   A Fifty-Year Follow-Up.**
        Lexington, Mass.:   D.C. Heath, 1982.

        A sequel to the classic "The Jack Roller:
        A Delinquent Boy's Own Story."

        KEYWORDS:   historical, methods

652.    Janeksela, M., and M. Miller.   "An Explora-
        tory Study of Delinquency, Criminal
        Offenses, and Juvenile Status Offenses Via
        the Cross Validation."   **Adolescence**
        20(1985):161-69.

        The authors report the results of their
        exploratory study of thirty variables that
        may have an effect on delinquency, criminal
        offenses, and juvenile status offenses.
        The study is based on secondary data.

KEYWORDS: academic achievement, anomie, number of children, parental supervision, two parent vs. single parent

653.  Jarosz, M. "Disintegration of the Family in the Etiology of Deviant Behavior." **Deviant Behavior** 2(1980):1-14.

Results indicate that families experiencing shrinking alimonies have much worse material and housing conditions than average Polish families and that this syndrome of psychological, social, and material factors is associated with delinquency.

KEYWORDS: cross-cultural, education, intra-familial conflict, prevention

654.  Jason, L., De Amicis, L., and B. Carter. "Prevention Intervention Programs for Disadvantaged Children." **Community Mental Health Journal** 14(1978):272-78.

The author describes a 6-year effort aimed at developing educational interventions for a group of economically disadvantaged children.

KEYWORDS: both parents, economic depriva-tion, education, intelligence, intervention, residence

655.  Jensen, G. (ed.). **Sociology of Delinquency: Current Issues.** Beverly Hills: Sage, 1981.

This volume attempts to identify important theoretical and empirical issues for the sociology of delinquency in the 1980's.

KEYWORDS: ethnicity, methods, peers vs. parents

656.  Joe, D., and N. Robinson.  "Chinatown's
      Immigrant Gangs:  The New Young Warrior
      Class."  **Criminology** 18(1980):337-45.

      The authors examine the characteristics and
      processes of four gangs operating in the
      Chinatown of Vancouver, Canada, over a
      three-year period (1975-1978).

      KEYWORDS:  generations, immigration,
      parental discipline, parental modeling,
      parental supervision, policy, values

657.  Johnson, R.E.  **Juvenile Delinquency and its
      Origins.**  Cambridge:  Cambridge University
      Press, 1979.

      An excellent overview of the causal images
      contained in the major theoretical orienta-
      tions in search of an understanding of
      juvenile delinquency.  The author focuses
      on social class, the family, school,
      perceptions of the future, delinquent
      peers, delinquent values, deterrence, and
      parental support.

      KEYWORDS:  delinquent vs. non-delinquent,
      education, family background, methods,
      parent-child, parental support, peers vs.
      parents, perceptions, social class, social
      control, theory, values

658.  Johnson, T.  "Family Therapy with Families
      Having Delinquent Offspring."  **Journal of
      Family Counseling** 3(1975):32-37.

659.  ————.  "The Juvenile Offender and His
      Family."  **Juvenile Justice** 26(1975):31-34.

660.  Johnstone, John W.C.  "Juvenile Delinquency
      and the Family:  A Contextual Interpreta-
      tion."  **Youth and Society** 9(1978):299-314.

Variation in the quality of family life is more strongly related to less serious norm violations than to "hard core" delinquency. For the more serious delinquent, family economic deprivation and the community are more strongly related than family structure or family functioning.

KEYWORDS: economic deprivation, integration, peer influences, social class, values, violence

661.  ———.  "Delinquency and the Changing American Family." **Critical Issues in Juvenile Delinquency.** Edited by Shicher, D., and D. Kelly. Lexington: Lexington Books, 1980, pp. 83-97.

The author states that fewer and fewer social scientists claim the family as a major determinant of delinquency among American children and adolescence. This is so even though this view is ideologically incompatible with our national heritage and values, and the author argues, it is questionable whether the public at large accepts this view.

KEYWORDS: both parents, divorce effects, economic deprivation, father absence, generations, intervention, parental rejection, parental support, residence, restructured families, single parent, social class

662.  ———.  "Youth Gangs and Black Suburbs." **Pacific Sociological Review** 24(1981):355-75.

The author presents evidence that refutes the supposition that there is an absence of gang activity outside the inner-city.

KEYWORDS: economic deprivation, ethnicity, single parent, urban-rural

663.    ————.  "Recruitment into a Youth Gang."
        **Youth and Society** 14(1983):281-300.

        Unusual data for gang research consisting
        of self-reported experiences of adolescents
        involved in street gangs.  Perhaps the
        author's most important conclusion is that
        gang membership represents a last option,
        not a preferred one, for most urban youth.

        KEYWORDS:  community, economic deprivation,
        education, ethnicity, father absence,
        family cohesion, gangs, peer influence,
        residence, social control


664.    Jurich, A.P., C. Polson, J. A. Jurich, and R.
        Bates.  "Family Factors in the Lives of
        Drug Users and Abusers."  **Adolescence**
        20(1985):143-59.

        Drug users were less likely to come from
        families where there was a communication
        gap and more likely to come from families
        which used democratic disciplinary techniq-
        ues.

        KEYWORDS:  drug use, interaction, intra-
        familial conflict, parent-child, parental
        discipline, mother vs. father


665.    Kaplan, H., Martin, S., and C. Robbins.
        "Pathway to Adolescent Drug Use:  Self-
        Derogation, Peer Influence, Weakening of
        Social Controls, and Early Substance Use."
        **Journal of Health and Social Behavior**
        25(1984):270-89.

        Longitudinal data is used to test a model
        that accounts for the adoption of drug use
        by adolescents.

        KEYWORDS:  drug use, longitudinal, peers
        vs. parents, social control

666.    Kellam, S., and M. Ensminger. "Theory and
        Method in Child Psychiatric Epidemiology."
        **Studies of Children.** Edited by F. Earls.
        New York:  Neal Watson Academic Publica-
        tions, 1980.

        The authors focus on identifying theoreti-
        cal constructs and examine how epidemiology
        fits into an overall framework for under-
        standing research and service in mental
        health and illness.

        KEYWORDS:  aggression, drug use, education,
        family background, intervention,
        longitudinal, male-female, methods, theory

667.    Kellam, S., Ensminger, M., and M. Simon.
        "Mental Health in First Grade and Teenage
        Drug, Alcohol, and Cigarette Use."  **Drug
        and Alcohol Dependence** 5(1980):273-304.

        Among females, higher levels of psychiatric
        symptoms in first grade predicted, to some
        extent, lower teenage drug use.  Teenage
        antisocial behavior was an important
        mediator of teenage drug use for first-
        grade shy-aggressive males and somewhat
        less important for first-grade aggressive
        males.

        KEYWORDS:  aggression, drug use, family
        background, IQ, male-female

668.    Knight, B., Osborn, S., and D.J. West.
        "Early Marriage and Criminal Tendency in
        Males."  **British Journal of Criminology**
        17(1977):348-60.

        The authors have collected information
        relevant to two questions.  Are males who
        marry early characterized by delinquent
        tendencies or related social character-
        istics?  Is early marriage followed by
        changes in delinquent habits or in related
        social behavior?

KEYWORDS: age at marriage, aggression,
parental criminal record, self-reported
delinquency, work

669.  Knight, B., and D.J. West.  "Temporary and
      Continuing Delinquency."  **British Journal
      of Criminology** 15(1975):43-50.

      The authors investigate some of the factors
      which distinguish young men who give up
      delinquency on reaching adulthood from
      those who continue to be active delin-
      quents.

      KEYWORDS: intelligence, longitudinal,
      parental criminal record, peers vs.
      parents, recidivism, self-reported delin-
      quency, sibling criminal record, social
      class

670.  —————.  "Criminality and Welfare Dependency
      in Two Generations."  **Medicine, Science and
      the Law** 17(1977):64-67.

671.  Kozloff, M.  "Systems of Structures Exchange:
      Changing Families of Severely Deviant
      Children."  **Sociological Practice** 2(1976):
      86-104.

      The author describes the results of a three
      year project developed to evaluate a system
      for training parents to modify the
      exchanges in the family so that beneficial
      behavioral change would be manifest in both
      them and their children.

      KEYWORDS: interaction, parent-child,
      values

672.  Krohn, M.  "Social Status and Deviance:
      Class Context of School, Social Status, and
      Delinquent Behavior."  **Criminology**
      18(1980):303-18.

The authors address the social class to
delinquent behavior relationship on samples
of students from small towns to large urban
areas.

KEYWORDS: education, social class, self-
reported delinquency

673. Landau, S.F.  "Juveniles and the Police:  Who
is Charged Immediately and Who is Referred
to the Juvenile Bureau?"  **British Journal
of Criminology** 21(1981):27-46.

The author examines whether social control
agencies discriminate between juveniles
based on non-legal characteristics.

KEYWORDS: discrimination, ethnicity, male-
female, recidivism, social class, social
control, violence

674. Lang, D., Papenfuhs, R., and J. Walters.
"Delinquent Females Perceptions of their
Fathers."  **The Family Coordinator** (October
1976):475-81.

Delinquents from a sample of Georgia and
Oklahoma juveniles indicated that they were
not close to their fathers, and that their
fathers were neither very interested in
them, loving, kind, nor understanding.
More favorable perceptions were reflected
if fathers were head of the family, average
or above in terms of masculinity, and if
daughters felt loved by fathers.

KEYWORDS: delinquent vs. non-delinquent,
father-daughter, mother-daughter, parental
discipline, perception

675. Lee, L.  "Reducing Black Adolescent Drug Use;
Family Revisited."  **Child and Youth
Services** 6(1983):57-59.

The author presents the family as a major source in preparing children to cope with the pressures to experiment with drugs.

KEYWORDS: both parents, drug use, education, ethnicity, religion

676.   Leigh, Geoffrey K., and Gary W. Peterson (eds.). **Adolescents in Families.** Cincinnati: South-Western Publishing Company, 1986. In press.

This is a collection of original papers on issues relating adolescence to the family. Includes section on minority patterns (black, adolescent, rural) as well as a wide range of issues.

KEYWORDS: blacks, conflict, delinquency, divorce, occupation achievements, rural, sex roles

677.   Lemelle, A.J. "Killing the Author of Life: or, Decimating 'Bad Niggers'." **Journal of Black Studies** (1986): in press.

This paper is a theoretical perspective of deviance in American Society where the role of the black male juvenile delinquent is viewed as a central force in the transformation of high industrial culture from the history of alienated labor to a period of non-repressed labor.

KEYWORDS: alienation, culture, education, ethnicity, racism, work

678.   Lessin, S., and T. Jacob. "Multichannel Communication in Normal and Delinquent Families." **Journal of Abnormal Psychology** 12(1984):369-84.

Significant results reveal that parents of non-delinquent sons emit more inconsistent communication patterns than parents of

delinquent sons, in the form of negative
verbal, positive facial, and interpersonal
relationships.

KEYWORDS:  delinquency vs. non-delinquency,
interaction, parent-child

679.   Lewis, D., and S. Shanok.  "Medical Histories
       of Delinquent and Nondelinquent Children:
       An Epidemiological Study."  **American
       Journal of Psychiatry** 134(1977):1020-25.

       The authors conclude that the number,
       reasons, and timing of hospital contacts
       significantly differentiated the delinquent
       from the nondelinquent child.  Prenatal
       difficulties did not differentiate the
       delinquent child from the nondelinquent
       child.

       KEYWORDS:  intra-familial conflict, medical
       histories, parental support

680.   Liska, A., and M. Reed.  "Ties to Conventional
       Institutions and Delinquency:  Estimating
       Reciprocal Effects."  **American Sociological
       Review** 50(1985):547-60.

       The authors examine the relationship
       between juvenile delinquency and ties to
       conventional institutions, defined by them
       as attachment to parents and school.
       Findings show a negative effect of attach-
       ment on delinquency.

       KEYWORDS:  education, family cohesion
       methods, social control, violence

681.   Lowney, J.  "Correspondence between Attitudes
       and Drinking and Drug Behavior:  Youth
       Subculture Over Time."  **Adolescence**
       19(1984):903-12.

       A longitudinal study to analyze the
       correspondence between attitudes of the

youth subculture theories and overt
behavior patterns.

KEYWORDS: drug use, politics, religion,
subcultures, values

682.  Lyerly, R., and J. Skipper.  "Differential
      Rates of Rural-Urban Delinquency."
      **Criminology** 19(1981):385-99.

      The authors attempt to explain the differ-
      ences of rural-urban delinquency rates
      utilizing social control theory.

      KEYWORDS: education, family background,
      peers vs. parents, social control, urban-
      rural

683.  Lysaghy, T., and J. Burchard.  "The Analysis
      and Modification of a Deviant Parent-Youth
      Communication Pattern."  **Journal of
      Behavior Therapy and Experimental Psychi-
      atry** 6(1975):339-42.

684.  Maloney, D., Fixsen, D., and E. Phillips.
      "The Teaching-Family Model:  Research
      Dissemination in a Service Program."
      **Children and Youth Services Review** 3(1981):
      343-55.

      The authors describe a teaching-family
      model as a residential model used for the
      care and treatment of emotionally disturb-
      ed, predelinquent, and delinquent adoles-
      cents.

      KEYWORDS: both parents, mother-father
      agreement, residence

685.  Marchant, H., and H. Smith.  **Adolescent Girls
      at Risk.**  Oxford, England:  Pergamon Press,
      1977.

The author describes the Kitbury Girls
Project which attempted to reach deviant
and delinquent adolescents who were defined
as at risk.

KEYWORDS: academic achievement, intra-
familial conflict, parental mental health,
work

686. Martin, L., and P. Snyder.  "Jurisdiction
     over Status Offenses:  Should That be
     Removed from the Juvenile Court."  **Crime
     and Delinquency** 21(1976):44-47.

     The authors imply that the removal of
     status offenses from the jurisdiction of
     the juvenile court would cause a reduction
     of services for families under stress.

     KEYWORDS: intra-familial conflict,
     punishment, rehabilitation

687. McBroom, W., F. Reed, C. Burns, J. Hargraves,
     and M. Trankel.  "Intergenerational
     Transmission of Values:  A Data-Based
     Reassessment."  **Social Psychology Quarterly**
     48(1985):150-63.

     Results show family structure to be
     important in predicting parent-child
     agreement.

     KEYWORDS: drug use, interaction, parent-
     child, two parents vs. single parent,
     values

688. McCarthy, J., and D. Hoge.  "The Dynamics of
     Self-Esteem and Delinquency."  **American
     Journal of Sociology** 90(1984):396-410.

     The results show that the effect of self-
     esteem on subsequent delinquent activity is
     negligible, although there are consistent
     but weak negative effects of delinquent
     behavior on subsequent self-esteem.

KEYWORDS: male-female, parental education, self-esteem, self-reported

689.   McCord, W., and McCord, J., and I. Zola. **Origins of Crime**. New York: Columbia University Press, 1959.

A classic U.S. study showing that convicted delinquents tended to come from poor areas; to have parents with lax or erratic discipline; to have parents who were rejecting, criminal, or absent.

KEYWORDS: economic deprivation, parental criminal record, parental discipline, parental rejection, parental supervision, two parents vs. single parent

690.   McDermott, D. "The Relationship of Parental Drug Use and Parent's Attitude Concerning Adolescent Drug Use to Adolescent Drug Abuse." **Adolescence** 19(1984):89-97.

The authors argue that adolescents who use drugs are significantly more likely to have one or more parents who use drugs, and that adolescents who perceive their parents as having permissive views about drug use by youths are significantly more likely to use drugs than those who perceive their parents as holding non-permissive views.

KEYWORDS: delinquent vs. non-delinquent, drug use, parent-child

691.   McHenry, P., Tishler, C., and C. Kelley. "The Role of Drugs in Adolescent Suicide Attempts." **Suicide and Life-Threatening Behavior** 13(1983):166-75.

Drug histories are presented of 46 adolescent suicide attempters and their parents and are compared with a non-attempters-parent group.

KEYWORDS: both parents, delinquent vs.
non-delinquent, drug use

692. McKissack, I. "Early Socialization: The
     Base Line in Delinquency Research."
     **International Journal of Criminology and
     Penology** 3(1975):43-51.

693. Meadow, A. "Self-Concept, Negative Family
     Affect, and Delinquency." **Criminology**
     19(1981):434-48.

     The authors examine the relationship
     between negative self-concept and family-
     other affect and delinquency.

     KEYWORDS: affect, delinquent vs. non-
     delinquent, ethnicity, family background,
     intra-familial conflict, labeling, social
     class, social control

694. Menard, S., and B. Morse. "A Structuralist
     Critique of the IQ Delinquency Hypothesis:
     Theory and Evidence." **American Journal of
     Sociology** 89(1984):1347-78.

     The hypothesis that IQ is an important
     variable in explaining delinquency is
     examined theoretically and empirically.
     The conclusion is that the IQ-delinquency
     hypothesis contributes nothing to existing
     delinquency theory.

     KEYWORDS: academic achievement, intelli-
     gence, labeling, parent-child, peer
     influence, self-reported delinquency,
     theory, work

695. Millham, Spencer. "The Therapeutic Implica-
     tions of Locking Up Children." **Journal of
     Adolescence** 4(1981):13-26.

     The therapeutic implications of placing
     young people in security are discussed in

relation to the clients themselves, to
their care givers and to the wider provi-
sion of services for troubled juveniles.

KEYWORDS: education, historical, rehabilitation, violence, work

696.    Mirande, A.    "Deviance and Oppression:    The
        Application of Labeling to Racial and
        Ethnic Minorities."    **International Journal
        of Contemporary Sociology** 15(1978):375-96.

697.    Montmarquette, C., and M. Nerlove.
        "Deterrence and Delinquency:    An Analysis
        of Individual Data."    **Journal of Quantita-
        tive Criminology** 1(1985):37-58.

        Self-reported data on the commission of
        three crimes are analyzed in relation to
        perceived probabilities of arrest for more
        than 3,000 french speaking teenagers in the
        Montreal educational system.    The authors
        conclude that there is clear evidence of a
        negative association between the subjective
        probability of arrest for each crime and
        the frequency of commission of the crime.

        KEYWORDS: deterrence, drug use, methods,
        perceptions, self-reported delinquency

698.    Moore, J.    **Homeboys:    Gangs, Drugs, and
        Prison in the Barrios of Los Angeles.**
        Philadelphia:    Temple University Press,
        1978.

        This book is a research collaboration
        between the academic world and chicano ex-
        convicts and gang members.    The research
        was conducted in 1974 and 1975.    The author
        examines the persistence and influence of
        the neighborhood chicano youth gangs.
        Policy issues are also addressed.

KEYWORDS: drug use, gangs, hispanics, methods, policy, social class, social control, work

699.  Moore, J., Vigil, D., and R. Garcia. "Residence and Territoriality in Chicano Gangs." **Social Problems** 31(1983):182-94.

The authors suggest that not all gang members live in the areas they defend, and they believe this non-resident membership reflects the nature of improvised chicano settlements in Los Angeles.

KEYWORDS: residence, subculture

700.  Muehlbauer, G., and L. Dodder. **The Losers: Gang Delinquency in an American Suburb.** New York: Praeger, 1983.

The authors describe the origins and development of a suburban American gang.

KEYWORDS: both parents, community, gangs, peers vs. parents, subculture

701.  Nye, F.I. **Family Relationships and Delinquent Behavior.** New York: Wiley, 1958.

A classic study reporting that high self-reported delinquents tend to come from large families, do not living with both parents, receive erratic punishment from their parents, feel rejected by their parents, and rate their parents' marriages unhappy.

KEYWORDS: intra-familial conflict, number of children, parental discipline, parental rejection, self-reported delinquency, two parents vs. single parent

702.    Norland, S., N. Shover, W. Thornton, and J.
        James. "Intrafamily Conflict and Delin-
        quency." **Pacific Sociological Review**
        22(1979):223-40.

        The authors address two questions. Is the
        relationship between family conflict and
        delinquency stronger for girls than for
        boys? Is conflict in the home directly
        related to delinquency or is the relation-
        ship mediated by other variables? The
        total effect of family conflict on delin-
        quency was found to be stronger for females
        than for males. The relationship of family
        conflict to delinquency for females is
        indirect through reduced identification
        with parents, adoption of more relativistic
        beliefs about the law, reduced parental
        supervision, and increased exposure to
        social support for delinquency.

        KEYWORDS: aggression, economic depriva-
        tion, family cohesion, intra-familial
        conflict, male-female, parental supervi-
        sion, peer influence, social class, values


703.    Offer, D., Marohn, R., and E. Ostrov. **The
        Psychological World of the Juvenile
        Delinquent.** New York: Basic Books, 1979.

        The authors identify significant aspects of
        the delinquents' psychological world that
        are important in understanding their
        behavior.

        KEYWORDS: family background, hyper-
        activity, interaction, self-esteem, values


704.    Offord, David R. "Family Backgrounds of Male
        and Female Delinquents." **Abnormal
        Offenders, Delinquency, and the Criminal
        Justice System.** Edited by Guinn, J., and
        D.P. Farrington. New York: John Wiley and
        Sons, 1982, pp. 129-51.

The authors summarize the findings of a
study of male and female delinquents aimed
at learning more about the extent to which
certain factors within the family play a
role in the production of delinquent
behavior.

KEYWORDS: number of children, parental
criminal record, parental mental illness,
school performance, self-esteem, social
class

705.  Olweus, Dan. "Stability of Aggressive
      Reaction Patterns in Males: A Review."
      **Psychological Bulletin** 86(1979):852-75.

      A review of sixteen studies on the
      stability of aggressive behavior and
      reaction patterns. The author points out
      the great variation among the studies in
      sample composition, in definition of
      variables, in method of data collection,
      and in the ages and intervals studied.

      KEYWORDS: age roles, aggression, both
      parents, education, intelligence, social
      class

706.  Osborn, S. "Moving Home, Leaving London and
      Delinquent Trends." **British Journal of
      Criminology** 20(1980):54-61.

      In this report the author investigates
      various aspects of the relationship between
      moving home and delinquency.

      KEYWORDS: delinquent vs. non-delinquent,
      family moves, intelligence, longitudinal,
      number of children, parental criminal
      record, residence

707.  Osborn, S., and D.J. West. "The Effective-
      ness of Various Predictors of Criminal
      Careers." **Journal of Adolescence** 1(1978):
      101-17.

Data accumulated from a long term follow up
of a sample of normal boys is utilized to
test the value of social background factors
as predictors of a delinquency career
extending into adult life.

KEYWORDS: education, family background,
intelligence, longitudinal, number of
children, parental criminal record, self-
reported delinquency, sibling criminal
record, social class

708.  ———. "Conviction Records of Fathers and
Sons Compared." **British Journal of
Criminology** 19(1979):120-33.

This paper is based on data from the
Cambridge Study in Delinquent Development
and follows some preliminary investigations
previously reported.

KEYWORDS: family background, father-son,
generations, labeling, parental criminal
record, recidivism, self-reported delinquency, violence

709.  ———. "Marriage and Delinquency:  A Post-
script." **British Journal of Criminology**
18(1979):254-56.

This is an extension of a previous report
on marriages and delinquency.  The analysis
of marital status and delinquency bears no
significant relationship to age at first
marriage.

KEYWORDS: age at marriage, recidivism,
spouse criminal record

710.  ———. "Do Young Delinquents Really
Reform." **Journal of Adolescence** 3(1980):
99-114.

A group of male delinquents and a control
group of non-delinquents are interviewed

around the age of 24. The delinquents had
been seen previously at age 21 and both
categories had been seen at 18.

KEYWORDS: delinquent vs. non-delinquent,
father-son, longitudinal, parental criminal
record, recidivism

711.   Oustin, J.   "Delinquency, Family Background,
       and Educational Attainment."  **British
       Journal of Criminology** 24(1984):2-26.

       Data are based on official records, meaning
       analysis is related to youth and contact
       with the police rather than to wider
       delinquent groups.  Findings support
       earlier research, suggesting that delin-
       quent youths are from lower social class
       homes and are more likely to become
       officially recorded delinquents.

       KEYWORDS: delinquents vs. non-delinquents,
       education, ethnicity, intelligence,
       longitudinal, male-female, methods, work

712.   Paperny, D., and R. Deisher.   "Maltreatment
       of Adolescents:  The Relationship to a
       Predisposition Toward Violent Behavior and
       Delinquency."  **Adolescence** 18(1983):499-
       514.

       The authors review the importance and
       family dynamics of abuse which are related
       to delinquent behavior.  The distinction is
       made between child abuse and adolescent
       abuse.

       KEYWORDS: intervention, intra-familial
       conflict, parental discipline, social
       class, violence

713.   Parker, H., and H. Giller.   "More or Less the
       Same:  British Delinquency Research Since
       the Sixties."  **British Journal of Crimino-
       logy** 21(1981):230-45.

The authors review the literature focusing
on juvenile delinquency, its etiology,
correction, and control over the last 15
years. They suggest that despite claims to
the contrary, it is not criminology that
has been radicalized but merely some of the
criminologists.

KEYWORDS: historical, interaction,
labeling, methods, political rehabilitation, social class, social control

714. Patterson, G. **Coercive Family Processes.**
Eugene, Oregon: Castalia, 1981.

715. Patterson, G., and T. Dishion. "Contributions of Families and Peers to Delinquency." **Criminology** 23(1985):63-79.

A model is presented that explains the
contribution of parents and peers to
delinquent behavior. The model was tested
on a sample of 136 7th and 10th grade
adolescent males by using the structural
modeling approach and LISREL IV analysis
program.

KEYWORDS: both parents, intelligence,
methods, parent-child, parental supervision, peers vs. parents

716. Patterson, G., and M. Stouthamer-Loeber.
"The Correlation of Family Management
Practices and Delinquency." **Child Develop-
ment** 55(1984):1299.

Both problem solving and reinforcement do
not relate strongly with delinquent
behavior. Their role in a model of how
family management skills interact with
child behavior is more related to positive
child behavior. Lack of parental monitor-
ing and parental disciplining are significant in accounting for delinquent behavior.

KEYWORDS: family cohesion, parental
discipline, parental support

717.  Perez, J.  **The Roots of Adolescent
      Delinquency.** New York:  Van Nostrand
      Reinhold, 1978.

      A detailed case study of one family and the
      family's history as a basis for understand-
      ing the delinquent.

      KEYWORDS: education, family background,
      generations, parental mental health, peers
      vs. parents, transmission, values

718.  Perez, P.  "Correlates and Changes Over Time
      in Drug and Alcohol Use within a Barrio
      Population." **American Journal of Community
      Psychology** 8(1980):621-36.

      The determinants of drug and alcohol use
      were explored in a group of Mexican-
      American youths from an East Los Angeles
      housing project.

      KEYWORDS: drug use, peer influence, self-
      concept, subculture

719.  Phillips, B.  **Patterns of Juvenile Crime.**
      London:  Peel Press, 1980.

      An attempt to establish the origins of
      crimes and backgrounds of 449 juveniles in
      England.

      KEYWORDS: family background, male-female

720.  Poole, E., and R. Regoli.  "Parental Support,
      Delinquent Friends, and Delinquency:  A
      Test of Interaction Effects." **Journal of
      Criminal Law and Criminology** 70(1979):
      188-93.

721.   Rahav, G.   "Family Size and Delinquency."
       Sociology and Social Research 66(1981):
       42-51.

       The survey of the literature, the author
       claims, seems to indicate that delinquents
       tend to come from larger families.  This
       trend is observable even when some
       confounding background variables are
       controlled.

       KEYWORDS:  cross-cultural, ethnicity,
       intelligence, number of children, parent-
       child, parental discipline, social class

722.   ————.   "Culture, Conflict, Urbanism, and
       Delinquency."  Criminology 18(1981):523-
       30.

       The study was undertaken to test the
       relationships between urbanization, socio-
       cultural composition, and juvenile delin-
       quency in Israel.

       KEYWORDS:  community, cross-cultural,
       recidivism, social structure

723.   Rankin, J.   "The Family Context of Delin-
       quency."  Social Problems 30(1983):466-79.

       The author concludes that studies which
       suggest that broken homes are not an
       important causal factor are misleading.  He
       feels that these types of studies present
       inadequate operational definitions of both
       family context and delinquency.  When
       family context is defined more explicitly,
       the number of absent biological parents as
       well as the presence of a stepparent
       strongly affects some types of juvenile
       delinquency.

       KEYWORDS:  biological vs. adoptive parents,
       both parents, divorce effects, male-female,
       two parents vs. single parent

724.    Rankin, J., and L. Wells.  "The Preventive
        Effects of the Family on Delinquency."
        **Handbook of Crime and Delinquency Preven-
        tion.**  Edited by E. Johnson.  Wesport, Conn.:
        Greenwood Press, 1986.  In press.

725.    Reardon, B., and P. Griffing.  "Factors
        Related to the Self-Concept of Institution-
        alized, White, Male, Adolescent Drug
        Abusers."  **Adolescence** 18(1983):29-41.

        Significant predictors of S's self-concept
        are both mother/adolescent relationship and
        father/adolescent relationship, the number
        of S's prior status offenses, and the S's
        preference for non-depressant drugs.

        KEYWORDS:  drug use, parent-child, self-
        concept

726.    Reckless, W.  "A New Theory of Delinquency
        and Crime."  **Federal Probation** 25(1961):
        42-46.

        A classic study putting forth the 'contain-
        ment' theory which proposed that there
        appears to be a personality factor that
        acts as an inner 'containment' or barrier
        against an individual's decision to become
        involved in delinquent behavior, and that
        favors the development of a socially
        acceptable lifestyle.

        KEYWORDS:  theory

727.    Reckless, W., Dinitz, S., and E. Murray.
        "The 'Good Boy' in a High Delinquency
        Area."  **Journal of Criminal Law, Crimino-
        logy and Police Science** 48(1957):18-25.

        A classic study focusing on sixth-grade
        boys in high delinquency areas who had not
        and were not expected to become delinquent.

KEYWORDS:   delinquent vs. non-delinquent,
family background, mother-son, peers vs.
parents, theory, values

728.    Reeves, D.   "Parental Power and Adolescent
        Drinking."   **Psychological Reports** 55(1984):
        161-62.

        Questionnaire data collected from 191
        adolescents indicate that maternal power
        was negatively associated with adolescent
        drinking.   Parental power was not signifi-
        cant.   Adolescent drinking was positively
        related to parental drinking.

        KEYWORDS:   education, parent-child, power

729.    Richards, P.   "Quantitative and Qualitative
        Sex Differences in Middle Class
        Delinquency."   **Criminology** 18(1981):473-80.

        The author examines sex differences in
        middle class delinquency using self-
        reported data drawn from junior and senior
        high school students from an affluent
        suburb of a large midwestern city.

        KEYWORDS:   male-female, methods, social
        class

730.    Riley, D., and M. Shaw.   **Parental Supervision
        and Juvenile Delinquency.**   Home Office
        Research Study No. 83.   London:   Her
        Majesty's Stationery Office, 1985.

        This report is based on a maternal survey
        of young teenagers of 14 and 15 and their
        parents.   The major focus is on parental
        supervision and its part in preventing
        delinquency.

        KEYWORDS:   education, methods, parental
        discipline, parental supervision, single
        parent

731.  Robins, L., West, P., and B. Herjanic.
      "Arrests and Delinquency in Two Genera-
      tions:  A Study of Black Urban Families and
      Their Children."  **Journal of Child Psycho-
      logy and Psychiatry** 16(1975):125-40.

      The effect of parent's arrests explained
      50% of the variance in both boys' and
      girls' delinquency.  The father's adult
      arrests were a more important prediction
      than his delinquency, suggesting an
      environmental rather than a genetic effect.

      KEYWORDS:  genetics, mother vs. father,
      parental criminal record

732.  Rodman, H., and P. Grams.  "Juvenile
      Delinquency and the Family:  A Review and
      Discussion."  In the President's Commission
      on Law Enforcement and Administration of
      Justice.  **Task Force Report:  Juvenile
      Delinquency and Youth Crime.**  Washington,
      D.C.:  U.S. Government Printing Office,
      1967.

      The authors compiled about 250 references
      on the role of the family in the etiology
      of juvenile delinquency.  They began in the
      twenties and thirties with the work of such
      people as Burgess, the Gluecks, Healy,
      Park, Shaw and McKay, Sutherland, and
      Thrasher, and identify pertinent research
      through 1967.

      KEYWORDS:  family background, family
      structure, methods, theory

733.  Rojek, D., and G. Jensen (eds.).  **Readings in
      Juvenile Delinquency.**  Lexington, Mass.:
      D.C. Heath, 1982.

      A collection of readings on various
      delinquency issues.

      KEYWORDS:  economic deprivation, family
      background, genetics, heredity, labeling,

methods, prevention, social control, urban-
rural

734.   Rollins, B., and D. Thomas.   "A Theory of
       Parental Power and Child Compliance."
       **Power in Families.**   Edited by Cromwell, R.,
       and D. Olson.   New York:   Halsted Press,
       1975, pp. 38-61.

       The authors believe that there is evidence
       accruing from parent-child research which
       can be useful for parents in their attempts
       to effectively influence their children to
       comply with parental desires.   To this end,
       a theory of parental influence in the
       socialization of children is presented.

       KEYWORDS:   compliance, parental control,
       parental support, power

735.   Rowe, David.   "Biometrical Genetic Models of
       Self-Reported Delinquent Behavior:   A Twin
       Study."   **Behavior Genetics** 13(1983):473-
       89.

       Adolescent twins reported delinquent acts
       on an anonymous questionnaire.   Monozygo-
       tic (MZ) twins were more alike in their
       rates of delinquent behavior than dizygotic
       twins, and this result held for both sexes.

       KEYWORDS:   environment, genetics, male-
       female, methods, parental education, social
       class

736.   Rowe, David., and D.W. Osgood.   "Heredity and
       Sociological Theories of Delinquency:   A
       Reconsideration."   **American Sociological
       Review** 49(1984):526-40.

       An analysis of genetic variation is united
       with sociological theory.   In particular, a
       twin study of the covariation between
       delinquent behavior and association with
       delinquent peers is used to demonstrate the

value of a behavioral genetic analysis for
developing social theory.

KEYWORDS: environment, genetics,
interaction, peers vs. parents, self-
reported delinquency

737.  Rutler, M.  **Changing Youth in a Changing
      Society:  Patterns of Adolescent Develop-
      ment and Disorder.**  Cambridge, Mass.:
      Harvard University Press, 1980.

      The author begins with a complete survey of
      the problems of youth, showing disorders
      peak during the teen years, and then
      addresses historical questions about
      whether adolescent disorders are becoming
      more frequent.

      KEYWORDS: academic achievement, education,
      environment, family background, genera-
      tions, heredity, historical, peer groups

738.  Sagl, A., and Z. Eisikovits.  "Juvenile
      Delinquency and Moral Development."
      **Criminal Justice and Behavior** 8(1981):79-
      93.

      The authors examine the moral development
      of 249 male and female, delinquent and non-
      delinquent adolescents, ranging in age from
      13 to 17.

      KEYWORDS: delinquent vs. non-delinquent,
      male-female, social class

739.  Sanderson, H.  "Dependency on Mother in Boys
      Who Steal."  **British Journal of Criminology**
      17(1977):180-84.

      Boys who had been stealing at least three
      times in the past six months, were compared
      with clinical referrals and normal controls
      with poor school progress.  Boy stealers
      were less dependent on their mothers.

KEYWORDS:   mother-son, social class

740.   Sarason, Irwin G.   "A Cognitive Social
       Learning Approach to Juvenile Delinquency."
       **Psychopathic Behavior.**   Edited by Hare, D.,
       and D. Schalling.   New York:   John Wiley
       and Sons, 1978, pp. 299-317.

       The author describes a cognitive social
       learning approach to juvenile delinquency
       and presents empirical evidence which
       suggests how this orientation is applicable
       to the rehabilitation of young offenders.

       KEYWORDS:   education, parental modeling,
       rehabilitation, social class, work

741.   Sas, L., Jaffe, P. and J. Reddon.
       "Unraveling the Needs of Dangerous
       Offenders:   A Clinical-Rational and
       Empirical Approach to Classification."
       **Canadian Journal of Criminology** 27(1985):
       83-96.

       The authors attempt to employ cluster
       analysis in validating a clinical-rational
       approach to the classification of dangerous
       young offenders based on the nature of
       their offense and their clinically
       predicted dangerousness.

       KEYWORDS:   aggression, divorce effects,
       education, parent-child, parental disci-
       pline, parental drug use, two parents vs.
       single parent

742.   Savelsberg, J.   **Foreign Juveniles:   Assimila-
       tive Integration, Delinquency and Criminal-
       ization, and the Youth Aid System.**
       Munchen:   Minerva Publication, 1982.

       This book deals with foreign juveniles,
       children of labor immigrants, and the local
       system of youth aid in the Federal Republic
       of Germany.   The author's central question

is:  What are the effects of the organiza-
tion of the local system of youth aid in
terms of delinquency and criminalization,
integration and assimilation of foreign
youth - and under what conditions could its
effects be more functional?

KEYWORDS:  cross-cultural, discrimination,
integration, labeling, theory, work

743.  ———. "Socio-Spatial Attributes of Social
Problems:  The Case of Crime and Delinquency."  **Population and Environment**
7(1984):163-81.

The author contends that the explicit
consideration of the category "space"
increases the explanatory power of sociological approaches to crime and
delinquency.  Results show that socio-
spatial structures and processes are
relevant factors for the explanation of
criminality.

KEYWORDS:  labeling, policy, residence,
theory

744.  Schaffer, B., and R. DeBlassie.  "Adolescent
Prostitution."  **Adolescence** 19(1984):689-
96.

The purpose of this paper is to explore the
conditions which lead to teenagers becoming
prostitutes and how our institutions and
legal system deal with them.

KEYWORDS:  drug use, economic deprivation,
education, intra-familial, number of
children, parental rejection, self-concept,
work

745.  Schwarz, J., and H. Getter.  "Parental
Conflict and Dominance in Late Adolescent
Maladjustment:  A Triple Interaction

Model." **Journal of Abnormal Psychology**
89(1980):573-80.

The authors indicate the triple interaction
of conflict, parental control, and gender
of child adds significantly to the prediction of adolescent neuroticism and major
psychopathology but not to the prediction
of social nonconformity.

KEYWORDS:  father-daughter, mother vs.
father, mother-son, parental control, power

746.   Shanker, A.  "Strict Parents Can Cut the
       Crime Rate."  **International Journal of
       Family Therapy** 3(1981):205-7.

       This study appears to show a clear link
       between laxness in parental supervision and
       delinquency in pre-adolescent boys residing
       in high crime areas.

       KEYWORDS:  both parents, environment,
       parental supervision, residence

747.   Shaw, M., and D. Riley.  "Families, Teenagers
       and Crime."  **Research Bulletin.**  London:
       Home Office Research and Planning Unit,
       1985, pp. 20-22.

       A survey of a representative sample of
       households in England and Wales consisting
       of 751 families with a girl or boy of 14 or
       15.  Interviews were held separately with
       the teenager and with a parent.

       KEYWORDS:  education, parent-child,
       parental supervision, peers vs. parents

748.   Shichor, D.  "Perceived 'Family Attractive-
       ness' Among Continuing and Non-Continuing
       Delinquents in Israel."  **Journal of
       Comparative Family Studies** 9(1978):327-34.

The concept of family attractiveness as a
possible causal variable in the explanation
of juvenile delinquency was explored among
juvenile delinquents in Israel.

KEYWORDS: delinquent vs. non-delinquent,
family background, values

749.  Shoemaker, Donald. **Theories of Delinquency:**
**An Examination and Explanations of**
**Delinquent Behavior.** New York: Oxford
University Press, 1984.

The author describes the empirical assump-
tions and key concepts, prominent contributions to the origins and development, and
research findings with respect to the
validity of major theories of juvenile
delinquency.

KEYWORDS: family background, labeling,
male-female, methods, social control

750.  Shoham, S.G.  "Family Variables and Stigma
Among Prostitutes in Israel." **Journal of**
**Social Psychology** 120(1983):  57-62.

Based on interviews with 67 prostitutes and
a like size comparison group.  The authors
put forth the argument that fathers send
negative labels which are internalized by
the young daughter out of which she
constructs her identity.

KEYWORDS: father-daughter, labeling, self-
concept

751.  Shover, N., S. Norland, J. James, and W.
Thornton.  "Gender Roles and Delinquency."
**Social Forces** 58(1979):162-75.

The authors compare the merits of two
theories of the relationship between
traditional sex roles and delinquency.
Both the theory of opportunity and social

controls and masculinity theory posit a
positive relationship between traditional
masculine role expectations and delinquency.  Opportunity and social controls
theory showed more empirical support.
Femininity is positively related to
attachment to conventional others.

KEYWORDS:  mother-child, social control,
theory

752.    Sipila, J.   "Community Structure and Deviant
        Behavior Among Adolescents."  **Youth and
        Society** 16(1985):471-97.

        The author attempts to detect typical
        structural features of a good community.
        Good communities or favorable environmental
        conditions were not found; a social
        structure good in one respect was generally
        poor in another.

        KEYWORDS:  community, discrimination,
        environment, integration, social class,
        social control, social structure, values

753.    Smith, R., and J. Walters.   "Delinquent and
        Non-Delinquent Males' Perceptions of their
        Fathers."  **Adolescence** 13(1978):21-28.

        The authors investigate the differences in
        delinquents' and non-delinquents' percep-
        tions of their fathers, and the relation
        between their perceptions and selected
        background and familial variables. Delin-
        quency was found to be associated with lack
        of parental support, lack of parental
        involvement with children, high maternal
        involvement, broken homes, and feelings of
        anomie.

        KEYWORDS:  anomie, mother-father, parent-
        child, parental support, single vs. two
        parents

754.  Sobel, H., and W. Sobel.  "Discriminalizing
      Adolescent Male Delinquents Through Use of
      Kinetic Family Drawings."  **Journal of
      Personality Assessment** 40(1976):91-94.

      The drawings of 20 male adolescent delin-
      quents were compared to a group of 20 non-
      delinquent male adolescents.

      KEYWORDS:  delinquent vs. non-delinquent,
      family background


755.  Solnick, J., C. Braumann, M. Bedlington, and
      M. Wolf.  "The Relationship Between Parent-
      Youth Interaction and In-Group Homes."
      **Journal of Abnormal Child Psychology**
      9(1981):107-20.

      The results of this study indicate an
      inverse linear relationship between self-
      reported delinquency and observational
      measures of youths proximity and talking to
      their group home parents.  There is a
      relationship between delinquency and
      frequency of parent-child interaction.

      KEYWORDS:  interaction, methods, parent-
      child, parental supervision


756.  Spergel, I.  "Violent Gangs in Chicago:  In
      Search of Social Policy."  **Social Service
      Review** 58(1984):199-226.

      A study of two types of violent gang
      subcultures in Chicago.  The author
      proposes a community intervention model for
      dealing with gang problems.

      KEYWORDS:  community, gangs, intervention,
      policy, subculture


757.  Stanton, A.M.  **When Mothers Go to Jail.**
      Lexington, Mass.:  D.C. Heath, 1980.

The author explores the consequences of a
parent's incarceration on children.

KEYWORDS:  delinquent vs. non-delinquent,
parental criminal record, mother-daughter,
mother-son

758.   Stewart, C., and M. Zaengleinsenger.  "Family
       Delinquency, Family Problems, and Parental
       Interaction."  **Social Casework** 65(1984):
       428.

759.   Stewart, M., C. Cummings, S. Singer, and C.
       Susan DeBlois.  "The Overlap Between
       Hyperactive and Unsocialized Aggressive
       Children."  **Journal of Child Psychology and
       Psychiatry** 22(1981):35-45.

       The present study was designed to define
       the relationship between the supposed
       syndrome of hyperactivity and that of
       aggressive conduct disorder.  The authors
       did not find any differences between
       children with conduct disorder who were
       hyperactive and those who were not.

       KEYWORDS:  aggression, family background,
       hyperactivity, intelligence, number of
       children, school performance, social class

760.   Stillion, J., McDowell, E., and J. Shamblin.
       "The Suicide Vignette Experience:  A Method
       for Measuring Adolescent Attitudes Toward
       Suicide."  **Death Education** 8(1984):65-90.

       Results are presented to validate a new
       approach (SAVE Scale) for measuring suicide
       attitudes among adolescents.

       KEYWORDS:  methods, theory

761.   Susser, M., Watson, W., and K. Hopper.
       **Sociology in Medicine.**  New York:  Oxford
       University Press, 1985.

Though the overall focus of this text is to
demonstrate the uses of the social sciences
in interpreting the origins and manifesta-
tions of human disease, there is relevant
material on child-rearing, adolescence,
peer groups versus parents, and crime and
adolescence.

KEYWORDS: birth order, child rearing,
divorce effects, education, ethnicity,
family structure, peers vs. parents, single
vs. two parents, social class, work

762.   Thomas, C., and C. Sieverdes. "Juvenile Court
       Intake: An Analysis of Discretionary
       Decision-Making." **Criminology** 12(1975):
       413-32.

763.   Thompson, W., and R. Dodder. "Juvenile
       Delinquency Explained? A Test of Contain-
       ment Theory." **Youth and Society** 15(1983):
       171-94.

       The authors operationalize seven components
       of containment theory. Containment theory
       is tested through self-reported delinquency
       of black and white males and females.

       KEYWORDS: ethnicity, methods, peers vs.
       parents, social control, theory, values

764.   Thompson, W., Mitchell, J., and R. Dodder.
       "An Empirical Test of Hirschi's Control
       Theory of Delinquency." **Deviant Behavior**
       5(1984):11-22.

       Findings indicate that Hirschi's
       contentions are only supported when
       delinquent companions are included. The
       findings appear more consistent with the
       social learning or differential association
       theory.

KEYWORDS: education, family cohesion,
male-female, peers vs. parents, social
control, values

765.  Thornton, W., and J. James. "Masculinity and
      Delinquency Revisited." **British Journal of
      Criminology** 19(1979):225-41.

      The authors explore the ways in which
      gender may explain the differential
      delinquency involvement of adolescents.
      Social control variables do not
      substantially change the relationship
      between the masculine expectations
      perceived by others and delinquency.

      KEYWORDS: male-female, methods, parental
      supervision, peer influence, self-reported
      delinquency, social control

766.  Thornton, W., Voigt, L., and W. Doerner.
      **Delinquency and Justice.** New York: Random
      House, 1986.

      Included in this introductory delinquency
      text are two chapters (Adolescence and
      Delinquency, Families and Delinquency) that
      extensively review the changing nature of
      the American family and how this might
      influence contemporary and future juvenile
      delinquency.

      KEYWORDS: historical, number of children,
      parental discipline, parental supervision,
      rehabilitation, self-concept, subculture,
      transmission, two parents vs. single parent,
      values, work

767.  Tittle, C., and W. Villemez. "Social Class
      and Criminality." **Social Forces** 56(1977):
      474-502.

      The authors examine social class variations
      in self-reported criminality. Their
      results are contrary to current theories

which postulate that there is an inverse
relationship between social class and
deviance.

KEYWORDS:  ethnicity, male-female, self-
reported delinquency, social class


768.   Tittle, C., Villemez, W., and D. Smith.  "The
       Myth of Social Class and Criminality:  An
       Empirical Assessment of the Empirical
       Evidence."  **American Sociological Review**
       43(1978):643-56.

       Thirty-five studies examining the relation-
       ship between social class and crime/delin-
       quency were reduced to comparable
       statistics.  Interpretation of results is
       discussed with all evidence leading to
       serious doubts about the adequacy of
       theories of deviance that contain assump-
       tions of class differences.

       KEYWORDS:  ethnicity, historical, methods,
       residence, social class


769.   Traub, S., and C. Little (Eds.)  **Theories of
       Deviance**.  Itasca, Ill.:  F.E. Peacock
       Publishers, 1985.

       The authors present primary theoretical
       works from diverse perspectives within
       sociology.  The selections included in this
       book represent the mainstream approaches in
       the sociology of deviance.  These key
       passages are presented in original form and
       thus make up the foundation of which
       current research concerning deviance
       emanates from.

       KEYWORDS:  methods, theory


770.   Trommsdorff, G., Burger, C., and T. Fuchsle.
       "Social and Psychological Aspects of Future
       Orientation."  **Studies in Decision Making**.

Edited by M. Irle. New York: Walter de
Gruyter, 1982, pp. 167-94.

The authors state that the dominance male
delinquents accord the self in their future
orientation indicates that, in comparison
to non-delinquents, delinquents may give
their social environment too little
consideration and thus develop a relatively
poor understanding of social expectations,
norms, values, and institutions.

KEYWORDS: child rearing, delinquent vs.
non-delinquent, social class, social
structure, theory, values

771.  Ubrici, D.K.  "The Effects of Behavioral and
Family Interventions on Juvenile Recidivism."  **Family Therapy** 10(1983):25-36.

A review of the effectiveness of behavioral
and family intervention in preventing
juvenile recidivism. The author analyzes
treatment components which contribute to
positive outcomes are presented.

KEYWORDS: family cohesion, intervention,
prevention, recidivism

772.  Valone, K., Goldstein, M., and J. Norton.
"Parental Expressed Emotion and Psycho-
physiological Reactivity in an Adolescent
Sample at Risk for Schizophrenia Spectrum
Disorders."  **Journal of Abnormal Psychology**
93(1984):448-57.

The results show that the parental
expressed emotion measure is identifying
discernable family emotional environments
associated with the subsequent onset of
schizophrenia.

KEYWORDS: both parents, interaction,
parental rejection

773.  Virkbunen, M.  "Parental Deprivation and
      Recidivism in Juvenile Delinquents."
      **British Journal of Criminology** 16(1976):
      378-84.

      The author attempts to clarify the
      relationship between parental deprivation
      and recidivism of juvenile delinquents.
      Results show that the absence of the
      mothers or the mother substitute did not
      prove to be as significant as absence of
      father or father substitute.

      KEYWORDS:  aggression, biological vs.
      adoptive parents, divorce effects, parental
      deprivation, punishment, recidivism


774.  Voigt, L., and W. Thornton.  "The Rhetoric and
      Politics of Soviet Delinquency:  An
      American Perspective."  **Comparative Social
      Research.**  Edited by R. Tomasson.
      Greenich, Conn.:  Jai Press, 1985.

      The authors attempt to explain Soviet
      delinquency.  They argue that most Western
      analyses of Soviet criminology center
      around discussion of the applicability f
      Marxist thought to crime.  They suggest
      that Soviet criminologists generally do not
      use such explanations themselves but rely
      instead on a social control theory in which
      they have attempted to manipulate and
      control their basic social institutions
      (especially the family and school) in order
      to inculcate and forward socialist princi-
      ples and doctrines and eliminate delin-
      quency.

      KEYWORDS:  cross-cultural, historical,
      social control, theory


775.  ————.  "Family Forests and Delinquency."
      Unpublished paper presentation at the
      Society for the Study of Social Problems,
      Washington, D.C., 1985.

The authors review self-report data from
the Louisiana Youth Survey with respect to
alternative family structures (e.g., single
parent families, joint custody families,
and traditional nuclear families) and
delinquency involvement.

KEYWORDS: family cohesion, parental
discipline, self-reported delinquency,
social control, two parents vs. single
parent

776. ─────. "Soviet Attitudes Toward Family
Policy." Unpublished paper presented at
the Southern Sociological Society, North
Carolina, 1984.

The authors review the family in the
U.S.S.R. as it has been subjected to
planned social change since the 1917
Revolution. A reassessment of the history
of Soviet family policy and its effects on
cultural values suggests that the relationship between the family and Soviet emigres
indicate that the State's efforts to offer
supplementary socialization for Soviet
children are often met by ambivalence on
the part of children and families and that
many problems including delinquency have
not been eliminated by family policies.

KEYWORDS: cross-cultural, historical,
policy, divorce effects

777. Wadsworth, M. **Roots of Delinquency: Infancy,
Adolescence and Crime**. New York: Barnes
and Noble Books, 1979.

The author contributes to the debate about
the usefulness of empirical work in crime
and delinquency.

KEYWORDS: delinquent vs. non-delinquent,
education, emotional disorder, family
background, methods, work

778.  Walker, B., and M. Mehr.  "Adolescent
      Suicide-A Family Crisis:  A Model for
      Effective Intervention by Family Thera-
      pists."  **Adolescence** 18(1983):285-92.

      The author presents a model of crisis
      intervention counseling which emphasizes
      and delineates a treatment plan for
      adolescent suicidal patients and their
      families.

      KEYWORDS:  interaction, parent-child


779.  Weinrott, M., Jones, R., and J. Howard.
      "Cost-Effectiveness of Teaching Family
      Programs for Delinquents:  Results of a
      National Evaluation."  **Evaluation Review**
      6(1982):173-201.

      Analysis shows that teaching-family model
      homes are seven percent less expensive to
      operate on a per diem basis and cost
      approximately 20 percent less per client.

      KEYWORDS:  community, education, family
      background


780.  Wells, L., and J. Rankin.  "Self-Concept as a
      Mediating Factor in Delinquency."  **Social
      Psychology Quarterly** 46(1983):11-22.

      Family relationships is one variable
      utilized.  It is measured by a global
      summary index, formed by the average of
      four smaller indices of parent-son
      interaction:  closeness to father, close-
      ness to mother, parental reasoning and
      communication with son, and parental
      punishment.  Self-esteem correlates
      moderately well with family relationships.

      KEYWORDS:  blacks, education, interaction,
      intervention, parent-child, polity, self
      concept, self esteem, social class

781.  ———.  "Broken Homes and Juvenile Delin-
      quency:  An Empirical Review."  **Criminal
      Justice Abstracts** 17(1985):249-72.


782.  ———.  "The Broken Homes Model of Delin-
      quency:  Analytic Issues."  **Journal of
      Research in Crime and Delinquency** (1986):
      in press.


783.  Welsh, R.  "Severe Parental Punishment and
      Delinquency:  A Developmental Theory.
      **Journal of Clinical Child Psychology**
      5(1976):17-20.

      The authors strongly suggest that severe
      parental punishment leads the future
      delinquent to gradually become habituated
      to the punishment, and start to exhibit
      strong "conditionability" to aversive
      stimuli.

      KEYWORDS:  aggression, child rearing,
      delinquent vs. non-delinquent, parental
      discipline, parental supervision


784.  West, D.J.  **The Delinquent Way of Life.**
      London:  Heinemann Educational Books,
      1977.

      A systematic survey sample of four hundred
      males recruited, at age eight, from a
      working-class neighborhood in London, and
      followed up to age 25, by which time a
      third of the group had acquired a criminal
      conviction record.

      KEYWORDS:  intelligence, parental criminal
      record, parental rejection, number of
      children, social class


785.  ———.  **Delinquency.**  Cambridge, Mass.:
      Harvard University Press, 1982.

An overview of the Cambridge University
Institute of Criminology study to obtain a
better understanding of the reasons why
youngsters become delinquents, and to
acquire evidence about the transmission of
deprivation through families from one
generation to the next.

KEYWORDS: drug use, education, generations, intelligence, methods, number of
children, parental criminal record,
parental rejection, sibling criminal
record, social class

786. West, D.J., and D.P. Farrington. **The
     Delinquent Way of Life.** London: Heinemann
     Educational Books, 1977.

787. Wiatrowski, M., Griswold, D., and M. Roberts.
     "Social Control Theory and Delinquency."
     **American Sociological Review** 46(1981):
     525-41.

     The authors develop and test multivariate
     models of social control theory while
     simultaneously considering how the four
     bond elements (attachment, commitment,
     involvement, and belief) operate in
     relation to delinquency.

     KEYWORDS: education, family background,
     social class, social control, values

788. Wilkinson, K., Stitt, B., and M. Erikson.
     "Siblings and Delinquent Behavior: An
     Exploratory Study of a Neglected Family
     Variable." **Criminology** 20(1982):223-40.

     The authors examine the relationship
     between sibling structure (sex of sibling
     and birth order) and self reported
     delinquency. An interaction effect between
     birth order and sex of sibling relative to
     rates of delinquency is indicated.

KEYWORDS: birth order, divorce effects, drug use, family background, parental supervision, social class, social control, violence

789. Wilson, Harriet. "Juvenile Delinquency, Parental Criminality and Social Handicap." **British Journal of Criminology** 15 (1975): 241-50.

Juvenile delinquency is correlated with parental criminality. The findings show low family income, large family size, and parental criminality to be conducive to delinquency.

KEYWORDS: delinquent vs. non-delinquent, education, number of children, parental criminal record, social class

790. ————. "Parental Supervision: A Neglected Aspect of Delinquency." **British Journal of Criminology** 20(1980):203-35.

The purpose of the research seems to aim at the establishment of a causal relationship between specific methods of parenting and resultant functioning of children.

KEYWORDS: child rearing, community, education, number of children, parental criminal record, parental support, social class

791. ————. "Parents Can Cut the Crime Rate." **New Society** 59(1980):456-58.

The author examines the association between parental supervision and delinquency in families living in deprived inner-city, high crime areas.

KEYWORDS: delinquent vs. non-delinquent, number of children, parental supervision

792.  Woodson, R.  A Summons to Life:  Mediating
      Structures and the Prevention of Youth
      Crime.  Cambridge, Mass.:  Ballinger
      Publishing Co., 1982.

      The author turns attention toward the
      family as our most basic institution and
      aid in the prevention of juvenile crime.

      KEYWORDS:  community, family background,
      prevention

793.  Wright, W., and M. Dixon.  "Community
      Prevention and Treatment of Juvenile
      Delinquency."  Crime and Delinquency
      14(1977):35-67.

794.  Yang, K.  "Problem Behavior in Chinese
      Adolescents in Taiwan:  A Classificatory-
      Factorial Study."  Journal of Cross-
      Cultural Psychology 12(1981):179-93.

      The authors attempt to provide an empirical
      basis for a better structure definition of
      problem behavior in Chinese adolescents.

      KEYWORDS:  ethnicity, male-female, methods

795.  Zatz, Marjorie.  "Los Cholos:  Justice
      Processing of Chicano Gang Members."
      Social Problems (1986):  in press.

      Results indicate that application of the
      label "gang member" does not have an
      independent impact on processing, but the
      type of complaint, the offense, schooling,
      and prior record, in particular, operate
      differently for gang and non-gang youths in
      their effects on rates of movement to case
      disposition.

      KEYWORDS:  gangs, labeling, subculture

796.  Zorber, E.  "The Socialization of Adolescents
      into Juvenile Delinquency."  **Adolescence** 16
      (1981):321-30.

      The author discusses the socialization
      process of adolescents into juvenile
      delinquency by examining various phenomenon
      such as labeling, and age roles.

      KEYWORDS:  age roles, family background,
      labeling, self-concept, social structure

# AUTHOR INDEX

# SUBJECT INDEX